THE IMPACT OF SUPREME COURT DECISIONS

The Impact of Supreme Court Decisions

EMPIRICAL STUDIES

SECOND EDITION

EDITED BY

THEODORE L. BECKER
UNIVERSITY OF HAWAII

MALCOLM M. FEELEY
NEW YORK UNIVERSITY

NEW YORK   OXFORD UNIVERSITY PRESS
London   1973   Toronto

"Does anybody know . . . where we can go to find light on what the practical consequences of these decisions have been?"

FELIX FRANKFURTER

Preface to the Second Edition

Becker first imagined this volume while teaching at New York University in the summer of 1967. At that time, "impact analysis" was only occasionally discussed by a few political scientists, but the ever increasing number of studies made it obvious that it was an idea whose time had come. So it was clear that there was room for a book assembling the best examples of this type of research. Since that time (and we like to believe it was partly due to the publication of the first edition of this volume) impact analysis has gained a wide audience and has developed into an attractive sub-field within the area of public law. This trend represents a continued interest in an empirically based jurisprudence.

Because of the great and rapid changes in this field we felt the need for a number of changes in this second edition. The most important addition, one that we feel reflects the growing significance of impace analysis, is the introduction of an entirely new section: Toward a Theory of Impact. The three articles included therein demonstrate that interest in impact has matured and gone beyond the descriptive stages to a concern with the development of generalizations and "theory." While the actual results of "theory building" are considerably less impressive than the rhetoric about "theory building" these articles nevertheless reflect the latest controversies and problems posed by the growth of impact analysis.

Other changes have been made in order to illustrate the wide variety of types of "impact" that can occur. Now included are examples and analyses of the attempts of two Presidents to disturb directly the very nature of the Court, an example of the "self-correcting" mechanisms possessed by the Court itself, and a discussion of the over-all effectiveness of the Court in resisting popular majorities. Finally, this second edition represents our attempts to present the best of the more recent work in this area.

The task of putting a reader together has been known to have its bad days. Most of the lonelier moments in preparing this second edition were experienced by one Joel Rubin. However, we will wait to analyze the impact upon him. This is just, as he must be held at least partially accountable for any errors of judgment our colleagues discover in using this volume. Such are the consequences of contemporary acknowledgments, as irresponsibility is the advantage of modern-day obscurity—even for the powerless.

THEODORE L. BECKER
Honolulu

MALCOLM M. FEELEY
New York City

Contents

Editors' Introduction

There are at least two major reasons for pursuing impact analysis of the Supreme Court's decisions. First, the United States Supreme Court occupies a unique and paradoxical position in a society claiming to be democratic. The American high court has at its command tremendous powers, unparalleled by any other court in history, yet it is not subject to the same type and degree of public pressure and scrutiny as are the other popularly elected branches of the national government. The esoteric language of law and the shrouds of secrecy and formality that cloak the Court's decisions tend to isolate all but the most important decisions of this "least dangerous branch." Few know and fewer care. But what is worse is that even fewer think about *consequences* flowing from such decisions. Since the Court makes extremely important decisions, should we assume that they are self-executing? We know they are not—yet we do not know the kinds of effects these decisions have on our government and society. After all, this is a society pledged to the "rule of law" is it not? And the Court's decisions are "law." However, to the degree that the Court's mandate is disregarded, in one way or another, we have the "rule of men." The degree and the circumstances of this "impact" are the sort of information about the government that all Americans have the right to know, and the sort of problem that should attract social science research.

Additionally, as Professor Arthur S. Miller has reminded us, justices themselves are frequently forced to make decisions despite their abiding ignorance of the past and likely future impact of their actions. A "jurisprudence of consequences," as he terms it, would provide judges—as well as other policy-makers—with valuable information by which to evaluate the results of their behavior and, perhaps, to guide future decisions. After all, we can assume that the Court cares about who listens and who does not, about who evades and defies and under what conditions, and about what (and the degree of) political consequences they can expect from certain types of decisions. We believe the Court should be receptive to such studies. We would also hate to think that the Justices adhere to some outmoded notions, that they act in a political vacuum. We doubt that they do, particularly those on the Warren and Nixon courts.

In addition to the politically relevant reason for the study of the impact of Supreme Court decisions, there are valid academic reasons. Political science is interested in developing a general theory about political behavior. Certainly, then, research into "the law"—whether the source be the Court, the legislature, or the executive—must be a key undertaking in any such theory. Because of this, one area of the development of political science research is called "policy analysis," i.e. the study of the effects of policies. Clearly, the study of the impact of Supreme Court decisions falls comfortably within "policy analysis."

Within the tangle of recent conceptual discussions on public policy analysis, Randall Ripley's thinking and discussion appeal to us as perhaps the most explicit and the simplest. He suggests that policy analysis should examine three areas: (1) the statement of *goals*; (2) the *action* taken to *implement* these goals; and (3) the social *outcomes* or *consequences* of implementing these actions.

Ripley defines a *policy statement* to be "a declaration of intent on the part of the government to do something." But, he warns, "all too often students and scholars who have declared an interest in policy have stopped with the policy statements and assumed that it is the whole of policy." This warning is right on target for students of public law, who all too often—as Justice Holmes said time and time again—have wallowed contentedly in the policy statements (that is, the Court's opinions) and assumed that they could understand political realities from them and them alone.

Policy action, according to Ripley, is the actual manifestation of policy, i.e. the actual governmental actions, "what the government does, as distinguished from what it has said it is going to do." Among other aspects, it entails the mechanisms of policy-statement evasion even within lower, or co-ordinate, or the same branches of government. And *policy outcomes* include "the consequences that accrue to society as a result, either direct or indirect, of the government's actions or inaction. The impact of the government on society, either intended or unintended, is an outcome."

What is most beneficial in relying on these concepts is that they present an analysis of *consequences for society* as a whole as the primary and ultimate intellectual goal for analysis. Many people in our society are questioning the social value of even our most hallowed (and isolated) institutions, which include the courts and the universities. So, it is appropriate that social scientists should examine the complex interrelationships between the people and the government. It is important work—self-justifying and needed.

What the Supreme Court says is one thing. What other echelons of government do about it is more directly related to the citizenry, and it is this latter interaction that characterizes the substance of many of the empirically based studies included in this volume— although they may not explicitly base their analysis on Ripley's framework, or they may ignore the jargon of public policy analysis completely. Many of them begin by examining the formal statements of purpose found in specific Court decisions and then contrast them with the subsequent behavior of the various actors required to carry out the Court's ruling. But what is more, many of them go on to examine, in a broader context, the impact of the Court on society, both directly and indirectly. As with all American governmental policies, one suspects there may be a rather wide gap between what the Court says *ought* to be done and what in fact *is* actually done. And this is borne out to a large extent by the representative studies we have included.

Unfortunately, though, no contemporary selection of readings could add up to a *comprehensive* assessment of the high Court's impact on mid-twentieth-century American life. The reason for this is simple enough: too little research has been undertaken and too little is known. For example, although political scientists have recently spent considerable effort examining the Court's major civil liberties decisions and their consequences, virtually no systematic attention has been paid to some less politically glamorous areas in which the Court also makes policy. Even such weighty topics as the consequences and potential consequences of the Court's rulings in the economic realm, and anti-trust policy in particular, have received virtually no attention from contemporary political scientists, despite their obvious importance for American society. Nevertheless, the studies reprinted in this volume *do* represent a cross section of the best empirical research to date on the Court's impact, and they can profitably be used as models for extending the analysis of the Court's impact into other areas.

Finally, we would like to explain why we have organized this book the way we have. The reader will quickly see that the sections in this volume correspond to various political locales in American government, e.g. Congress, other courts, state and local governments, the public, etc. This is so largely because the research itself rarely includes more than one specific political location of action. Most of the articles concern themselves with only one arena of the governmental process. So we are not subtly pushing any pet theory by our classification.

As a matter of fact, it is much too early in the development of the field to classify the available research through degree of compliance or types of evasion or defiance. Further, it would be equally too early to classify the literature according to what the researchers themselves believed are the chief extragovernmental factors (e.g. attitudes, social backgrounds, region, etc.) that might account for variations in impact. Thus, mainly out of necessity and deference to the authors, the sections of this volume continue to reflect the political locus of the effect of the Court's decisions, since it is a convenient and theoretically neutral way to put these studies together. As for "theory-building," we have saved that for a special section with which to conclude this volume.

One last word. While we would like to think that impact analysis plays some role in effecting desirable social change, being familiar with the nature of government, we are not terribly optimistic.

1 The Effect on the President and Congress

The Supreme Court is one of three constitutionally co-equal branches of the federal government. Still it was only owing to the political guile of Chief Justice John Marshall in 1803 that the Court managed to get and keep the vital power to declare acts of the President and laws of Congress unconstitutional. The vehicle for this judicial *coup* was the famous case of *Marbury v. Madison*. Since then, the ensuing political equilibrium that constitutes our legal "check and balance system" has been a delicate one, and it has been disturbed seriously and often throughout the years.

The long history of friction between the Court and the President endured well into the twentieth century.[1] It has been dramatized by classic quotations and by tragicomic proposals. One statement that has weathered the years is tough, old Andrew Jackson's "John Marshall has made his decision, now let him enforce it." One of the more prominent suggestions for changing the Court's very fiber was FDR's abortive Court-packing proposal of the late 1930's, proposed after much of his major New Deal economic legislation was ruled unconstitutional by a laissez-faire oriented Court. FDR's speech in which he presented his plan to the nation is reprinted in this section.

This struggle between the President and the high court has resurfaced in the 1960's and early 1970's as a consequence of an

1. See Glendon Schubert, *The Presidency in the Courts* (Minneapolis: University of Minnesota Press, 1957).

activist court. This time, however, the issues were not economic policies, but the civil libertarian decisions of the Warren Court. The 1964, and particularly the 1968, Republican presidential campaigns raised the Court's decisions as major political issues. Furthermore, as the election and subsequent actions of Richard M. Nixon have demonstrated, the controversy has penetrated more deeply than most campaign rhetoric. Nixon, beholden to the South in general and Senator Strom Thurmond (R., South Carolina) in particular for his nomination in 1968, has attempted to make good his debt by continuing to attack the Court. But the Court has suffered more than verbal abuse from the President: he has systematically set about to alter past decisions and remake the Court. The tactics: unprecedented public pronouncements criticizing the Court, directives to the federal bureaucracy to ignore certain rules pursuant to the enforcement of federal court rulings, the attempt to appoint—subsequently thwarted by the Senate's refusal to confirm—two lower court judges well known for their segregationist stances and decisions; the eventual appointment of four new Justices (at the time of this writing); and, because of the intransigence of some lower court judges, the recommendation to Congress that the federal courts' jurisdiction be restricted so that they could not decide certain types of issues. This last proposal—in the form of a nationally televised speech—is reprinted in this section. The eventual impact of these actions by the President can only be guessed at by contemporary historians.

Throughout history Congress also has exhibited profound reactions to the Court, continues to do so today, and promises to do much the same tomorrow. This is probably the reason why it still draws the undivided attention of many political scientists interested in studying the Court's effect: There is abundant sound and fury, and it signifies *something*.

Congress receives the impact of a Supreme Court decision directly and indirectly. The direct effect of a decision is experienced when the Court rebuffs a federal statute as being unconstitutional or construes a statute so far beyond what Congress wanted that it becomes apparent the Court felt the measure to be unwise or unreasonable. The indirect effect is experienced subsequent to a direct consequence on some state constituency; that is, when a state or local action has been declared unconstitutional. The Congressman himself may be offended (being "just plain homefolks" too); there may be widespread local indignation; some powerful interests might be hurt, and they are not loath or slow to convey their anguish to The Hill.

When a Supreme Court decision irks Congress directly or indirectly, Congress has ample power to retaliate. The weaponry it can field against the Court is impressive. Among the heavier artillery, Congress can initiate the constitutional amending process to undo a Court decision or to curtail the Court's power. In the medium range, it can redo a law that the Court has knocked down, or pare Court jurisdiction by statute. Sometimes the retribution could be classified as harassment or terrorism. For instance, Congress can direct darts and arrows at the place where it stings the most: The Pocketbook. Witness, for example, the House of Representatives frustrating a proposed pay increase for the Justices in 1965. As the reader plainly can see, Congress can really play it tough and rough. As the reader will see, it does.

The materials in this section cover a wide range of problems dealing with the Court's relationships with its co-equal branches. In his article, Stuart Nagel systematically classifies and analyzes extensive historical data in order to find out what factors contribute to Congressional effectiveness in curbing the Court by legislation. This historical survey is followed by a carefully constructed and detailed case study by William Beaney and Edward Beiser which focuses on one particular Court-curbing and intimidating effort within the Congress. Their essay contains much information on the sources of the Court's political strength in the face of a frontal assault on its institutional power. Following these social scientists' analyses, we let the politicians speak for themselves and in so doing point to at least one common bond—the attempt to alter *directly* the nature and functions of the Court—between two otherwise dissimilar Presidents, Franklin Roosevelt and Richard Nixon.

The last essay in this section focuses on the shared powers in United States national government, and the nature of Presidential-Congressional reaction to the Supreme Court. It is axiomatic that in a system of shared power, such as the United States national government, victors in conflict are likely to be a temporary coalition. This general principle certainly holds true for conflicts among the three branches of government, as is demonstrated in Robert Dahl's article, "The Supreme Court and Judicial Review: Performance," reprinted here. His central conclusion, which should comfort all advocates of popular democracy, is that the Court has never been able successfully to defend itself against the will of a determined majority, as indicated by the combined opposition of Congress and the President.

STUART S. NAGEL

Court-Curbing Periods in American History

Due to its unavoidable involvement in the political process, the Supreme Court has often been an object of congressional attack. Excellent descriptive studies have been made of certain periods of conflict between Congress and the Court,[1] but there is a lack of writing which systematically analyzes relations between Congress and the Court throughout American history. It is the purpose of this paper to analyze in a partially quantitative manner some of the factors which seem to account for the occurrence or nonoccurrence and for the success or failure of congressional attempts to curb the Court.

I. RESEARCH DESIGN

One hundred and sixty-five instances of bills designed to curb the Supreme Court were compiled along with information concerning their content, sponsor, and fate from a perusal of *The Congressional Record* and its forerunners and also from the previous literature in the field.[2] In order to keep the data within manageable limits, reso-

---

1. Walter F. Murphy concentrates on the problems of the Warren Court in his book, CONGRESS AND THE COURT (1962) as does PRITCHETT, CONGRESS VERSUS THE COURT (1960). Robert Jackson concentrates on the 1937 Court-packing plan in THE STRUGGLE FOR JUDICIAL SUPREMACY: A STUDY OF A CRISIS IN AMERICAN POWER POLITICS (1941). . . .

2. *Ibid.* See also Culp, *A Survey of Proposals to Limit or Destroy the Power of Judicial Review by the Supreme Court of the United States*, 4 IND. L.J. 386,

From the *Vanderbilt Law Review*, 18: 3 (June 1965), pp. 925–44. Reprinted by permission of the publisher and the author.

Stuart S. Nagel is an Associate Professor of Political Science at the University of Illinois (Urbana).

9

lutions and constitutional amendments were not included although they are introduced frequently and often contain proposals which would substantially reduce the powers of the Court.[3] Relatively narrow bills designed to reverse a single decision were also excluded. Relying on the distribution of bills as well as the consensus of historians, seven time periods as shown in Table 1 were labeled high-frequency Court-curbing periods. This identification is both quantitative and qualitative. For example, the first period covering the years from 1802 to 1804, had only two instances of overt congressional attempts to curb the Court, one of which was the unsuccessful impeachment of Justice Chase. While it may well be a quantitatively marginal period, most writers agree that this was a time of high friction between the Federalists on the bench and the Jeffersonians in Congress and the Administration.

Table 1

HIGH AND LOW FREQUENCY PERIODS OF COURT-CURBING IN AMERICAN HISTORY

	High-Frequency				Low-Frequency		
	Years	# of Bills	% of 165		Years	# of Bills	% of 165
1.	1802–1804	2	1%	1.	1789–1801	0	0%
2.	1823–1831	12	7	2.	1805–1822	0	0
3.	1858–1869	22	13	3.	1832–1857	1	1
4.	1893–1897	9	5	4.	1870–1892	8	5
5.	1922–1924	11	7	5.	1898–1921	6	4
6.	1935–1937	37	22	6.	1925–1934	2	1
7.	1955–1957	53	32	7.	1939–1954	2	1
	Total:	146	87%			19	12%

474 (1929); Warren, *The Early History of the Supreme Court of the United States in Connection with Modern Attacks on the Judiciary*, 8 Mass. L.Q. 1 (1922).

3. Twenty-five joint resolutions were proposed in 1937 while thirty-three constitutional amendments were introduced during the two year period from 1935 to 1937. Several attempts have been made, for example in 1867 and 1871, to establish via Constitutional amendment a new court representing all the states which would have jurisdiction over constitutional questions. A joint resolution in 1861 demanded the abolition of the federal judicial system.

A criterion by which to judge the relative success or failure of any one Court-curbing period is more difficult to establish. A total of only nine out of the 165 bills regulating the Court have passed Congress. This group of "absolutely successful" bills, representing approximately five per cent of the total instances, is too small to work with for the purposes of this study. Three criteria of "relative success" will therefore be used. First, *how many* anti-Court bills during each period were reported from committee, the lowest stage of the legislative process aside from introduction? Second, *what per cent* of the bills introduced were reported out of committee? The third criterion of success, as shown in Table 2, is that of determining whether a congressional attack has had the effect of changing within the immediate future the pattern of voting behavior of the Court on the issues which originally provoked the attack. In four of the seven attacks, the Court did retreat from its previous controversial policy by executing a tactical abstention from further similar provocation (as was the case in the years following the 1804 conflict) or by effecting a reversal of policy (as was the case in 1937). At the climax of the seventh period, the Court drew back from its stand on one of the issues which antagonized Congress—namely a broad interpretation of free speech —but remained firm on its policies toward segregation and criminal procedure which were also under congressional fire.

Table 2

RELATIVE SUCCESS OF SEVEN HIGH-FREQUENCY COURT-CURBING PERIODS

Years	Number of Bills Out of Committee	Per cent of Bills Out of Committee	Judicial Retreat	Composite Success	Rank Order of Composite Success
1. 1802–04	1	50%	Yes	Yes	3
2. 1823–31	3	25	Yes	Yes	4
3. 1858–69	11	50	Yes	Yes	1
4. 1893–97	1	11	No	No	7
5. 1922–24	2	18	No	No	6
6. 1935–37	6	16	Yes	Yes	2
7. 1955–59	2	4	Partial	No	5
	Avg. = 3.7 (N = 26)	Avg. 25% per period	Usually Yes	Usually Yes	

The fourth column in Table 2 provides a composite index of over-all success. Thus, a high-frequency period can be considered success-ful if it is above average on the number of bills that were reported out of committee (*i.e.*, four or more); if it is above average on the per cent of successful bills (*i.e.*, 25% or above); and if it was cli-maxed by retreat of the Court on the majority of the issues involved. A period will be termed relatively successful if it is above average on at least two of these three criteria. Using this composite standard, four of the seven high-frequency periods have been classified as rela-tive overall successes, and each period has been given a rough success ranking as shown in the last column of Table 2.

The variables influencing the occurrence and success of the seven Court-curbing periods seem to fit into a model like the psychological model of stimulus-organism-response. In the political phenomenon of Court-curbing, the stimulus is represented by judicial provocation. The organism is represented by the political system which may con-tain certain catalytic or conditioning factors which shape the percep-tion of the provocation and the response. The response manifests itself in certain types of Court-curbing bills and Presidential action. This response may feed back on the judiciary and thereby stimulate judicial counter-action. Having this overall model in mind helps one to see better the interrelations between the more specific variables discussed in this paper.

II. JUDICIAL PROVOCATION

A. *Quantity of Judicial Review*

To what extent does a high quantity of judicial review of legislative acts provoke Court-curbing regardless of the type of interests in-volved? Table 3 shows that almost 50 of the total 86 instances of judicial nullification of federal statutes in American history have occurred during or within three years prior to the seven Court-curbing periods. Thus, over half of the instances of judicial nulli-fication have occurred during a time span equaling less than one-third of the history of the Supreme Court. The use of judicial review for the first time in *Marbury v. Madison*,[4] was certainly an irritant in the Federalist-Jeffersonian dispute over relative amounts of judicial and executive power in the early 1800's. The nullification of state bankruptcy and debtor laws as well as the invalidation of a Maryland act taxing the Bank of the United States provoked the wrath of congressmen in the 1820's.[5] The 1858 Dred Scott case [6] nullified a federal statute, and congressional anticipation of judicial review of Reconstruction legislation led to the court-packing and restrictions on habeas corpus in the 1860's. The 1890's attack was precipitated in part by the invalidation of a federal income tax law, and nullification of federal and state economic legislation led to another Progressive attack on the Court in the 1920's. The judicial review of fifteen New Deal statutes was a prime causative factor in the 1930's conflict. In the 1950's, portions of federal and state laws were held unconstitutional, and proposed legislation such as the Jenner bill was clearly aimed at several decisions. In short, all the periods of intense Court-curbing have been provoked to some degree by the judicial review of legislative acts. Nullification of federal statutes, however, seems to provide a greater provocation than nullification of state statutes since judicial review of state statutes seemed to be a prime factor only in

Table 3

OCCURRENCE OF JUDICIAL REVIEW DURING AND 3 YEARS PRIOR TO THE
HIGH-FREQUENCY COURT-CURBING PERIODS

Years	Instances of judicial review of federal acts during or 3 years prior
1802–04	1
1823–31	0 *
1858–69	5
1893–97	3
1922–24	13
1935–37	15
1955–59	5
Total:	42

* Judicial review of state acts present
4. 5 U.S. (1 Cranch) 137 (1803).
5. 17 U.S. (4 Wheat.) 316 (1819).
6. 60 U.S. (19 How.) 393 (1857).

the 1820's Court-curbing period and partially in the 1950's. Congress is apparently more protective of its own lawmaking than it is of the various state legislative bodies.

If the seven periods are divided into the periods of relatively high judicial review of federal legislation and relatively low . . . a slightly greater proportion of the relatively high review periods involved relatively successful Court-curbing bills than did the relatively low review periods. Thus, the intensity of judicial review may be a partial determinant of the success of controversial Court-curbing bills as well as a determinant of the introduction of Court-curbing bills. There are, however, more important determinants of Court-curbing success as will be shown later.

B. *Subject of the Provoking Cases*

The specific issues over which conflict has occurred whether from judicial review cases or other cases can be divided into four categories —economic regulation, civil liberties, federal-state relations, and general separation of powers. Table 4 indicates that first, economic regulation has been involved to some extent in four of the seven high-frequency periods. Civil liberties and federal-state relations have each been at issue in two periods, while general separation of powers at the national level has been the main controversy in only the earliest period.

Trends in the frequency or occurrence of certain issues are apparent. For example, the attacks during the first half of the nineteenth century were largely concerned with federal-state relations and separation of powers, a fact which can be explained in part by the youth of the country. At this time, the power distribution between the parts of the newly established federal system was not at all clear, this question being a dividing point between the two political parties as well as a major public issue. From the latter half of the nineteenth century through 1937, the basic issue in Congress-court relations was that of economic regulation. Conflict over civil liberties has occurred intermittently but particularly in recent years.

From the data in Table 4 one might also be able to say that Court-curbing bills are more likely to succeed where federal-state relations

Table 4

INTERESTS INVOLVED IN COURT-CURBING DURING AMERICAN HISTORY

Issues	Period	Overall Success
1. Economic Interests		
a. Business Regulation	1930's	Yes
	1890's	No
	1820's	Yes
b. Labor Relations	1890's	No
	1920's	No
c. Taxes	1890's	No
2. Civil Liberties		
a. Segregation	1950's	No
b. First Amendment	1950's	Partial
	1860's	Yes
c. Criminal Procedure	1950's	No
	1860's	Yes
3. Federal-State Relations		
	1800's	Yes
	1820's	Yes
4. Separation of Powers in the National Government	1800's	Yes

or separation of powers represent the prime subject matters involved. On the other hand, where intensely held economic interests or civil libertarian interests are involved, the likelihood of Court-curbing success is decreased.

C. *Unanimity of Provoking Cases*

Does the degree of conflict within the Supreme Court influence the occurrence of congressional Court-curbing? The degree of conflict within the Court can be measured by the degree of unanimity in key decisions at a given time. Using the statements of various writers and congressmen as to what cases provoked the anti-Court bills, the voting split on these controversial decisions was determined. The average degree of unanimity for all the periods was 76% which means that there was an average of two to three dissents in the cases provoking the attacks. This number contrasts with the higher degree of unanimity normally found in the totality of Supreme Court cases. The results of Table 5 support the hypothesis that during periods in which there is a relatively high (*i.e.*, above average) degree of disagreement between members of the Court (and thus high controversy), congressional attack is more likely to occur.

Table 5

DEGREE OF UNANIMITY IN THE SUPREME COURT AND THE EFFECT ON
OCCURRENCE AND SUCCESS OF COURT-CURBING

Periods	Degree of Unanimity		Relative Success
1800's	100%	relatively high	Yes
1820's	89	rel. high	Yes
1860's	59	rel. low	Yes
1890's	72	rel. low	No
1920's	69	rel. low	No
1930's	69	rel. low	Yes
1950's	76	rel. high	No
	Avg. = 76%		

Contrary to what one might expect Table 5 shows that a slightly greater proportion of the high unanimity (rather than the low unanimity) periods involved relatively successful Court-curbing bills. However, the high unanimity in the 1800's and the 1820's does not necessarily indicate complete unity on the part of the Court. It may merely indicate that dissenting had not yet become an established practice.

*   *   *

III. CONGRESSIONAL AND PRESIDENTIAL RESPONSE

A. *Congressional Response*

Several courses of action are available to the congressmen seeking to attack the policies of the Supreme Court. At the local level, he can participate in nullification movements to register disapproval of a particular decision. In Congress, he can attempt retaliation via the fiscal powers, introduce restrictive constitutional amendments, sponsor legislation to overturn a statutory interpretation, initiate joint resolutions or investigations, or, if a Senator, he can attempt to block a Presidential nominee for the bench. Although these methods account for a good share of the activity during congressional attacks on the Court, this paper and the following table is concerned only with specific bills designed directly or indirectly to change some general policy of the Court.

Table 6

TYPES OF BILLS PROPOSED TO CURB THE SUPREME COURT

	Frequency		*Relative Success*	
	Number	% of 165	Number	% of Type
1. Judicial Review				
a. Special concurrence needed	41	25%	5	12%
b. Miscellaneous regulate	5	3	0	0
c. Abolish	3	2	0	0
Total:	49	30%	5	10% Avg.
2. Personnel				
a. Qualifications	24	15	0	0
b. Size of Court	13	8	5	38
c. Retirement	7	4	3	43
d. Appointing	4	2	1	25
e. Give states equal representation	1	½	0	0
Total:	49	29½%	9	18% Avg.
3. Jurisdiction				
a. Regulate and define general appellate jurisdiction	23	14	3	13
b. Repeal Supreme Court jurisdiction over state	3	2	1	33
c. Limit jurisdiction in special cases:				
1) Habeas corpus appeals	3	2	2	67
2) Reconstruction	1	½	0	0
3) Public schools	7	4	0	0
4) Other specific areas	8	5	1	12
Total:	45	27½%	7	16% Avg.

Table 6 (*continued*)

TYPES OF BILLS PROPOSED TO CURB THE SUPREME COURT

	Frequency		Relative Success	
	Number	% of 165	Number	% of Type
4. Procedure				
a. General reorganization	6	4	3	50
b. Amend judicial code	4	2	2	50
c. Amend rules of practice and procedure	1	½	0	0
d. Facilitate decisions on con- stitutional questions	1	½	0	0
Total:	12	7%	5	42% Avg.
5. Curtail Contempt or Injunction Powers	4	2	3	75
6. Miscellaneous				
a. Let lower court ignore non- legalistic Sup. Ct. decisions	2	1	0	0
b. Change doctrine of pre- emptive federalism	1	½	1	100
c. Postpone meeting of Court	1	½	1	100
d. Impeachment	1	½	1	100
e. Give some body direct review over Sup. Ct. decisions	1	½	0	0
Overall Total:	165	100%	32	19% Avg.

After the congressman has decided to attack the power of the judges and to do it through legislative means, he still has a range of alternatives from which to choose. Table 6 indicates that about 30% of the Court-curbing bills dealt with regulating or abolishing judicial review which particularly includes bills requiring special concurrences to declare statutes unconstitutional. Another 29% dealt with matters of Court personnel, particularly qualifications (like lengthy prior judicial experience) for holding a Supreme Court judgeship. Within this 29% are also included thirteen bills designed to increase or decrease the size of the Court so as to allow a new President to make new appointments or to keep him from making new appointments. About 28% of the bills attempted to restrict the court's appellate jurisdiction, and the relatively few remaining bills dealt with various procedural and miscellaneous matters.

Some measures have been peculiar to one time period. Bills curtailing the contempt and injunction powers were predominant, for example, during the period of the Progressives' attack on the Court, particularly before the enactment of the Clayton Act.[7] Bills pertaining to the appellate jurisdiction of the Court in respect to public schools, and bills abolishing the doctrine of pre-emptive federalism were characteristic of the 1955–1959 conflict. The broad historic trend has been away from bills which would remove or circumscribe a broad area of the Court's power and toward those bills which would limit a small, more specific part of the Court's functions. For example, the only serious attempt at impeachment occurred in 1804. Bills advocating the repeal of the 25th section of the Judiciary Act of 1789 which would be tantamount to removing the Court's appellate jurisdiction over state courts were concentrated in the first half of the nineteenth century. Unsuccessful bills providing for equal representation of the states on the Court were proposed prior to 1870, and thus those groups favoring such a change have recently resorted to a constitutional amendment via a constitutional convention. In contrast, many bills proposed during the intense conflict in 1937 were designed to effect changes in the quorum, retirement of Justices, and size of the Court. In the attack on the Warren Court, many bills prescribed limitation of jurisdiction in special cases dealing with subversion, public schools, and (after 1961) reapportionment. More extreme bills in the earlier years may be attributable to the fact that in the early nineteenth century, the rule of the judicial branch of the government was not yet established, and the obvious partisanship of some justices during the very early years was a hindrance to the growth of the judicial myth. In addition, history has shown that bills removing comparatively smaller amounts of the Court's power have the greatest prospect of success. Astute congressmen may well have taken note of this fact. One, however, should note that although the severity of bills during the Warren and Roosevelt courts was lower than in prior periods, the quantity of bills was higher. This possibly indicated a more widespread discontent toward specific decisions and a lack of cohesive leadership by the anti-Court forces which kept these forces from centering on one or a few bills.

7. 64 Stat. 1125 (1950), 15 U.S.C. § 12 (1958).

With regard to the matter of success, ten of the twenty-three categories of bills had a higher percentage of relative success (*i.e.*, got out of committee) than the average of 19%. These ten types of bills included repealing jurisdiction over state supreme courts, limiting jurisdiction in regard to habeas corpus appeals, changing the rules concerning retirement and the size of the Court, restricting the Court's procedure, and limiting the Court's contempt and injunction powers. Most of the ten types could be considered as limited means of curbing the Court. The substantially higher rate of success for the relatively milder bills can be explained by the fact that during all the time periods, there has been a sizeable opposition in Congress to any attempts to curb the Supreme Court—a factor which necessitates compromise.

B. *Presidential Response*

To what extent have Presidents become involved in Court-curbing and what effect has their participation had on the outcome of congressional court conflicts? Four Presidents have been openly critical of the Court during the high-frequency periods, *i.e.*, Jefferson, Jackson, Lincoln, and Roosevelt, but not Eisenhower or the Presidents of the 1920's or 1890's. Presidents have been hesitant to openly initiate Court-curbing legislation. FDR's Court-packing plan of 1937 was an exception, but it was only one of numerous anti-Court bills introduced in the 1930's. This presidential reluctance is possibly due to a fear of alienating the Court's numerous defenders in Congress and the public (as well as a respect for the independence of the judiciary), and in some instances to a favorable presidential attitude toward the Court's policies.

With regard to the success of individual bills, Roosevelt's Court-packing bill was reported out of committee unfavorably. This is attributable to inadequate cultivation of support in Congress and among the public and to reversals by the Court itself. In view of the Court's retreat, however, the Roosevelt period can be considered a relative success. Presidents also have administrative weapons to either thwart or aid orders of the Supreme Court, and ultimately via his appointive power the President can change the Court's policies.

Nevertheless, with the astute use of his tools of leadership, the President can be a powerful figure both in the initiation and successful outcome of Court-curbing bills. With his active support Court-curbing legislation is probably more likely to pass, and without it, such legislation is more likely to fail.

*   *   *

WILLIAM M. BEANEY
EDWARD N. BEISER

Prayer and Politics: The Impact of Engel and Schempp on the Political Process

*   *   *

. . . [I]t seems obvious that students of our legal system should not be satisfied with an acceptance of the official theory that court decisions, and particularly Supreme Court decisions that affect important public policy issues, are universally accepted as the law. It is grossly misleading and dangerous to treat law as a significant form of social control by concentrating on the rules handed down by courts. The realist persuasion in legal philosophy, if it has done nothing else, has warned us against ignoring the ways in which law affects or may leave untouched the daily lives of those to whom it ostensibly applies.

When a court decision impinges on an activity of only a few persons, the tracing of impact is a simple and obvious process. A *Steel Seizure* case,[1] for example, poses a single question with respect to consequences: Did the United States relinquish control of the seized mills to their private corporate owners? But seldom will the question and the answer be so simple. Some decisions, such as those affecting the right of free speech of a curbstone orator, may have few consequences beyond resolving the specific dispute because of the varying contexts in which official action curtailing speech takes place. The impact of decisions affecting behavior of law en-

1. Youngstown Sheet & Tube Co. v. Sawyer, 343 U.S. 579 (1952).

From *Journal of Public Law,* 13: 2 (1964), pp. 475–503. Reprinted by permission of the publisher and the authors.

William M. Beaney is a Professor of Law at the University of Denver. Edward N. Beiser is an Assistant Professor of Political Science at Brown University.

forcement officials are difficult to trace because of the difficulty of observing post-decision conduct. If any conclusions are to be reached they must inevitably be based on the judgment of a few well-placed observers, or on the frequency of future cases where a breach of the rule of the earlier decision can be documented.

These preliminary remarks are intended to serve as qualifications of the present brief study of some of the principal political and governmental responses to *Engel v. Vitale*,[2] in June 1962, outlawing the use of a Regent's prescribed prayer in New York public schools, and the decision of *School Dist. v. Schempp* [3]—*Murray v. Curlett* [4] in June 1963, prohibiting the reading of Bible passages or saying of prayers as religious exercises in public schools throughout the nation . . . A careful state-by-state study of what has occurred since these Court pronouncements has not been undertaken because of limitations of time and resources. What follows is based on data available in newspaper and other printed accounts, supplemented by interviews with those possessing first-hand knowledge of various facets of this subject.

THE NEW YORK PRAYER CASE

The reaction to the Court's decision declaring unconstitutional the use in public schools of a prayer prepared by the New York Regents was not long in forthcoming. And, at least in Congress, it was as one-sided as it was violent. Senator Talmadge (D. Ga.) denounced the decision as "unconscionable . . . an outrageous edict. . . ." [5] Congressman Williams (D. Miss.) insisted that the decision constituted "a deliberately and carefully planned conspiracy to substitute materialism for spiritual values and thus to communize America." [6] Congressman Sikes' (D. Fla.) description of the Court's action as infamous was probably closer to the mood of Congress than Senator Sparkman's (D. Ala.) milder comment: "a tragic mistake." [7] And

2. 370 U.S. 421 (1962).
3. 374 U.S. 203 (1963).
4. *Ibid.*
5. 108 CONG. REC. 11675 (1962).
6. *Id.* at 11734.
7. *Id.* at 11775, 11844.

Congressman Becker (R. N.Y.), who was to become the leader of the opposition to the Court on this issue, informed his colleagues that *Engel* was "the most tragic decision in the history of the United States." [8]

The immediate congressional reaction stressed what was to become one of the major themes of opponents of the Court's decisions: any opposition to religious activities in the public schools was an attack upon religion and upon God Himself. For Senator Robertson (D. Va.) this was the most extreme ruling the Supreme Court had ever made in favor of atheists and agnostics.[9] And Congressman Abernathy (D. Miss.) insisted that it would be "most pleasing to a few atheists and world Communism." [10] . . .

*   *   *

Congressional reaction was expressed in several other forms as well. Congressman Haley (D. Fla.) offered an amendment to a judiciary appropriations bill to earmark out of the Supreme Court's appropriations funds to purchase "for the personal use of each justice a copy of the Holy Bible," but his resolution was rejected 47-66.[11] And on September 27, the House voted unanimously to place the motto "In God We Trust" behind the Speaker's desk. Lest the motivation behind this sudden religious impulse escape anyone, Congressman Randall (D. Mo.) pointed out that "we have given perhaps not directly but yet in a not so subtle way" our answer to the Supreme Court's decision.[12]

The type of Congressional action which posed the most serious threat to the Court's holding, and with which this article will be primarily concerned, was the introduction of proposed amendments to the Constitution to allow public schools to conduct religious exercises. Congressman Frank Becker (R. N.Y.) introduced his amendment the day after *Engel* was decided. His language is typical of this

8. *Id.* at 11719.
9. *Id.* at 11708.
10. *Id.* at 11718.
11. 108 CONG. REC. 14360 (1962).
12. *Id.* at 21102.

type of proposal: "Prayers may be offered in the course of any program in any public school or other public place in the United States." [13]

Twenty-two senators and fifty-three representatives introduced amendments in response to *Engel,* as indicated in the following table: [14]

Table 1

MEMBERS OF CONGRESS INTRODUCING ANTI-*Engel* AMENDMENTS.
87TH CONGRESS, 2D SESSION.

Party Affiliation	House	Senate
Republicans	26	12
Southern Democrats	19	8
Non-Southern Democrats	8	2
Total	53	22

Congressional hostility toward the Court's decision was further demonstrated at hearings conducted by Senator Eastland's Judiciary Committee, just one month after *Engel* was decided. Testimony by various senators shows that they were acutely aware that the Court was soon to consider the constitutionality of Bible reading and the recitation of the Lord's Prayer in public schools, and that it was fully expected that both practices would be prohibited. Thus one of the joint resolutions before the committee anticipated the Court's action in *Schempp,* by proposing to amend the Constitution to allow prayer and Bible reading in public schools. It is interesting to note that in their general frame of reference as well as in their specific resolutions, the senators were significantly affected not only by what the Court had done—but by what it might be expected to do in the future.

*   *   *

13. Quoted in *Hearings on Prayer in Public Schools and Other Matters Before the Senate Committee on the Judiciary,* 87th Cong., 2d Sess. 71 (1962) [hereinafter cited as 1962 *Senate Hearings*].
14. "Southern Democrats" includes representatives of the eleven states of the old Confederate States of America. This is the usage of V. O. Key in SOUTHERN POLITICS (1949).

The short Senate Judiciary Committee hearings, with Senator Eastland, the chairman, absent, provided a field day for opponents of the Court. While the critical statements of such organizations as the American Legion and Young Americans For Freedom were countered by statements submitted by such groups as the American Civil Liberties Union, Anti-Defamation League, The Baptist Joint Committee on Public Affairs, and others, the oral testimony of the witnesses was unanimous in opposing the Court's action. The principal theme of the several witnesses—as had been the case in the initial congressional reaction—was that the decision represented a concerted attack on God and on religion in American life. Bishop Pike, for example, insisted that the result of the decision was "secularism, whether by intent or by default. I am not implying for a moment that the proponents or supporters of the decision of the Supreme Court intentionally wish an atheistic result. Nevertheless, when it is by default we simply *cut off the whole spiritual dimension of life,* and without even a reference to it. What we have left is actually a secularist view of life." [15]

The Eastland Committee hearings also provided a platform for those who had other bones to pick with the Court. There were repeated references in the testimony to persistent abuses by the Supreme Court of its judicial function. It is hardly coincidental that the overwhelming majority of congressmen and senators who participated in these hearings were Southerners. Table 1 indicated that more than half of the amendments to the Constitution introduced to reverse *Engel* were introduced by representatives of the 11 states of the former Confederacy. And Bishop Pike—the one non-congressional witness at the hearings—began his testimony with a strong states' rights argument.[16] Apart from allowing opponents of the Court and of the *Regents' Prayer* decision to vent their spleen, the hearings accomplished nothing. No final report was issued, nor was any legislation proposed.

15. 1962 *Senate Hearings* 56. (Emphasis added.)
16. *Id.* at 51. Bishop Pike misstated the text of the 10th amendment in his comment that the amendment "makes clear that those things not *specifically* given to the federal government by authority, are reserved to the States and the people." (Emphasis added.)

The reaction of the late President Kennedy differed significantly. In response to a question at his regular news conference, he said:

> The Supreme Court has made its judgment. Some will disagree and others will agree. In the efforts we're making to maintain our Constitutional principles, we will have to abide by what the Supreme Court says. We have a very easy remedy here, and that is to pray ourselves. We can pray a good deal more at home and attend our churches with fidelity and emphasize the true meaning of prayer in the lives of our children. I hope, as a result of that decision, all Americans will give prayer a greater emphasis.[17]

The late President Hoover, however, voiced a strong dissent:

> The interpretation of the Constitution is a disintegration of one of the most sacred of American heritages. The Congress should at once submit an amendment to the Constitution which establishes the right to religious devotion in all government agencies—national, state, or local.[18]

*   *   *

THE RESPONSE TO THE LORD'S PRAYER AND
BIBLE READING DECISIONS [19]

When the decision in *Schempp* was handed down on June 17, 1963, the immediate reaction was less violent than those who had experienced the stormy reaction to *Engel* had anticipated. . . .

*   *   *

. . . In any event, the generally milder initial reaction to the 1963 decision was to prove illusory to those who thought that this portended widespread acceptance of the Court's ruling. Both in the affected states and in Congress, unmistakable evidence of resistance and opposition in various forms soon appeared and battle was joined.

*   *   *

17. *CLSA Bull.* 3.
18. *Ibid.*
19. School Dist. v. Schempp, 374 U.S. 203 (1963).

THE BECKER AMENDMENT

In light of popular support for the continuation of Bible reading and prayers in the public schools, and the obvious reluctance of many states to abandon practices which have been in effect for several decades, it was hardly to be expected that Congress would stay out of the controversy engendered by the 1963 decision. The initial congressional reaction, though largely reflecting opposition, was more restrained than that of a year earlier when the *Regents' Prayer* decision was handed down. There was some of the damning language which followed the earlier decision. Congressman O'Konski (R. Wis.), for example, suggested mental tests for the Justices, and Senator Ellender (D. La.), continuing a long standing quarrel with the Court, referred to the "eight silly old men." [20] Senator Thurmond (D. S.C.) called it "another major triumph of secularism and atheism which are bent on throwing God completely out of our national life," while his colleague Senator Robertson (D. Va.) insisted that "we will become as Godless a nation as is the Soviet Union." [21] Striking a more positive note, Senator Johnston (D. S.C.) urged teachers to defy the decisions, and Congressman Ashmore (D. S.C.) moved that "In God We Trust" be placed in the Supreme Court building in much the same spirit that had led the House to place that motto behind the Speaker's desk a year earlier.[22] By and large, however, the violent outburst which had followed *Engel* was missing.

But whatever personal views members of Congress may have held, those of their constituents were made increasingly clear by a barrage of letters and petitions heavily weighted against the prayer and Bible reading decisions. And this unusually heavy flood of mail was soon followed by Congressional action in the form of numerous bills proposing amendments to the Constitution intended to reverse the *Schempp* decision. A comparison of Tables 1 and 2 indicates that almost twice as many members of Congress felt impelled to introduce such amendments as had been the case after *Engel*. In all, 146 amendments were introduced as of March 24, 1964. We are thus

20. Arnold Forster (Director of civil liberties division, ADL), *Memorandum to All ADL Regional Offices*, July 11, 1963, p. 6.
21. *Ibid.*
22. *Ibid.*

Table 2 [23]

PARTY AFFILIATION OF AUTHORS OF CONSTITUTIONAL AMENDMENTS TO
REVERSE *Schempp*. 88TH CONGRESS, 2D SESSION.

Party Affiliation	House	Senate
Republicans	64	15
Southern Democrats	30	8
Non-Southern Democrats	19	4
Total	113	27

faced with an interesting paradox: popular reaction to *Engel* was much greater than the outcry after *Schempp;* yet at the same time positive political action was much more significant after *Schempp* than it had been a year earlier. Several factors may help us to understand this situation. First, as indicated above, the 1963 decisions directly affected a much wider segment of the American public than had the *Regents' Prayer* case. Thus while the immediate outcry from public figures may have been greater after *Engel,* the *Schempp* decision was much more likely to stir up a widespread wave of opposition. Second, while it was not likely that Congressional action in response to *Engel* could have been taken in time to affect the 1962 Congressional elections, the elections of 1964 were constantly in the minds of Congressmen as Congress convened after the summer 1963 recess. And finally, we must interject into the 1963/64 situation the effects of the untiring efforts of Congressman Frank Becker (R. N.Y.).

Although the Senate had chosen to act following *Engel,* through its Judiciary Committee, the House was to be the center of the fight between supporters and opponents of amendments following *Schempp.* And the battle focused increasingly on the efforts of Representative Becker to push through such an amendment, and those

23. "Southern Democrats" represent the 11 states of the former Confederacy. The table is based on the *Congressional Record,* 88th Congress, both sessions. One might have expected many Southerners would have introduced such resolutions. It is important to realize that the pattern of behavior among Southern Congressmen was far from uniform. As indicated below, there were Southern states in which resentment against the Court would be expected to be high, in which the Congressmen did not feel called upon to introduce such amendments.

of Representative Emmanuel Celler (D. N.Y.), powerful chairman
of the House Judiciary Committee, to forestall any attack on the
Court's ruling. Becker had proposed an amendment after *Engel,* and
on the day after the 1963 decision was handed down, he introduced
another. Firmly convinced that the Court had struck a serious blow
against the religious training of the nation's youth, Becker devoted
all his personal efforts to a crusade to convince the public and his
colleagues that the great majority of Americans favored and were
entitled to the continuation of religious ceremonies in the public
schools. A devout Catholic, Congressman Becker had been educated

Table 3

NUMBER OF CONGRESSMEN INTRODUCING AMENDMENTS TO REVERSE
Schempp. 88TH CONGRESS, 1ST & 2D SESSIONS.

State	Democrats	Republicans
Alabama	3 out of 8	—
Arkansas	0 out of 4	—
Florida	5 out of 10	1 out of 2
Georgia	3 out of 10	—
Louisiana	1 out of 8	—
Mississippi	5 out of 5	—
North Carolina	7 out of 7	2 out of 2
South Carolina	4 out of 6	—
Tennessee	0 out of 3	3 out of 3
Texas	2 out of 19	0 out of 2
Virginia	0 out of 6	2 out of 2
Total	30 out of 86	8 out of 11

Note that almost all Southern Republicans introduced "anti-Court" amendments. But compare the behavior of Congressmen from Mississippi and North
Carolina with that of Democrats from Virginia and Arkansas. The authors
attempted to correlate the above indicated pattern with such factors as V. O.
Key's "Black Belt" thesis; income distribution; presence of an opposition party;
and religious affiliation of both Congressmen and population, without success.
Whatever caused this interesting pattern, it warns us to avoid the danger of
viewing the South monolithically in this matter.

in public schools, as had his children, and he regarded as wholly
salutary the modest practices by which the public schools recognized
the roles of God and of religion. Becker's zeal was reinforced by his
conception of the opponents he was combatting: "I certainly believe

that the atheists intend to bury religion. . . ." [24] Since he did not intend to seek re-election in 1964, Becker was prepared to devote virtually his entire energies to the task at hand. He made numerous public addresses, carried on a heavy correspondence, and made himself available as a leader in the fight to get an amendment through both Houses of Congress. Recognizing that the Chairman of the Judiciary Committee was unalterably opposed to any such amendment and would not let such a bill out of his committee unless compelled to do so, Becker sought to unite those who agreed with him on one form of amendment, and, by introducing a discharge petition either to force the holding of hearings, or to get his amendment out of Celler's committee and to the floor, where he anticipated favorable action by the required two-thirds of the House. With the unprecedented number of almost 115 fellow amendment seekers, he thought his chances of success were high, since only 218 signatures were necessary to discharge the bill from the committee. Becker faced two major difficulties from the start: one was the ingrained reluctance of many members to sign a discharge petition on any subject, particularly where the powerful Judiciary Committee was involved, the other was the coincidence of this issue and the Civil Rights Bill, eventually enacted in 1964, which tended to divide supporters of a prayer amendment.[25]

The bill which was to become identified in the public's mind as the "Becker Amendment" was not the bill introduced originally by the Representative, but was the product of a drafting effort by six members of Congress designated to perform this task following a meeting of amendment supporters in late August, 1963.[26] The amendment proposed in House Joint Resolution 693, introduced on September 10, 1963, provided that:

24. Hearings on School Prayers Before the House Committee on the Judiciary, 88th Cong., 2d Sess. 2008 (1964) [hereinafter cited as 1964 House Hearings].
25. Note that the battle over Becker's discharge petition probably hurt the attempt to discharge the Civil Rights Bill from the House Rules Committee at about the same time. Many Congressmen who were afraid to "fight God" but who opposed Becker refused to sign his petition on the grounds that as a matter of principle they never signed discharge petitions. This prevented some from signing the civil rights discharge petition.
26. RNS, Aug. 26, 1963. The six were Becker, W. Baring (D. Nev.), W. Cramer (R. Fla.), D. Fuqua (D. Fla.), H. R. Kornegay (D. N.C.), and D. Latta (R. Ohio).

Sec. 1. Nothing in this Constitution shall be deemed to prohibit the offering, reading from, or listening to prayers or Biblical scriptures, if participation therein is on a voluntary basis, in any governmental or public school, institution or place.

Sec. 2. Nothing in this Constitution shall be deemed to prohibit making reference to, belief in, reliance upon, or invoking the aid of God or a Supreme Being in any governmental or public document, proceeding, activity, ceremony, school, institution, or place, or upon any coinage, currency, or obligation of the United States.

Sec. 3. Nothing in this article shall constitute an establishment of religion.

Ratification by three-fourths of the state legislatures within seven years was required by the last section of the proposed amendment.

During this period petitions and letters continued to pile up in congressional offices, and especially in those of members of the House Judiciary Committee. The campaign on behalf of an amendment to overcome the Court's decisions now had a clearer focus. From now on the battle was to be waged exclusively in terms of the Becker Amendment.

Although the volume of mail favoring the Becker Amendment continued to mount and members of the House continued to sign Becker's discharge petition, supporters of the decision did not view the matter seriously. The natural congressional opposition to discharge petitions under any circumstances and the feeling that the Judiciary Committee and especially its chairman could not be stampeded, along with the relative mildness of the initial reactions to the 1963 decision, led usually well-informed observers to believe that the Becker Amendment would peacefully die in committee. But support for the amendment from constituents of all types continued to mount, largely as a result of the activities of Congressman Becker and of organizations supporting his position. The *New York Times* reported that "largely through his efforts, it is conceded widely in Congress that Congressional mail on this issue has grown to flood proportions, exceeding the mail of the civil rights controversy." [27] Congressman Lionel Van Deerlin (D. Cal.) wrote that his colleagues "are being inundated with constituent mail, the great bulk of which favors such an amendment." [28] A form letter used by Congressman R. G. Ste-

27. N. Y. Times, April 23, 1964, p. 14, col. 5.
28. Personal letter to Mr. Dore Schary, in the ADL files.

phens (D. Ga.) to reply to constituents apologized for the fact that
a printed reply was being used, but said that it was necessitated by
the fact that he had had over one thousand letters on the subject.
On February 18, the House Republican Policy Committee voted to
support the Becker Amendment.[29] Congressman Alec G. Olson (D.
Minn.) informed a constituent that he believed "this is a result of
the large volume of mail running in favor of this amendment. In my
case, I have received correspondence which is at least 200 to 1 in
favor of such an amendment. . . ." [30] Gradually the number of signatures on the discharge petition rose so that eventually it contained
almost 170 names.[31] And, the *Wall Street Journal* reported, "it is no
secret that many more members including some hostile to the proposal and others adverse to the irregular procedure, have warned
Mr. Celler that pressure from home would force them to sign unless
he made some move." [32]

How is it that the members of Congress—who were surely well
aware that much of the mail they were receiving was "inspired"
—were sensitive to public sentiment to the extent that the *Wall
Street Journal* pointed out that "for the most part, even lawmakers
adamant in their opposition have kept silent in public"? [33] The
answer is probably to be found in the way the issue was phrased by
Becker and his supporters. In an election year, no Congressman
wanted to be placed in a position of appearing to vote against God,
which was exactly the role into which supporters of the Court were
being forced. . . .

Early in 1964 it became apparent that Congressman Celler would
have to schedule hearings, in order to avoid having the bill taken out
of his committee. And indeed, by the middle of February he reacted
to the Republican Policy Committee's demand for hearings by dryly

29. N. Y. Times, Feb. 19, 1964, p. 21, col. 3.
30. Letter to Mr. Merrill Keller, St. Paul, Minn., March 13, 1964, in ADL
files.
31. It is impossible to know exactly how many signatures appear on a discharge petition at a given moment, as this figure is never officially released,
and members can withdraw their names at any time. The *Wall Street Journal*
reported that 166 signatures were said to have been obtained. This appears to
square with other published reports, and with Becker's claims. Wall Street
Journal, April 22, 1964, p. 1, col. 4.
32. *Id.* at 1.
33. *Ibid.*

remarking that a staff study was in progress, and that hearings would be scheduled when it was completed.[34] Opponents of the Becker Amendment who had previously been relatively inactive suddenly realized that if they did not stop Becker's juggernaut at the Committee hearings, their worst fears would be fulfilled. Meeting in New York on St. Patrick's Day, 1964, an *ad hoc* committee consisting of representatives of numerous Protestant, Jewish, and civil liberties groups opposed to the amendment decided that at that time the Becker Amendment had an excellent chance of receiving the approval of a majority of the Judiciary Committee, that if reported out favorably it was likely to pass easily in the House, and that while the Senate might delay passage of the bill, it would eventually pass there as well, an estimate concurred in by close students of the situation not present at the meeting.

Faced with this prospect, the members of the *ad hoc* group decided to coordinate their organizational efforts. It was agreed that probably the most important function the group could play would be to mobilize leaders of the religious community to oppose the Becker Amendment, in order to make it "respectable" and "safe" for Congressmen to oppose the Becker proposal. . . .

*   *   *

Although any effort to summarize briefly or evaluate the testimony of the contending forces is inevitably highly subjective, a few observations reflecting the authors' impressions may be of some value. The arguments of the Becker supporters followed the pattern previously established: the people favor such practices; the Court's decisions are an attack on God and on religion; this country was founded on a belief in God, and cannot exist without it; majorities have rights, and they need not always bow to the will of an "atheistic" minority.

*   *   *

Equally impressive, and perhaps almost as significant, was the testimony of legal scholars who attacked the amendment. . . .

34. N. Y. Times, Feb. 19, 1964, p. 21, col. 5.

The testimony of the opponents of the amendment was intended to sway the opinion of wavering congressmen. Which version of the *Bible* would be used? Would the *Koran* qualify under the amendment? Who would decide which prayers to say? Could the "Ave Maria" be employed? And again and again they returned to the basic theme: "thou shalt not touch the Bill of Rights."

The Becker Amendment movement, while endorsed widely, was essentially a one-man crusade. Although various organizations lent their support, and vigorous statements were made by several witnesses, the strategy used and the calibre of the witnesses did not match the efforts of the anti-amendment forces. To one who tries to read the pro-Becker testimony objectively, it seems that in the minds of many witnesses popular support for continuance of school prayers and Bible reading was regarded as the decisive factor. With notable exceptions, such as Charles Wesley Lowry,[35] many pro-Becker witnesses seemed to have adopted the simple equation—The people want prayers in schools; the Court took them away; we, on behalf of the people, must restore them. When the Chairman or other Committee members attempted to draw them out as to the effects of the various provisions of the amendment, they were often unable to follow the subtleties of the questioner. They frequently seemed annoyed by the complexities of issues framed by opponents.

Press coverage of the hearings was relatively full, and though the public was unable to gain a very coherent notion of the trend of the debates, it appears that the testimony of the anti-Becker church leaders and that of the legal authorities opposing the measure dominated the reports, especially in the later sessions. This may help to explain the increase in the anti-Becker mail, and a number of editorials throughout the nation urging that the amendment not pass.[36]

The real test of the effectiveness of the opposition lay in the impact on members of the Judiciary Committee. Although any judgment must be made with considerable reservation, it would seem that the direction of change of views of committee members was almost exclusively in one direction—against the amendment. At the beginning of the hearings, as noted above, the *ad hoc* committee had

35. *1964 House Hearings*, 1125.
36. See, *e.g.*, N. Y. Herald Tribune, May 10, 1964, p. 22, col. 1, editorial entitled "It's not a vote against God."

estimated that the Becker Amendment would easily win a majority in the committee; by the end of May, they expected that the Becker Amendment would probably be opposed by as many as 20 of the 35 members. By that time it was doubtful that any amendment then in prospect could attract a majority of the committee. It was apparent that the drive for a discharge petition had passed its crest; not only could it not gain the necessary 218 signatures, but members who had signed the petition were prepared to remove their names should the total approach 210. And even if a bill were discharged, it was doubtful that it could obtain a majority in the House, much less the required two-thirds majority. The *Wall Street Journal* doubted that as many as 8 members of the committee still supported an amendment.[37]

The use of public hearings as a means of shaping the thinking of committee members has been increasingly discounted by political analysts in recent years. They have tended to view them as a show with little relevance to the actual struggle over important public issues. The Becker Amendment hearings would appear to cast serious doubt as to the validity of these conclusions, for, as we have seen, the hearings had a significant impact *both* on Congressional opinion and on public opinion. The Becker hearings point to many aspects of the legislative process which students of future contests would do well to keep in mind. A combination of factors: expert, if belated, planning by opponents; their ability to gain the support of heavier "guns" at the hearings; and the natural advantage that our political system provides those opposing legislative action, was all too much for the Becker cause, regardless of its popular support. Also, the skillful operation of an experienced committee chairman and ally was of inestimable value to the anti-amendment forces.

*   *   *

37. Wall Street Journal, June 16, 1964, p. 3, col. 2.

Presidential Reactions to the Supreme Court: Altering Personnel and Power

Sometimes the Supreme Court, through a series of decisions, can drive a President to distraction when he would rather concentrate on other matters. But our highest court is a very important branch of government, and by determining that certain kinds of federal or state actions are "unconstitutional" it can upset many a Presidential applecart. For example, Supreme Court decisions can rankle large numbers of political supporters of the President and cause them to pressure him to "do something." Also, a stubbornly adverse Court can force him to alter important parts of his master political strategy. Thus, at some point Presidents may decide to confront those nine men across the way in order to get future Court decisions more to their liking.

The first method a President considers in tackling the Court is one that offers the least resistance, although it too is fraught with political peril. This approach is to appoint new Justices more closely in tune with his political philosophy and program. One major flaw in this tactic is that there has to be an opening on the high bench—a Justice must die or retire. Another problem is that Presidents make mistakes in assessing how a man will act on the Court once he is there. Still another is that Presidents run into politically hostile Senates—and the Senate has the constitutional power to deny his appointments to the Supreme Court. President Nixon twice ran the Senate gauntlet unsuccessfully while trying to change Messers Haynesworth and Carswell into Justices Haynesworth and Carswell.

A President has other means at his disposal even if no immediate vacancy has occurred or if he would rather not take a chance on

37

what some new man might do once he became an Associate Justice. He can try to change the size of the Court, since there is no constitutional floor or ceiling on how many Justices there need to be. He can try to increase the size through Congressional legislation. Or, he can try to shrink the size of the Court once a Justice leaves the bench. This way he would not be taking a risk of disturbing some newly favorable balance on the smaller Court. Another means of potentially altering future decisions on the Court is to limit selectively its appellate jurisdiction so that it loses the power to hear certain types of cases.

All these tactics were successfully utilized during the nineteenth century. On several occasions the Court's size was expanded or contracted in order to reduce Southern influence and representation. Likewise, during the Civil War, President Lincoln asked for and received Congressional legislation limiting the high court's appellate jurisdiction. This power was upheld in the controversial Supreme Court decision of Ex parte McCardle.[1]

While the prestige of the Supreme Court was not as great in the nineteenth century as it has become, many similar maneuvers by opponents of the Court are used up to the present day. And Presidents have not been too shy to try and pack the Court—and lower federal courts as well—into its "proper" place. Two twentieth-century attempts to change the Court, by Presidents Franklin Roosevelt and Richard Nixon, are illustrated in the speeches reprinted below.

FDR requested, in a "fireside chat" to the nation, that the size of the Court be increased in order that his New Deal legislation would be given a clean bill of health by the New Court. While this "Court packing plan" was not accepted by Congress, his speech and subsequent efforts at securing the passage of the legislation are generally regarded as influencing at least two Justices' views so that their "switch in time saved nine." While campaigning for the presidency in 1968, Richard Nixon repeatedly attacked the Warren Court's activist decisions, and vowed to appoint "strict constructionists" to any vacancies on the Court. Even after several Nixon appointments and some friendly decisions in some areas, the Court still upheld lower court orders to bus school children for the purposes of overcoming state and local segregation.[2] Since much of his political con-

1. 7 Wall 566 (1869).
2. *Swann v. Charlotte-Mecklenburg Board of Education* 403 U.S. 912 (1971).

stituency strongly opposed this, the President decided to try another tactic, and in a nationally televised broadcast asked Congress to re-strict the jurisdiction of the federal courts to make them powerless to order any more school busing—at least for a specified period of time. This issue, of course, lives on.

* * *

Franklin D. Roosevelt

A "FIRESIDE CHAT" DISCUSSING THE PLAN FOR REORGANIZATION OF THE JUDICIARY. WASHINGTON, D.C. MARCH 9, 1937

The American people have learned from the depression. For in the last three national elections an overwhelming majority of them voted a mandate that the Congress and the President begin the task of providing that protection—not after long years of debate, but now.

The Courts, however, have cast doubts on the ability of the elected Congress to protect us against catastrophe by meeting squarely our modern social and economic conditions.

We are at a crisis in our ability to proceed with that protection. It is a quiet crisis. There are no lines of depositors outside closed banks. But to the far-sighted it is far-reaching in its possibilities of injury to America.

I want to talk with you very simply about the need for present action in this crisis—the need to meet the unanswered challenge of one-third of a Nation ill-nourished, ill-clad, ill-housed.

Last Thursday I described the American form of Government as a three horse team provided by the Constitution to the American people so that their field might be plowed. The three horses are, of course, the three branches of government—the Congress, the Executive and the Courts. Two of the horses are pulling in unison today; the third is not. Those who have intimated that the President of the United States is trying to drive that team, overlook the simple fact that the President, as Chief Executive, is himself one of the three horses.

It is the American people themselves who are in the driver's seat.

It is the American people themselves who want the furrow plowed.

It is the American people themselves who expect the third horse to pull in unison with the other two...

In the last four years the sound rule of giving statutes the benefit of all reasonable doubt has been cast aside. The Court has been acting not as a judicial body, but as a policy-making body.

When the Congress has sought to stabilize national agriculture, to improve the conditions of labor, to safeguard business against unfair competition, to protect our national resources, and in many other ways, to serve our clearly national needs, the majority of the Court has been assuming the power to pass on the wisdom of these Acts of the Congress—and to approve or disapprove the public policy written into these laws.

That is not only my accusation. It is the accusation of most distinguished Justices of the present Supreme Court. I have not the time to quote to you all the language used by dissenting Justices in many of these cases. But in the case holding the Railroad Retirement Act unconstitutional, for instance, Chief Justice Hughes said in a dissenting opinion that the majority opinion was "a departure from sound principles," and placed "an unwarranted limitation upon the commerce clause." And three other Justices agreed with him. ...

In the case holding the A.A.A. unconstitutional, Justice Stone said of the majority opinion that it was a "tortured construction of the Constitution." And two other Justices agreed with him.

In the case holding the New York Minimum Wage Law unconstitutional, Justice Stone said that the majority were actually reading into the Constitution their own "personal economic predilections," and that if the legislative power is not left free to choose the methods of solving the problems of poverty, subsistence and health of large numbers in the community, then "government is to be rendered impotent." And two other Justices agreed with him.

In the face of these dissenting opinions, there is no basis for the claim made by some members of the Court that something in the Constitution has compelled them regretfully to thwart the will of the people.

In the face of such dissenting opinions, it is perfectly clear, that as Chief Justice Hughes has said: "We are under a Constitution, but the Constitution is what the Judges say it is."

The Court in addition to the proper use of its judicial functions has improperly set itself up as a third House of the Congress—a super-legislature, as one of the justices has called it—reading into the Constitution words and implications which are not there, and which were never intended to be there.

We have, therefore, reached the point as a Nation where we must take action to save the Constitution from the Court and the Court from itself. . . .

What is my proposal? It is simply this: whenever a Judge or Justice of any Federal Court has reached the age of seventy and does not avail himself of the opportunity to retire on a pension, a new member shall be appointed by the President then in office, with the approval, as required by the Constitution, of the Senate of the United States.

That plan has two chief purposes. By bringing into the judicial system a steady and continuing stream of new and younger blood, I hope, first, to make the administration of all Federal justice speedier and, therefore, less costly; secondly, to bring to the decision of social and economic problems younger men who have had personal experience and contact with modern facts and circumstances under which average men have to live and work. This plan will save our national Constitution from hardening of the judicial arteries.

The number of Judges to be appointed would depend wholly on the decision of present Judges now over seventy, or those who would subsequently reach the age of seventy.

If, for instance, any one of the six Justices of the Supreme Court now over the age of seventy should retire as provided under the plan, no additional place would be created. Consequently, although there never can be more than fifteen, there may be only fourteen, or thirteen, or twelve. And there may be only nine.

Is it a dangerous precedent for the Congress to change the number of the Justices? The Congress has always had, and will have, that power. The number of Justices has been changed several times before, in the Administrations of John Adams and Thomas Jefferson—both signers of the Declaration of Independence—Andrew Jackson, Abraham Lincoln and Ulysses S. Grant.

I suggest only the addition of Justices to the bench in accordance with a clearly defined principle relating to a clearly defined age limit. Fundamentally, if in the future, America cannot trust the Congress it elects to refrain from abuse of our Constitutional usages, democracy will have failed far beyond the importance to it of any kind of precedent concerning the Judiciary.

*   *   *

Two groups oppose my plan on the ground that they favor a constitutional amendment. The first includes those who fundamentally object to social and economic legislation along modern lines. This is the same group who during the campaign last Fall tried to block the mandate of the people.

Now they are making a last stand. And the strategy of that last stand is to suggest the time-consuming process of amendment in order to kill off by delay the legislation demanded by the mandate.

To them I say: I do not think you will be able long to fool the American people as to your purposes.

The other group is composed of those who honestly believe the amendment process is the best and who would be willing to support a reasonable amendment if they could agree on one.

To them I say: we cannot rely on an amendment as the immediate or only answer to our present difficulties. When the time comes for action, you will find that many of those who pretend to support you will sabotage any constructive amendment which is proposed. Look at these strange bed-fellows of yours. When before have you found them really at your side in your fights for progress?

*   *   *

During the past half century the balance of power between the three great branches of the Federal Government, has been tipped out of balance by the Courts in direct contradiction of the high purposes of the framers of the Constitution. It is my purpose to restore that balance. You who know me will accept my solemn assurance that in a world in which democracy is under attack, I seek to make American democracy succeed. You and I will do our part.

Richard M. Nixon

A MESSAGE TO CONGRESS ON SCHOOL BUSING:
17 MARCH 1972

In this message, I wish to discuss a question which divides many Americans. That is the question of busing...

I want to do so in a way that will enable us to focus our attention on a question which unites all Americans. That is the question of how to ensure a better education for all of our children.

In the furor over busing, it has become all too easy to forget what busing is supposed to be designed to achieve: equality of educational opportunity for all Americans.

Conscience and the Constitution both require that no child should be denied equal educational opportunity. That Constitutional mandate was laid down by the Supreme Court in *Brown v. Board of Education* in 1954. The years since have been ones of dismantling the old dual school system in those areas where it existed—a process that has now been substantially completed.

As we look to the future, it is clear that the efforts to provide equal educational opportunity must now focus much more specifically on education: on assuring that the opportunity is not only equal, but adequate, and that in those remaining cases in which desegregation has not yet been completed it be achieved with a greater sensitivity to educational needs.

Acting within the present framework of Constitutional and case law, the lower Federal courts have ordered a wide variety of remedies for the equal protection violations they have found. These remedies have included such plans as redrawing attendance zones, pairing, clustering and consolidation of school districts. Some of these plans have not required extensive additional transportation of pupils. But some have required that pupils be bused long distances, at great inconvenience. In some cases plans have required that children be bused away from their neighborhoods to schools that are inferior or even unsafe.

The maze of differing and sometimes inconsistent orders by the various lower courts has led to contradiction and uncertainty, and often to vastly unequal treatment among regions, States and local school districts. In the absence of statutory guidelines, many lower court decisions have gone far beyond what most people would consider reasonable, and beyond what the Supreme Court has said is necessary in the requirements they have imposed for the reorganization of school districts and the transportation of school pupils.

All too often, the result has been a classic case of the remedy for one evil creating another evil. In this case, a remedy for the historic evil of racial discrimination has often created a new evil of disrupting communities and imposing hardship on children—both black and white—who are themselves wholly innocent of the wrongs that the plan seeks to set right.

The 14th Amendment to the Constitution under which the school desegregation cases have arisen provides that "Congress shall have power to enforce, by appropriate legislation, the provisions of this article."

Until now, enforcement has been left largely to the courts—which have operated within a limited range of available remedies, and in the limited context of case law rather than of statutory law. I propose that the Congress now accept the responsibility and use the authority given to it under the 14th Amendment to clear up the confusion which contradictory court orders have created, and to establish reasonable national standards.

The legislation I propose today would accomplish this.

It would put an immediate stop to further new busing orders by the Federal courts.

It would enlist the wisdom, the resources and the experience of the Congress in the solution of the vexing problems involved in fashioning school desegregation policies that are true to the Constitutional requirements and fair to the people and communities concerned.

It would establish uniform national criteria, to ensure that the Federal courts in all sections and all States would have a common set of standards to guide them.

These measures would protect the right of a community to maintain neighborhood schools while also establishing a shared local and Federal responsibility to raise the level of education in the neediest neighborhoods, with special programs for those disadvantaged children who need special attention.

At the same time, these measures would not roll back the Constitution, or undo the great advances that have been made in ending school segregation, or undermine the continuing drive for equal rights.

Specifically, I propose . . .

The Student Transportation Moratorium Act of 1972. This would provide a period of time during which any future, new busing orders by the courts would not go into effect, while the Congress considered legislative approaches—such as the Equal Educational Opportunities Act—to the questions raised by school desegregation cases. This moratorium on new busing would be effective until July 1, 1973, or until the Congress passed the appropriate legislation, whichever was sooner. Its purpose would not be to contravene rights under the 14th Amendment, but simply to hold in abeyance further busing orders while the Congress investigated and considered alternative methods of securing those rights—methods that could establish a new and broader context in which the courts could decide desegregation cases, and that could render busing orders unnecessary.

Together, these two measures would provide an immediate stop to new busing in the short run, and constructive alternatives to busing in the long run—and they would give the Congress the time it needs to consider fully and fairly one of the most complex and difficult issues to confront the Nation in modern times.

THE STUDENT TRANSPORTATION MORATORIUM ACT

In times of rapid and even headlong change, there occasionally is an urgent need for reflection and reassessment. This is especially true when powerful, historic forces are moving the Nation toward a conflict of fundamental principles—a conflict that can be avoided if each of us does his share, and if all branches of Government will join in helping to redefine the questions before us.

Like any comprehensive legislative recommendations, the Equal Educational Opportunities Act that I have proposed today is offered as a framework for Congressional debate and action.

The Congress has both the Constitutional authority and a special capability to debate and define new methods for implementing Constitutional principles. And the educational, financial and social complexities of this issue are not, and are not properly, susceptible of solution by individual courts alone or even by the Supreme Court alone.

This is a moment of considerable conflict and uncertainty: but it is also a moment of great opportunity.

This is not a time for the courts to plunge ahead at full speed.

If we are to set a course that enables us to act together, and not simply to do more but to do better, then we must do all in our power to create an atmosphere that permits a calm and thoughtful assessment of the issues, choices and consequences.

I propose, therefore, that the Congress act to impose a temporary freeze on new busing orders by the Federal courts—to establish a waiting period while the Congress considers alternative means of enforcing 14th Amendment rights. I propose that this freeze be effective immediately on enactment, and that it remain in effect until July 1, 1973, or until passage of the appropriate legislation, whichever is sooner.

This freeze would not put a stop to desegregation cases; it would only bar new orders during its effective period, to the extent that they ordered new busing.

This, I recognize, is an unusual procedure. But I am persuaded that the Congress has the Constitutional power to enact such a stay, and I believe the unusual nature of the conflicts and pressures that confront both the courts and the country at this particular time requires it.

It has become abundantly clear, from the debates in the Congress and from the upwelling of sentiment throughout the country, that some action will be taken to limit the scope of busing orders. It is in the interest of everyone—black and white, children and parents, school administrators and local officials, the courts, the Congress and the executive branch, and not least in the interest of consistency in Federal policy, that while this matter is being considered by the Congress we not speed further along a course that is likely to be changed.

The legislation I have proposed would provide the courts with a new set of standards and criteria that would enable them to enforce the basic Constitutional guarantees in different ways.

A stay would relieve the pressure on the Congress to act on the long-range legislation without full and adequate consideration. By providing immediate relief from a course that increasing millions of Americans are finding intolerable, it would allow the debate on permanent solutions to proceed with less emotion and more reason.

For these reasons and also for the sake of the additional children faced with busing now I urge that the Congress quickly give its approval to the Student Transportation Moratorium Act.

No message to the Congress of school desegregation would be complete unless it addressed the question of a Constitutional amendment.

There are now a number of proposals before the Congress, with strong support, to amend the Constitution in ways designed to abolish busing or to bar the coutrs from ordering it.

These proposals should continue to receive the particularly thoughtful and careful consideration by the Congress that any proposal to amend the Constitution merits.

It is important to recognize, however, that a Constitutional amendment—even if it could secure the necessary two-thirds support in both Houses of the Congress—has a serious flaw: it would have no impact this year; it would not come into effect until after the long process of ratification by three-fourths of the State legislatures. What is needed is action now; a Constitutional amendment fails to meet this immediate need.

Legislation meets the problem now. Therefore, I recommend that as its first priority the Congress go forward immediately on the legislative route. Legislation can also treat the question with far greater precision and detail than could the necessarily generalized language of a Constitutional amendment, while making possible a balanced, comprehensive approach to equal educational opportunity.

The Supreme Court and Judicial Review: Performance

An examination of the cases in which the Supreme Court has held *federal* legislation unconstitutional leads to a number of observations.

The Uncertain Line Between Policy and Constitutionality

To begin with, the boundary between decisions about *policy* and decisions about *constitutionality* has proved a difficult one for the Court to discover and abide by. Since the Court's claim to legitimacy rests on the validity of this distinction, it is always at pains to insist that its decisions are made purely on constitutional grounds and have nothing to do with the views the justices may hold on matters of public policy. The record, however, suggests otherwise. In an earlier day it was perhaps easier to believe that the Constitution is so clear and certain rights are so natural and self-evident that their fundamental validity is as much a matter of definite knowledge, at least to all reasonable creatures, as the color of a ripe cherry. But today we know that the line between abstract right and policy is extremely hard to draw. A court can and does make policy decisions by going outside established 'legal' criteria found in precedent, statute, and Constitution. In this respect the Supreme Court occupies a most peculiar position, for it is an essential characteristic of the institution that from time to time its members decide cases where constitutional criteria are not adequate in any realistic sense to the task. The distinguished legal scholar and member of the Court, the late Mr.

Justice Frankfurter, once described the business of the Supreme Court in these words:

> It is essentially accurate to say that the Court's preoccupation today is with the application of rather fundamental aspirations and what Judge Learned Hand calls "moods," embodied in provisions like the due process clauses, which were designed not to be precise and positive directions for rules of action. The judicial process in applying them involves a judgment . . . that is, on the views of the direct representatives of the people in meeting the needs of society, on the views of Presidents and Governors, and by their construction of the will of legislatures the Court breathes life, feeble or strong, into the inert pages of the Constitution and the statute books.[1]

Very often, then, the cases before the Court involve alternatives about which there is severe disagreement in the society, as in the case of segregation or economic regulation; the very setting of the case is, then, 'political.' Moreover, these are usually cases where competent students of constitutional law, including the learned justices of the Supreme Court themselves, disagree; where the words of the Constitution are general, vague, ambiguous, or not clearly applicable; where precedent may be found on both sides; and where experts differ in predicting the consequences of the various alternatives or the degree of probability that the possible consequences will actually ensue.

If the Court were assumed to be a 'political' institution, no particular problems would arise, for it would be taken for granted that the members of the Court would resolve questions of fact and value by introducing assumptions derived from their own predispositions or those of influential clienteles and constituents. However, since much of the legitimacy of the Court's decisions rests upon the belief that it is not a political institution but exclusively a legal one, to accept the Court as a political institution would solve one set of problems at the price of creating another. Nonetheless, if it is true that the nature of the cases arriving before the Court is sometimes of the kind I have described, then the Court cannot act strictly as a legal institution. It must, that is to say, choose among controversial

1. Justice Felix Frankfurter, "The Supreme Court in the Mirror of Justices," *University of Pennsylvania Law Review*, 105 (April, 1957) 781–796, at p. 793.

alternatives of public policy by appealing to at least some criteria of acceptability on questions of fact and value that cannot be found in or deduced from precedent, statute, and Constitution.

Court versus Congress and President: Minor Victories

A second conclusion to emerge from the record is that the Court rarely wins its battles with the president and Congress on matters of *major* policy, particularly if successive presidents and Congresses continue to support the policy the Court has called unconstitutional. The Court wins skirmishes; in a long war it may win a battle; it does not win continuing wars with Congress. On this point the evidence is overwhelming:

Court versus past Congresses. More than half the decisions in holding federal acts unconstitutional were decided by the Supreme Court more than four years after the legislation was enacted. Thus the Court frequently does not confront *current* legislative majorities so much as past majorities.

Court versus current Congresses. Where the Court confronts the major policies of a current president and Congress, it nearly always loses. In about two-thirds of the cases involving major policies of current law-making majorities, the Court's decision has, in effect, been reversed by congressional action—often simply by rewriting the law. Dramatic evidence is provided by twelve decisions in which a Supreme Court controlled by a conservative majority declared various aspects of FDR's New Deal unconstitutional. Of these, four involved trivial or minor policies. One involved a major New Deal policy contrivance, the NRA; it seems fair to say, however, that President Roosevelt and his advisers were relieved by the Court's decision of a policy that they had come to find increasingly embarrassing. In view of the tenacity with which FDR held to his major program, there can hardly be any doubt that, had he wanted to pursue the policy objective involved in the NRA codes, as he did for example with the labor provisions, he would not have been stopped by the Court's special theory of the Constitution. As to the seven other cases, whatever some of the eminent justices might have thought during their fleeting moments of glory, they did not succeed in interposing a barrier to the achievement of the objectives of the legislation; and in a few years most of the constitutional dogma on which they rested their opposition to the New Deal had been unceremoniously swept under the rug.

Court versus Congress and President: Major Delays

Nonetheless, although the Court loses most of its battles against a persistent president and Congress, the fact is that on some matters it has delayed policies for more than a decade and even more than a generation. What is more, if the views that finally prevailed on the Court are correct, then its lengthy obstruction had no proper constitutional basis. For example:

Workmen's compensation. A congressional act requiring employers to compensate longshoremen and harbor workers injured on the job was invalidated by the Supreme Court in 1920. In 1922, Congress passed a new law which was, in its turn, knocked down by the Court in 1924. In 1927 Congress passed a third law, which was finally upheld in 1932. Thus the Court delayed workmen's compensation for twelve years.

Child labor. Two child labor cases represent the most effective battle ever waged by the Court against legislative policy-makers. The original legislation outlawing child labor, based on the commerce clause, was passed in 1916 as part of Wilson's New Freedom. Like Franklin Roosevelt later, Wilson was somewhat unlucky in his Supreme Court appointments; he made only three appointments during his eight years, and one of these was wasted, from a policy point of view, on Mr. Justice McReynolds. Had McReynolds voted 'right,' the subsequent struggle over the problem of child labor need not have occurred, for the decision in 1918 was by a Court divided five to four, McReynolds voting with the majority. Congress moved at once to circumvent the decision by means of tax power, but in 1922 the Court blocked that approach. In 1924, Congress returned to the engagement with a constitutional amendment that was rapidly endorsed by a number of state legislatures before it began to meet so much resistance in the states remaining that the enterprise miscarried. In 1938, under a second reformist president, new legislation was passed twenty-two years after the first; thus a Court with a New Deal majority finally accepted child labor legislation in 1941, and thereby brought to an end a battle that had lasted a full quarter-century.

Bastion of Minority Rights?

It might be thought, nonetheless, that the Court has had a splendid record in protecting the fundamental rights of otherwise defenseless minorities against encroachment by the president and Congress. In this view of the Court's role we would expect to find a considerable number of important cases in which the justices have declared laws passed by Congress or orders of the president unconstitutional on the ground that they impaired the rights of citizens granted by the first ten amendments (the Bill of Rights). In fact, however, on this score the record of the Supreme Court over its *whole* history is remarkably unimpressive. For it is only recently that the Court has done much to protect minority rights—or at any rate the rights of otherwise weak or defenseless minorities:

(1) There have been only two cases, both in the 1960s, in which the Court has ever held a provision of federal law unconstitutional as contrary to the fundamental liberties of religion, speech, press, and assembly guaranteed by the First Amendment. Both cases involved federal legislation directed toward alleged Communists.[2]

(2) In about ten cases, the Court has held congressional acts unconstitutional because they violated other provisions of the Bill of Rights, chiefly Amendments Four to Seven, and the Fourteenth Amendment. With the exception of several recent cases, an inspection of the issues in all the earlier cases indicates that the lawmakers

2. In 1965 in *Lamont* v. *Postmaster General* and *Fixa* v. *Heilberg* the Supreme Court struck down a provision of a comprehensive postal law passed in 1962 which required that "Communist political propaganda" must be withheld by the Post Office unless the addressee requested delivery. The Court held that the requirement infringed on the addressee's freedom of speech. In 1967 in *U.S.* v. *Robel* the Court in a 6-2 ruling held unconstitutional a provision of the Subversive Activities Control Act of 1950 that barred members of Communist action organizations from employment in defense facilities. Speaking for the Court, Chief Justice Earl Warren said that the provision was "an unconstitutional abridgment of the right of association protected by the First Amendment." He also noted, however, that nothing in the holding would "deny Congress the power under narrowly drawn legislation to keep from sensitive positions in defense facilities those who would use their positions to disrupt the nation's production facilities."

and the Court were not very far apart. Moreover, the issues were mainly of such a minor sort that it is doubtful whether the fundamental conditions of liberty in this country were altered by more than a hair's breadth as a result. In several recent decisions, however, the Court has denied validity to congressional acts limiting the freedom of unpopular political minorities, particularly Communists.[3]

(3) Over against these decisions we must put the fifteen or so cases in which the Court used the protections of the Fifth, Thirteenth, Fourteenth, and Fifteenth Amendments to preserve the rights and liberties of a relatively privileged group at the expense of the rights and liberties of a submerged group: chiefly slaveholders at the expense of slaves,[4] white people at the expense of nonwhites,[5] and property holders at the expense of wage earners and other groups. These cases, unlike some of the relatively innocuous ones previously discussed, all involved liberties of genuinely fundamental importance, where an opposite policy would have meant thoroughly basic shifts in the distribution of rights, liberties, and opportunities in the United States—where, moreover, the policies sustained by the Court's action have since been repudiated in every civilized nation of the Western world, including our own.

Protector of National Polyarchy Against State and Local Attacks

As our dialogue in the last chapter suggested, the problem of judicial

3. Thus in 1965, in *Albertson* v. *Subversive Activities Control Board,* a unanimous Court held that members of the Communist party of the United States could not be required to register as such with the Justice Department under provisions of the Subversive Activities Control Act. The requirement was held to violate the members' right against self-incrimination protected by the Fifth Amendment. In 1967, the Circuit Court of Appeals for the District of Columbia held unconstitutional on the same grounds a provision of the Act requiring party officers to register. The Justice Department did not appeal the ruling and thus its sixteen-year effort to enforce these provisions ended in total failure.

4. *Dred Scott* v. *Sandford,* 19 How. (U.S.) 393 (1857).

5. *United States* v. *Reese,* 92 U.S. 214 (1876); *United States* v. *Harris,* 106 U.S. 629 (1883); *United States* v. *Stanley* (Civil Rights Cases), 109 U.S. 3 (1883); *Baldwin* v. *Franks,* 120 U.S. 678 (1887); *James* v. *Bowman* 190, U.S. 127 (1903); *Hodges* v. *United States,* 203 U.S. 1 (1906); *Butts* v. *Merchants & Miners Transportation Co.,* 230 U.S. 126 (1913).

review from a democratic perspective arises in its most acute form with respect to *federal* legislation, not state and local actions. In the domain of state and local actions the record of the Court, although uneven over its whole history, in this century has been increasingly closer to the model suggested in the last chapter of protector of the national polyarchy. In innumerable cases it has declared unconstitutional state or local laws, practices, and actions held to infringe on fundamental rights guaranteed by the Constitution;[6] it has markedly enlarged the scope of those rights;[7] since the failure of a last-ditch conservative Court to halt the New Deal, the Court has provided a constitutional foundation for the vast new national powers employed by all subsequent administrations in behalf of their programs; and the Court has imposed the principle of one man, one vote on unwilling legislative bodies.

THE COURT AS A POLITICAL INSTITUTION

How can we explain the behavior of the Court over the long run? Why does it have such a spotty record as protector of the national polyarchy? Why has it moved more sharply in this direction in recent years, particularly against incursions by state and local governments? A large part of the answer lies in the fact that the Supreme Court is inescapably a participant in the larger political process of the American polyarchy.

6. For example, in *Julian Bond* v. *James "Sloppy" Floyd* (1966) a unanimous Court held that Julian Bond's exclusion from the Georgia House because of his statements against the war in Vietnam violated the First Amendment. In *Bachellar* v. *State of Maryland* a unanimous Court held that where it was impossible to determine whether convictions for disorderly conduct in blocking a public sidewalk resulted from the unpopular views of the defendants (they were arrested during a demonstration against the war in Vietnam), the convictions violated the First Amendment and must be reversed.
7. For example, in *Goldberg* v. *Kelly* (1970) by a vote of 5–3 the Court held that a welfare recipient was denied due process under the Fourteenth Amendment because his public assistance payments were terminated with no opportunity for him to have a hearing. In *Pickering* v. *Board of Education* (1968) the Court unanimously held that a public school teacher may not be dismissed for criticizing the school board unless the criticism is knowingly or recklessly false.

Part of the Dominant Coalition

National politics in the United States, as in other stable polyarchies, is dominated by relatively cohesive alliances that endure for long periods of time. One recalls the Jeffersonian alliance, the Jacksonian, the extraordinarily long-lived Republican dominance of the post–Civil War years, and the New Deal alliance shaped by Franklin Roosevelt. Each is marked by a break with past policies, a period of intense struggle, followed by consolidation, and finally decay and disintegration of the alliance.

Except for short-lived transitional periods when the old alliance is disintegrated and the new one is struggling to take control of political institutions, the Supreme Court is inevitably a part of the dominant national alliance. It becomes so for an exceedingly simple reason: the eminent justices of the United States Supreme Court are mortal. They grow old. Sooner or later they retire or die. As they leave the Court new justices acceptable to the current coalition take their place.

Over the whole history of the Court, one new justice has been appointed on the average of every twenty-three months. Thus a president can expect to appoint two new justices during one term of office; and if this were not enough to tip the balance on a normally divided Court, he would be almost certain to succeed in two terms. For example, Hoover made three appointments; Roosevelt, nine; Truman, four; Eisenhower, five; Kennedy in his brief tenure, two. Presidents are not famous for appointing justices hostile to their own views on public policy; nor could they expect to secure confirmation of a man whose stance on key questions was flagrantly at odds with that of the dominant majority in the Senate. When Nixon violated this assumption in 1970 by his attempt to appoint first Clement Haynsworth and then George Carswell, he was twice defeated. Typically, justices are men who, prior to appointment, have engaged in public life and have committed themselves publicly on the great questions of the day. As the late Mr. Justice Frankfurter pointed out, a surprisingly large proportion of the justices, particularly of the great justices who have left their stamp upon the decisions of the Court, have had little or no prior judicial experience.

Nor have the justices—certainly not the great justices—been timid men with a passion for anonymity. Indeed, it is not too much to say that if justices were appointed primarily for their 'judicial' qualities without regard to their basic attitudes on fundamental questions of public policy, the Court could not play the influential role in the American political system that it does in reality.

It is reasonable to conclude, then, that the policy views dominant on the Court will never be out of line for very long with the policy views dominant among the law-making majorities of the United States. And it would be most unrealistic to suppose that the Court would, for more than a few years at most, stand against any major alternatives sought by a law-making majority. The judicial agonies of the New Deal will, of course, come quickly to mind; but President Franklin D. Roosevelt's difficulties with the Court were truly exceptional. Generalizing over the whole history of the Court, one can say that the chances are about two out of five that a president will make one appointment to the Court in less than a year, two out of three that he will make one within two years, and three out of four that he will make one within three years. President Roosevelt had unusually bad luck: he had to wait four years for his first appointment; the odds against this long interval are about five to one. With average luck, his battle with the Court would never have occurred; even as it was, although his 'court-packing' proposal did formally fail, by the end of his second term in 1940 Roosevelt had appointed five new justices and he gained three more the following year.

As an element in the leadership of the dominant alliance, the Court tends to support the major policies of the alliance. Acting solely by itself with no support from the president and Congress, the Court is almost powerless to affect the course of national policy.

The Supreme Court is not, however, simply an *agent* of the alliance. It is an essential part of the political leadership and possesses some bases of power of its own, the most important of which is the unique legitimacy attributed to its interpretations of the Constitution. This legitimacy the Court jeopardizes if it flagrantly opposes the major policies of the dominant alliance; such a course of action, as we have seen, is one in which the Court will not normally be tempted to engage.

It follows that within the somewhat narrow limits set by the basic policy goals of the dominant alliance, the Court *can* sometimes make national policy. Its discretion, then, is not unlike that of a powerful committee chairman in Congress who cannot, generally speaking, nullify the basic policies substantially agreed on by the rest of the dominant leadership, but who can, within these limits, often determine important questions of timing, effectiveness, and subordinate policy. Thus the Court is least effective against a current law-making majority—and evidently least inclined to act. It is most effective when it sets the bounds of policy for officials, agencies, state governments, or even regions, a task that has come to occupy a very large part of the Court's business.[8]

The main objective of presidential leadership is to build a stable and dominant aggregation of minorities with a high probability of winning the presidency and one or both houses of Congress. Ordinarily the main contribution of the Court is to confer legitimacy on the fundamental policies of the successful coalition.

But if this were the only function of the Supreme Court, would it have acquired the standing it has among Americans? In fact, at its best—and the Court is not always at its best—it does more than merely confer legitimacy on the dominant national coalition. For one thing, by the way it interprets and modifies national laws, perhaps but not necessarily by holding them unconstitutional, the Supreme Court sometimes serves as a guide and even a pioneer in arriving at different standards of fair play and individual right than have resulted, or are likely to result, from the interplay of the other political forces. Thus in recent years, as we have seen, the Court has modified by interpretation or declared unconstitutional provisions of federal law restricting the rights of unpopular and even widely detested minorities—military deserters, Communists, and alleged bootleggers, for example. The judges, after all, inherit an ancient tradition and an acknowledged role in setting higher standards of justice and right

8. "Constitutional law and cases with constitutional undertones are of course still very important, with almost one-fourth of the cases in which written opinions were filed (in recent years) involving such questions. Review of administrative action... constitutes the largest category of the Court's work, comprising one-third of the total cases decided on the merits. The remaining ... categories of litigation ... all involve largely public law questions" (Frankfurter, "The Supreme Court in the Mirror of Justices," p. 793).

than the majority of citizens or their representatives might otherwise demand. If the standards of justice propounded by the Court are to prevail, for reasons we have already examined they cannot be too remote from general standards of fairness and individual right among Americans; but, though some citizens may protest, most Americans are too attached to the Court to want it stripped of its power.

There are times, too, when the other political forces are too divided to arrive at decisions on certain key questions. At very great risk, the Court can intervene in such cases; and sometimes it may even succeed in establishing policy where the president and Congress are unable to do so. Probably in such cases it can succeed only if its action conforms to a widespread set of explicit or implicit norms held by the political leadership: norms which are not strong enough or are not distributed in such a way as to insure the existence of an effective law-making majority but are nonetheless sufficiently powerful to prevent any successful attack on the legitimacy and power of the Court. This is probably the explanation for the relatively successful work of the Court in enlarging the freedom of Negroes to vote during the past three decades, in its famous school integration decisions, and the reapportionment cases.

Legitimizers

Yet the Court does even more than this. Considered as a political system, polyarchy is a set of basic procedures for arriving at decisions. The operation of these procedures presupposes the existence of certain rights, obligations; liberties, and restraints; in short, certain patterns of behavior. The existence of these patterns of behavior in turn presupposes widespread agreement (particularly among the politically active and influential segments of the population) on the validity and propriety of the behavior. Although its record is by no means lacking in serious blemishes, at its best the Court operates to confer legitimacy, not simply on the particular and parochial policies of the dominant political alliance, but upon the basic patterns of behavior required for the operation of a polyarchy.

Yet in order to *confer* legitimacy, the Court must itself *possess* legitimacy. To the extent that the legitimacy of every political institution in the American polyarchy depends finally on its consistency with democratic principle, the legitimacy of judicial review and the

Court's exercise of that power must stem from the presumption that the Court is ultimately subject to popular control. The more the Court exercises self-restraint and the less it challenges the policies of law-making majorities, the less the need or the impulse to subject it to popular controls. The more active the Court is in contesting the policies of law-making majorities, the more visible becomes the slender basis of its legitimacy by democratic standards, and the greater the efforts will be to bring the Court's policies into conformity with those enacted by law-making majorities.

If the persistent temper of a dominant coalition is to use the Court as a privileged interest group or a protector of privileged interest groups, as in the period after the Civil War, no Court can long persist as protector of the national polyarchy. By yielding—and aging, retirement, and death make yielding ineluctable—the Court may gain the confidence and respect of the coalition's leaders in the White House and Congress. Yet it will lose the confidence and respect of those who search for its legitimacy in democratic principles. And at the next swing of the political pendulum, the Court may well find that it has impaired its own legitimacy.

Where the dominant coalition is prepared to allow or even encourage the Court to act as defender of the national polyarchy, the Court will gain in such legitimacy as it may draw from democratic principles. Yet in such periods, as in the others, the Court will rarely find it necessary to nullify any major policies of the dominant political coalition. Even as defender of the national polyarchy, then, its victories against the president and Congress are likely to be rare and transitory. Thus in this role—and it is hard to find grounds for legitimacy in any other—it will serve mainly as an arbiter in the federal system, protecting the fundamental requisites of polyarchy against incursions by minorities in states and localities. Although it has not always played this role well, and at times not even at all, it has probably performed better in recent decades than throughout most of its previous history.

In the end, however, we must not lose sight of the fact that the Court's power of judicial review over *national* legislation is, at best, an exceedingly weak guarantee of polyarchy in the United States. At its worst, the Court's power of judicial review has no claim to legitimacy according to democratic criteria.

SUMMARY

An examination of the performance of the Supreme Court in the actual cases in which it has declared federal laws unconstitutional indicates that:

(1) The line between decisions about the wisdom of policy and decisions about constitutionality has been a difficult one for the Court to discover and abide by.

(2) The Court has rarely succeeded in using judicial review to prevent the president and Congress from gaining any major policies on which they agree.

(3) However, in some instances the Court has delayed reforms for a decade or more. These include such matters as workmen's compensation and the abolition of child labor, which the Court finally accepted as constitutionally valid.

(4) Until recently, the Court has not made a significant contribution as protector of the rights of otherwise weak or defenseless minorities against incursions by the federal government.

(5) However, through judicial review the Court has made an important contribution, particularly in recent decades, as protector of the national polyarchy against encroachment by state and local governments.

These aspects of the Court's performance are largely to be explained as follows:

(1) Because members of the Court inevitably age, they retire or die and are replaced by new appointees.

(2) In making appointments, the president and Senate pay attention not only to the constitutional views of the candidate but also to the implications of his views or record for matters of public policy.

(3) Thus if a coalition persists for some time in controlling the presidency and Congress, it is certain to gain a majority of members of the Court who are sympathetic with the general policy views and goals of the dominant coalition.

(4) The extent to which the Court is, at the one extreme, a privileged interest group or, at the other, a defender of the national polyarchy depends, then, largely on the mood, temper, and outlook of the dominant forces in the presidency and the Congress.

(5) For this reason, the Court's power of judicial review over national legislation appears to be a rather weak guarantee of polyarchy.

According to traditional theories of formal organizational structure, when a superior issues a command it is expected that the order will be carried out by those below speedily and faithfully. Present-day experience, however, seems to indicate that this theory does not hold much water. Even the tightest organization, wherein ultimate authority formally resides in a single person (e.g., the President), there are great discrepancies between what the superior says he wants done and what even his most loyal subordinates actually do. This is essentially what Richard Neustadt means when he says that there are few "self-executing" Presidential orders.[1] In point of fact, present-day observers of organizations are now convinced that many factors must converge before rules, orders, edicts, fiats, commands, and the like are obeyed with strict or even substantially close adherence to the manifest intent of the man on top.

Traditional theory also has it that when the Supreme Court sneezes, lesser courts jump. In other words, the traditional theory on constitutional hierarchical relationships was at least as, if not more, rigid than theory on all other organizations. Indeed, this assumption of lower court lock-step compliance still serves as a central pillar for the anachronistic but persistent practice of many political scientists to describe (with loving detail) what the Supreme Court says, i.e., the field of "Constitutional Law"—and stopping there. The assumption remains that what the Court wills has everything to do with

1. Richard Neustadt, *Presidential Power* (New York: Wiley & Sons, 1960).

subsequent lower court realities despite the fact that modern organizational theories, modern theories on inter-court relations, and a
multitude of myth-shattering events of our recent past have raised
serious doubts about the validity of this, the most durable of formal
organizational theories.

Jack Peltason was the first "new breed" political scientist to go
about observing the impact of the Supreme Court's decision on lower
courts. In 1954 he had this to say:

> Defeated by the Supreme Court, the adversely affected interests
> can regain victory in the lower courts. The Supreme Court normally
> returns cases to trial judges via the intermediate appellate tribunals.
> It is these trial judges who have to interpret and apply the Supreme
> Court decisions, and they can do so in order to minimize the sig-
> nificance of their superior's orders. Between 1941 and 1951 out of
> 175 cases which the Supreme Court reversed and remanded to state
> tribunals there were forty-six cases involving further litigation. "In
> slightly less than half of these cases the party successful in the
> Supreme Court was unsuccessful in the state court following the
> remand." Thus even for the immediate parties, a Supreme Court
> victory is not cause for too much celebration. As between the
> interests, Supreme Court victory for one hardly means that the
> other lost the war.[2]

Some time later, Peltason focused his research on the federal judiciary of the South to see their reaction to the school desegregation
decisions of the Supreme Court.[3] What he saw prompted him to call
the resulting book, most aptly, *Fifty-eight Lonely Men*.[4]

At that time, the Supreme Court ordered that Southern school
officials desegregate their educational facilities with "all deliberate
speed." It became immediately incumbent on federal judges to determine the reasonableness of a gaggle of integration programs drummed
up by Southern officialdom, most of which were designed to coddle
age-old segregation practices. Some fourteen years later, published

2. Jack Peltason, *The Federal Courts in the Political Process* (New York:
Doubleday, 1955), p. 60.
3. In particular, of course, *Brown v. Board of Education* 347 U.S. 483 (1954).
4. *Fifty-eight Lonely Men* (New York: Harcourt, Brace & World, 1961).
See also, Leon Friedman (ed.), *Southern Justice* (New York: Pantheon, 1965).

statistics revealed that less than 3 per cent of Southern schools could in any way be classified as desegregated. One wag put it this way: "The Supreme Court got little speed and much deliberation." It was a way of saying what Peltason found out: the Court's mandate was really so vague, and gave the lower court judges so much discretion, that they could make decisions that were far more consistent with their own anti-integration attitudes and the like-minded social and political mores that prevailed in their own local communities than with the Court's highly publicized intentions. In effect, the Court was its own undoing; a man will not bring undue hardship upon himself and his family if he does not have to—even if he is a federal district court judge.

Generally speaking, the ambiguity of the command, the proximity of a subordinate to strong community pressures, and his preferences (personal attitudes) will influence execution. This seems to apply to trial judges as much as it does to the lower-echelon bureaucrat— though there may well be differences as yet unearthed. Peltason also found that as any of these factors might vary, so might the effective application of the Court's mandate. For instance, the Court of Appeals judges, also home-grown products of Southern culture, followed the Supreme Court far more assiduously than did their federal district court counterparts. One reason for this might have been that a circuit court is far better insulated from local pressures; few circuit judges hail from the seat where their court sits. As the influence of local pressures diminishes, it becomes less risky for the lower court judge to defer to the intent expressed in a highly provocative Supreme Court decision.

There have been some other highly insightful works on the impact of a Supreme Court decision on lower court judges. Two of them follow. Walter Murphy's article on "lower court checks" supplements Peltason's work by revealing an even wider variety of available methods by which *federal* judges can resist the Court's manifest desires. Moreover, Murphy describes a plentitude of options open to judges of *state* courts should they disagree also with the Court's constitutional interpretations or policy goals. Kenneth Vines elaborates on how "extra-legal factors" closely relate to highly disparate lower court decisions that are applying (supposedly) the same law (the Supreme Court decision). His work offers statistical support for

Peltason's thesis and covers all aspects of race relations, not simply that of school integration.

Thus, the Murphy and Vines articles embellish the modern theme that attitudes and strategies are as equally operant at lower court levels as they are in the Supreme Court itself. They present an intricate elaboration of how the Supreme Court cannot be said to control the lower courts and, indeed, the impact of the Supreme Court decision on lower courts now appears as intriguingly varied as it is on other governmental agencies. These essays illustrate why traditional court-hierarchy theory must look increasingly shopworn even to those who have treasured it most dearly.

Richard Neustadt has observed that the most severe limits on the President are the inherited commitments placed on him by previous officeholders, Congressional mandates, international agreements, and by other officials who share the government's power with him. In short, even a President is a prisoner of his role, history, and other political actors. Despite occupying the top executive office of the most powerful nation in the world, his options for action are severely limited. Presidents, like so many of us, frequently have to rely on indirect, slow, and incremental practices in order to get their way. Sometimes they succeed. Sometimes they do not.

The Supreme Court occupies a parallel position. The very life and language of the law are tied to the principle of *stare decisis,* the policy requiring judicial decisions to be directly derived from established precedent. In its extreme form, the traditional view of the judicial process is that the judge "finds the law" and never "makes it." But Supreme Court justices, like Presidents, do have strong views on public policy, and like Presidents they want to see them written into law as well. Also, like Presidents, they have a number of methods which allow them to ignore, modify, or dispose of previous commitments in order to get their way.

Two techniques which allow judges to overcome precedent are the *overruling* and *distinguishing* of cases. In the former, the Court explicitly states that a previous decision, which should be a controlling precedent, is an unwise or outmoded decision, and as a consequence no longer represents a decision to which the Court should be bound. Invariably this *overruled* decision is characterized as a past "error" which the present Court is "correcting" in order to set things right again. This technique, however, is a *direct* challenge to the law and must be used sparingly in that its use undermines the image of judges as objective finders and appliers of The Law. On the other hand, in distinguishing a case, all the Court must do is demonstrate that the controversy before it is significantly unlike any prior case and therefore the precedent of a prior case need not be applied in the present decision. By interpreting precedents either narrowly or broadly, the Court has considerable leeway in which to elude their grasp and strike out on a new course far more to its personal liking. This technique has the advantage of maintaining a formal adherence to precedent while at the same time ignoring or crippling it in fact.

The Supreme Court opinion reprinted in this section, *Harris v. New York,*[5] is a perfect illustration of the Court's *distinguishing* a past decision that a present majority thinks unwise. The past decision was the Warren Court's 1965 decision, *Miranda v. Arizona.*[6] The minority in the *Harris* case, it might be noted, was part of the earlier Warren Court majority in *Miranda.* This case might also be included as evidence of a President's impact on Supreme Court decision-making. Richard Nixon promised in the 1968 campaign that he would do his best to make the Court more responsive to "law and order" if elected. This is one clear instance of a President keeping his promise—and in double time.

* * *

5. 401 U.S. 222 (1971).
6. 384 U.S. 436 (1966).

WALTER F. MURPHY

Lower Court Checks on Supreme Court Power

Practicing politicians as well as students of politics have long recognized the check on presidential power imposed by the federal administrative machinery. High policy must be interpreted; it can sometimes be changed or even frustrated by the bureaucrats who apply laws and executive orders. Officials down the line have interests, loyalties, and ambitions which go beyond and often clash with the allegiance accorded a given tenant of the White House. Each bureaucrat has his own ideas about proper public policy, particularly in his field of special competence. If a career civil servant, he may identify only partially, if at all, the good of the governmental service, not to say the good of the public, with the ends sought by the Administration. And if he owes his appointment or promotion to other sources than the merit system, he may find a positive conflict between his loyalties to the President and to other politicians or political groups.

This conflict can occur at all administrative levels. Cabinet members may make up the President's official family, but some of them are at times his chief rivals for power within his own political party, or, more often, representatives of those rivals. Or the department heads may be so split with sibling political rivalry among themselves that common loyalty to their nominal leader may be subordinated to other values. An observer has lately written: "The conditions which a system of fragmented power sets for the success and the survival of a Cabinet officer encourage him to consolidate his own nexus of

From *The American Political Science Review,* 53 (Dec. 1959), pp. 1017–31. Reprinted by permission of the publisher and the author.

Walter F. Murphy is Professor of Politics at Princeton University and has been Chairman of the Department of Politics at Princeton since 1966.

power and compel him to operate with a degree of independence from the President." [1]

Internal friction or drag is is thus an inherent part of the executive process, a factor to be weighed in choosing among policy alternatives, much the same as congressional, or judicial, or pressure group resistance. Less obviously, but not necessarily less significantly, a similar bureaucratic factor must be reckoned with in the execution of Supreme Court decisions. Except in disputes between states or the rare litigation involving diplomats, the Supreme Court usually does not render either the initial or the final decision in a case. If it reverses a state decision, the Court remands the case to state courts for disposition "not inconsistent with this opinion"; and it frequently gives only slightly more precise directions in overruling federal tribunals. The Supreme Court typically formulates general policy. Lower courts apply that policy, and working in its interstices, inferior judges may materially modify the High Court's determinations.

I

As might be expected, state judges have a wider field in which to operate. Two technical rules help to enlarge their area of discretion. The first, already mentioned, is the vague criteria which the Supreme Court imposes when it overturns a state decision. Second, the Supreme Court will review only those state cases which were based on a substantial federal question. The Court has reiterated time and again its practice of not reviewing state decisions which have sufficient independent grounding in state law so that a reversal of the determinations of federal issues would not affect the final outcome of the case. . . .

Considering the perennial friction between state and national interests and outlooks, the different elements weighed in the appointment of state and federal judges, their allegiances (former if not current) to opposing political parties or to separate levels of party

1. Richard F. Fenno, Jr., "President-Cabinet Relations: A Pattern and a Case Study," *American Political Science Review* 52 (1958), pp. 388, 404. (Italics in original omitted.)

hierarchy, the different ambitions of the judges, and their varying conceptions of the role of the judiciary in a federal and democratic system, the wonder is that occasions of open conflict are the exception rather than the rule. Perhaps the use of the vague remand prescription acts as a psychological safety valve in allowing some of the pressure of resentment against reversal to be siphoned off in construing Supreme Court instructions.[2]

An additional safety valve is criticism of Supreme Court decisions, a practice in which judges who have been reversed engage only slightly less bitterly than disappointed litigants. The most serious recent verbal attack came when the 1958 Conference of State Chief Justices issued a sharp accusation that Justices of the Supreme Court were usurping state judicial power by confusing their own policy views with constitutional commands.[3] The Conference chose to launch this attack at the strategic moment when congressional assaults against the Supreme Court had reached a climax.

Both these devices permit exercise of power as well as escape of pressure. Criticism may persuade the Court of the error of its ways, or help convince Congress of a need for remedial legislation. The interpreting authority may even be stretched to accomplish a *de facto* overturning of Supreme Court decisions. A study published in 1954 reported that in eleven terms, some 46 Supreme Court reversals of state decisions required additional litigation. "In slightly less than half of these cases the party successful in the Supreme Court was unsuccessful in the state court following the remand."[4] This study also indicated that, with one exception,[5] the evasion had been accomplished by interpretation rather than by defiance. For example, when the High Court ruled in 1952 that Oklahoma's loyalty oath violated due process in not distinguishing between knowing and innocent

2. For historical accounts of state court defiance of Supreme Court decisions, see Charles Warren, "Federal and State Court Interference," *Harvard L. Rev.*, Vol. 43, p. 345 (1930); and Note, "Interposition v. Judicial Power," *Race Rel. L. Rep.*, Vol. 1, p. 465 (1956).
3. *Resolutions Adopted at the Tenth Annual Meeting of the Conference of Chief Justices* (Chicago: Council of State Governments, mimeo., 1958).
4. Note, "Congressional Reversal of Supreme Court Decisions, 1945–57," *Harvard L. Rev.* 73 (1958), p. 1324.
5. Ashcraft v. Tennessee, 322 U.S. 143 (1944); 327 U.S. 274 (1946). The intervening Tennessee decisions are unreported.

membership in proscribed organizations,[6] the Oklahoma court in which the case had begun read *scienter* into the state statute and sustained the judicially amended version.[7]

The line between evasion and defiance is always difficult to draw, and when in 1954 the Supreme Court declared Jim Crow legally dead,[8] the attitude of many segregationist state judges shifted perceptibly. Yet the manner in which Southern judicial resistance has been expressed is significant. These judges have criticized the *School Segregation* decisions on and off the bench; they were among the leaders of the movement in the 1958 Conference of State Chief Justices to reprimand the Supreme Court. They have given moral support and, one may guess, perhaps legal advice to Southern political leaders. But when pressed, no state supreme court has yet failed to concede that the School Segregation cases are the law of the land and binding on lower courts. Resistance of state supreme courts (and, though not universally, of state lower courts) has taken three specific forms: (1) refusing to expand the school decision to other areas; (2) upholding the constitutionality of state efforts to evade compliance; and (3), in line with the state chief justices' censure, balking at Supreme Court decisions in related areas of race and of federal-state relations.

*   *   *

II

There are both similarities and differences between the political relations of state courts and lower federal courts to the Supreme Court. Formal state-federal competition is absent, but it is often replaced by a local-national clash which can be almost equally as abrasive. This, in turn, is affected by the varying considerations in appointment of lower and Supreme Court judges. The Executive Department chooses district and, to a lesser extent, circuit judges in close cooperation with senators and national committeemen from the

6. Wieman v. Updegraff, 344 U.S. 183 (1952).
7. The lower court decision is unreported. The details can be found in the follow-up case of the same title, 301 P. 2d 1003 (Sup. Ct. of Okla., 1956).
8. Brown v. Board, 347 U.S. 483 (1954); 349 U.S. 294 (1955).

President's party and occasionally with congressmen from the state
or states involved. Even a senator from the opposition party may
enter the bargaining process. It would not be much of an exaggera-
tion to say, as President Taft once did, that at least as regards district
judges, the President's power is largely one of veto rather than of full
scale appointment.[9]

At the Supreme Court level there are still many political restrictions on the appointing power, but the President can weigh these
competing values on a national rather than on a local scale. Even if
Eisenhower's judicial probation-promotion policy remains in effect,
High Court members are likely to be different types of men from
those usually selected for the lower bench.

When the normal friction between trial and appellate judge is
added to these other factors, a substantial reservoir of potential conflict has been built up. On the other hand, several forces act to soften
this strife. First, and this bond unites federal with state judges as well
as the three levels of federal judges with each other, they are all
participants in the cult of the robe. They share the same holy mys-
teries and dispense the same sacred doctrine. No matter how fierce
their inter-court rivalries, common possession of this magic sets judges
apart from the rest of men and gives them interests and outlooks as
judges. Second, district, circuit, and Supreme Court judges are all
federal officials, in a sense joint competitors, whether they like it or
not, with state judges for power.

The concept of an independent judiciary, which can increase the
number of collisions between state and national tribunals, is balanced
within the national system by appellate court supervision which, if
it does not prevent conflict, does help keep that conflict from coming
out into the open. A state judge owes his appointment to local political groups and can be removed, if at all, only by state action. Federal
district and circuit judges are made even more independent by their
life tenure, but their inferior position in the hierarchical chain of
national authority subjects them to more strict Supreme Court sur-
veillance. Under its power as supervisor of the administration of
federal justice, the Supreme Court can set more exacting standards
for lower courts of the United States than for state tribunals.

9. Quoted in George H. Haynes, *The Senate of the United States: Its History
and Practice* (Boston, 1938), II, 722.

This makes federal court defiance less likely than state, but district and circuit judges are not mere pawns in the judicial game. They sometimes lash out in caustic criticism too. In 1958, for example, the Court of Appeals for the Ninth Circuit reversed the conviction of a pair of communist leaders on the basis of the Supreme Court's narrow interpretations of the Smith Act in *Yates* v. *United States.*[10] Judge Chambers remarked tartly that the court would have upheld the validity of the convictions on the basis of past practice had not the Supreme Court changed the law. "One may as well recognize that the Yates decision leaves the Smith Act, as to any further prosecutions under it, a virtual shambles—unless the American Communist Party should witlessly set out to reconstitute itself again with a new 'organization'." [11]

The reactions of a number of lower federal judges to the state chief justices' censure of the Supreme Court were no more subtle. The *U. S. News and World Report* polled all district and circuit judges, asking if they agreed or disagreed with the report of the state chief justices. Only 128 of 351 answered: 59 of them expressed approval, 50 disapproval, and 19 voiced no opinion.[12]

Another channel of criticism, more discreet but also more directly pointed toward securing remedial congressional action, is the Judicial Conference,[13] either at the national or circuit level. The Judicial Conference of the United States several times in recent years has endorsed bills to reverse Supreme Court decisions allowing relatively liberal opportunities for state prisoners to seek *habeas corpus* in federal courts.[14] But it was the Judicial Conference for the District of Columbia Circuit which struck one of the harshest blows with this weapon.

At the close of its 1956 term the Supreme Court had, in *Mallory*

10. 354 U.S. 298 (1957).
11. Fujimoto v. United States, 251 F. 2d 342, 342 (1958). The other two circuit judges specifically disassociated themselves from these comments on the Yates case.
12. October 24, 1958, pp. 36–37.
13. 28 U.S.C. §331 provides that every year the Chief Justice of the United States shall call a meeting of the chief judges of each circuit, the chief judge of the Court of Claims, and a district judge from each circuit. . . .
14. *Annual Report of the Proceedings of the Judicial Conference of the United States* (Washington, 1958), p. 28. Earlier recommendations are summarized in *House Report No. 1293 on H.R. 8361*, 85th Cong., 2d Sess. . . .

v. *United States*,[15] extended the application of its libertarian decision in the earlier *McNabb* case.[16] *McNabb* had ruled that confessions secured as a result of questioning during a prolonged period of delay between arrest and arraignment could not be used as evidence in a federal court. While the delay in *McNabb* had been several days, in *Mallory* less than eight hours had elapsed between arrest and confession. Nevertheless, the Court held that even this shorter period fell within the prohibition against "unnecessary delay" in arraignment imposed by Rule 5(a) of the Federal Rules of Criminal Procedure. Frankfurter's unanimous opinion conceded that "circumstances may justify a brief delay," but the police must "arraign the arrested person as quickly as possible so that he may be advised of his rights and so that the issue of probable cause may be promptly determined." [17] The Federal Rules were declared to allow "arresting officers little more leeway than the interval between arrest and the ordinary administrative steps required to bring a suspect before the nearest available magistrate." [18]

This decision, resulting as it did in the freeing of a chronic criminal who had just been found guilty of a brutal rape, stirred up a hornet's nest in Congress [19] as well as more tactfully expressed displeasure among lower court judges. At its next meeting, the Judicial Conference for the District of Columbia Circuit, the circuit in which *Mallory* had originated, endorsed pending legislation which would have rewritten Rule 5(a) so as to erase the *McNabb-Mallory* holdings.[20]

*   *   *

The Supreme Court had spoken in *Mallory,* and while its opinion obviously did not set precise or very narrow limitations on lower

15. 354 U.S. 449 (1957).
16. 318 U.S. 332 (1943).
17. 354 U.S. 449, 454 (1957).
18. *Ibid.*, at 453.
19. A number of bills to reverse the Mallory decision were introduced in the 85th Congress. H.R. 11477 passed both the House and Senate, but in somewhat different forms. The conference report was agreed to by the House, but was defeated in the Senate minutes before final adjournment when Senator Carroll (D., Colo.) raised a point of order which Vice President Nixon sustained.
20. *Washington Post & Times Herald*, May 9, 1958.

court discretion, it did impose broad restrictions on the number and kinds of decisional alternatives open to federal judges. On the other hand, many problems come before lower courts on which the Supreme Court has not yet passed judgment. In deciding such cases, these tribunals can do, once removed, what the Supreme Court itself occasionally does in an analogous situation. For the High Court's question "What would the Founding Fathers or Congress have willed had they foreseen the case at bar?" the lower courts can substitute "What would the Supreme Court have visualized the Framers or Congress as willing had the Supreme Court foreseen this case?" This kind of speculation comes close to giving oneself a blank check.

Further complications enter when judges sense shifts in Supreme Court policy. Two schools of thought tell lower courts how to handle such problems. One, represented by the late Jerome Frank, feels that "when a lower court perceives a pronounced new doctrinal trend in Supreme Court decisions, it is its duty, cautiously to be sure, to follow not to resist it." [21] In a footnote to this statement, Frank added: "To use mouth-filling words, cautious extrapolation is in order."

Judge John J. Parker provided one of the most dramatic occasions of an inferior court's declining to follow an explicit Supreme Court precedent. In 1940, in the Gobitis [22] case, the High Court had with only one dissenting vote sustained the authority of Pennsylvania to compel children of Jehovah's Witnesses attending public schools to salute the flag, despite First Amendment and First Commandment scruples. Just two years later a case with almost identical facts arose in West Virginia, but, in the teeth of Gobitis, Judge Parker held the regulation invalid. This was not defiance. Parker noted that three of the Gobitis majority had confessed error [23] and that two others had retired, leaving the flag salute supporters a minority of three. "Under such circumstances and believing, as we do, that the flag salute here required is violative of religious liberty when required of persons holding the religious views of plaintiffs, we feel that we would be recreant to our duty as judges, if through a blind following of a

21. Perkins v. Endicott Johnson, 128 F. 2d 208, 218 (1942). The Supreme Court affirmed this decision, 317 U.S. 501 (1943).
22. Minersville School District v. Gobitis, 310 U.S. 586 (1940).
23. Jones v. Opelika, 316 U.S. 584, 623–624 (1942).

decision which the Supreme Court itself has thus impaired as an authority, we should deny protection to rights which we regard as among the most sacred of those protected by constitutional guarantees." [24]

But prediction is a risky enterprise, and while Parker's nose-counting turned out to be correct, other guesses, however informed, can be and have been wrong.[25] . . .

*   *   *

The power of prediction evidently confers considerable latitude on its user. He may be discerning what he believes the future does hold, what he hopes the future will hold, or what he judges the future should hold. Such guessing can influence the Supreme Court, or Congress, and it can also embarrass both by creating not just one but, by the time certiorari is granted and the case heard on review, a whole series of *faits accomplis*. On the other hand, refusal to accord official recognition to changing doctrine can also confer power. Disavowal of authority may be used to conceal or at least to give good form to serious disagreement with Supreme Court policy. In South Carolina, District Judge George Bell Timmerman, Sr., father of the governor, twice after 1954 insisted on applying the rule of *Plessy* v. *Ferguson* [26] to bus segregation, asserting that the school cases had only involved education and not transportation. "One's education and personality," Timmerman said disdainfully, "is not developed on a city bus." [27]

24. Barnette v. West Virginia, 47 F. Supp. 251, 253 (1942). . . .
25. In Gardella v. Chandler, 172 F. 2d 402 (1949), Judge Frank thought that the Supreme Court had turned into an "impotent zombi" its 1922 decision (Federal Baseball Club v. National League, 259 U.S. 200) that professional baseball was beyond the scope of congressional regulatory power, and consequently outside the reach of the Sherman Act. In 1953, however, the Supreme Court continued baseball's anti-trust immunity, though not affirming all that the earlier case had implied. Toolson v. New York Yankees, 346 U.S. 356. . . .
26. 163 U.S. 537 (1896).
27. Flemming v. South Carolina Gas & Electric Co., 128 F. Supp. 469, 470 (1955). After the Court of Appeals reversed Timmerman, 224 F. 2d 752 (1955), he tried to salvage something by ruling that if not currently law, at least *Plessy* had been law at the time the bus dispute had begun. 1 *Race Rel. L. Rep.* 679 (1956). This, too, was reversed, 239 F. 2d 277 (1956). See also Timmerman's bitter statements dissenting in Bryan v. Austin, 148 F. Supp. 563 (1957). . . .

The authority to make findings of fact gives trial judges extensive power which appellate tribunals can only partially control.[28] And in the *School Segregation Cases*, the Supreme Court broadened the scope of this inherent authority by specifically directing the exercise of the widest sort of judicial discretion, guided only by the flexible formula "with all deliberate speed." This is obviously a grant of vast power, and the high bench has relied on the Courts of Appeals to supervise its exercise. At this writing, after four years of lower court administration of school segregation problems, the Supreme Court has consented to full-scale review of only one such decision,[29] and there it affirmed the Court of Appeals.

Such a policy constitutes a manifestation of faith as well as an invitation for assumption of power. And occasionally a judge will seize the full implications of this invitation. Flying directly in the face of the desegregation ruling, and even after one reversal by the Court of Appeals, District Judge William H. Atwell declined to order Dallas, Texas, to set a date for integration because this would cause "civil wrongs." Lest his own feelings be mistaken, Atwell declared: "I believe that it will be seen that the [Supreme] Court based its decision on no law but rather on what the Court regarded as more authoritative, modern psychological knowledge. . . . It will be recalled that in 1952, Mr. Justice Frankfurter said it was not competent to take judicial notice of Claims of social scientists.' "[30]

As a retired jurist called back for temporary service, Judge Atwell may have felt a wider margin of freedom than his more active brethren, but the significant fact remains that 48 months after the Supreme Court's implementation decision neither of the two Southern communities in which the original school cases began had yet been required to admit a single Negro child to a hitherto white school.[31] Indeed, although there had been several court orders for a

---

28. See especially Jerome Frank, *Courts on Trial: Myth and Reality in American Justice* (Princeton: Princeton University Press, 1950). . . .

29. Cooper v. Aaron, 3 L. ed. 2d 5 (1958).

30. Bell v. Rippy, 146 F. Supp. 485, 486 (1956). The earlier decision is reported at 133 F. Supp. 811 (1955), and the reversal, *sub nom.* . . .

31. In the case which originated in Prince Edward County, Virginia, the district judge in 1958 set 1965 as the date for compliance, 164 F. Supp. 786 (1958). The Court of Appeals reversed, and ordered admission of qualified Negro students to hitherto white schools in September 1959, 266 F. 2d 507 (1959). The county replied in June, 1959 by refusing to appropriate money for continued operation of public schools. . . .

"prompt start" on plans for eventual segregation, when the school year closed in June, 1959, the only two Deep Southern states to have even token public school integration in some localities were North Carolina and Virginia.

This is not to deny that most federal judges are trying their best to carry out desegregation in a sincere and workable manner, but even the most imaginative member of the realist school of jurisprudence could hardly conceive of a more fertile field for free play of judicial predilections, conscious and sub-conscious. As a reaction against this freedom and its resultant responsibility, there is evidence of a growing resentment among lower court judges in Southern and border states, a feeling that they have been left to engage in a violent emotional battle against prevailing white mores while the Justices in Washington refuse to stoop to such conflict by primly denying certiorari in segregation cases.

It is possible that the Court of Appeals for the Eighth Circuit in the August 1958 phase of the Little Rock campaign was trying to force the Supreme Court's hand when it took the somewhat unusual step of staying its own order to preserve the *status quo*.[32] If the case had not been immediately reviewed by the Supreme Court, the stay would have allowed Central High School to transfer its Negro students and to reopen as a segregated institution. This would have been an immense victory for Governor Faubus's obstructionist tactics.

If the Court of Appeals was trying to compel the High Bench to reiterate its principles and re-enter the fight, the circuit judges succeeded wonderfully well. Both the opinion of the Chief Justice and Frankfurter's concurrence spelled out the Court's constitutional authority and interpretation, as well as its policy intentions, in a far more powerful form than had either of the two previous school decisions.[33]

32. Cooper v. Aaron, 257 F. 2d 33 (1958).
33. Cooper v. Aaron, 3 L. ed. 2d 5 (1958).

KENNETH N. VINES

Federal District Judges and Race Relations Cases in the South

Among those nations with federal arrangements of political power, the United States is one of the few maintaining a national judiciary through the states.[1] Unlike other federal systems where federal judges adjudicate only at the appellate level, United States district judges have a large and continuing area of original jurisdiction. They decide thousands of cases each year and hold court in every state in the union.

The widespread location of a federal judicial power has important consequences for the operation of the American political process. In the first place, an important institution embodying national power is added to the political process at the state level. District courts initiate policy, they implement or may overrule policy made elsewhere in the political system. Further, political interests and factions in the several states may make political demands upon the federal courts as well as on federal legislators and administrators and all members of the state political system. Estimating their probable success, interested parties may choose to make claims in the first instance before the federal courts, or they may turn there as a last resort if efforts elsewhere in the political system have been unsuccessful.

* * *

1. Two others are Argentina and Mexico. Wiencyzslaw Wagner, *The Federal States and Their Judiciary* (Mouton and Co., 1959), pp. 165-72.

From the *Journal of Politics*, 26: 2 (May 1964), pp. 337-57. Reprinted by permission of the publisher and the author.

Kenneth N. Vines is a Professor of Political Science at the State University of New York (SUNY) at Buffalo.

An excellent opportunity to study the district courts may be found in the quantity of race relations cases which have occurred in recent years in the U.S. district courts in the South. Collectively, the cases involve important judicial policy making in the district courts. Cases concerning race relations have occurred in all eleven of the traditional states of the South, and, in varying quantities, in every judicial district.

The purpose of this paper is to explore the political activities of officials operating within a judicial environment, in a sensitive, crucial area of Southern politics. This will be done by an examination of race relations cases in Southern federal district courts. The disposition of cases will be described and the distribution of decisions related to judicial districts and to deciding judges. Finally, an attempt will be made to explain the similarities and differences in the decisions. The cases examined will include all race relations cases decided in the federal district courts of the eleven states of the traditional South from May 1954 to October 1962. Data concerning the disposition of these cases will be used in conjunction with information on the backgrounds and experiences of Southern district judges and with certain information on the judicial districts in which the cases were decided.

Political scientists have shown that a variety of political institutions are molded by their economic and social environment and that political behavior is related to the social backgrounds and political experiences of the participants. Legal theory supposes, however, that courts and judges, because of the myth of legal objectivity and the quasi-insulated position of the courts from the remainder of the political system, are not similarly influenced, except perhaps by their legal environment. Judicial analysts have frequently shown that judges do vary in their behavior but have not often attempted to explain the variations in judicial behavior. Through investigation of a homogeneous group of cases decided by judges in the context of a region with both social similarities and social differences, we have an opportunity to examine the behavior of judges against their social and political environment. Then we may see whether judges and courts are also molded by their social and political environment or whether legal theory correctly describes judicial behavior.

*　　*　　*

DISTRIBUTION OF CASES

The amount of race relations policy conflict settled in the Southern federal district courts is shown in Table 1. Most of the 291 [2] cases represent policy demands initiated by Negroes and offer proof that the federal judiciary has become an important arena for the handling of Negro claims in the political system, at the local and regional levels. During the same period of time we have evidence that other institutions in the state and regional political process handled few Negro claims.[3] The race relations cases in the Southern district courts highlight the possibility of access to the courts when other points in the political process are closed or unfavorable. Nor is this necessarily due to more favorable attitudes on the part of the district judges. Because claims are presented to courts according to fixed procedures and under stated and known jurisdictional criteria, cases can be heard irrespective of the attitudes of the judge.

Table 1 also describes the distribution of cases by period and subject matter. Cases on education were by far the most numerous type and accounted for more than half the total work of the courts during this period. . . .

As Table 2 indicates, Negroes, in spite of their reputation for success in the federal courts, won decisions in barely more than half (51.3 per cent) of all cases. Decisions in favor of Negroes varied, however, in different subject categories and during different periods. Only where the cases concerned education have Negroes won more than half the cases litigated before the Southern federal bar. Where agencies of the federal government have pushed and where higher court precedents are prominent, as in those cases involving voting, transportation, and desegregation of government facilities, Negro success is measured at or near the fifty per cent mark, indicating the

2. For a descriptive treatment of some of the more important cases on de-segregation, see J. W. Peltason, *Fifty-Eight Lonely Men* (Harcourt, Brace and World, 1961), and Robert Steamer, "The Role of the Federal District Courts in the Segregation Controversy," *Journal of Politics*, Vol. 22, pp. 417–38.
3. Cases concerned with remand and vacate orders are not included since, legally, these are directives to proceed and not genuine policy decisions although in practice remand orders are sometimes not followed by the district courts.

Table 1

DISTRIBUTION OF RACE RELATIONS DECISIONS IN SOUTHERN DISTRICT
COURTS BY SUBJECT AND PERIOD (N=291)

Subject	Percentage of Total Cases
Education	52.7
Government facilities	16.0
Voting	11.3
Transportation	8.3
Trial procedures	3.3
Employment	2.2
Other (other civil rights, criminal law, defense of Negro organizations)	6.2
	100.0
Period	
I — May 1954–1957 (43 months)	22.2
II — 1958–1960 (36 months)	38.9
III — 1961–Oct. 1962 (22 months)	38.9
	100.0

*   *   *

Table 2

PERCENTAGE OF RACE RELATIONS CASES FAVORING NEGROES BY SUBJECT
AND PERIOD OF DECISION (N=291)

Subject	Percentage Favoring Negroes
Education	60.7
Government facilities	47.7
Voting	48.4
Transportation	47.8
Trial procedures	11.1
Employment	16.7
Other	23.5
All cases	51.3
Period	
I — May 1954–1957	52.4
II — 1958–1960	44.9
III — 1961–Oct. 1962	57.0

influence of the legal environment. But in other areas not so well marked by precedent or government intervention, such as employment, defense of Negro organizations, and other civil rights, Negro interests have been much less successful in the adjudication of favorable policies.

The differential success of Negroes in different types of cases also suggests that more than the mere following of precedents from higher courts is involved. The directives from the Supreme Court in favor of Negro groups on the subject of transportation and voting are clearer than those on education; but the activities of opposing interest groups have been more energetic and inventive in the field of voting and especially in education. Yet the federal district courts have decided much more frequently in favor of Negro litigants in the field of education than in either of the two fields cited above. Apparently precedent alone, even from the U.S. Supreme Court, does not dictate the direction of the disposition of cases in the district courts.

The success of Negro interests seems related to the amount of litigation.

*   *   *

THE DISTRICTS

*   *   *

Federal district judges commonly come from the district which they serve. . . . Their ties with the judicial district in which they serve are consequently deep and of long standing. Moreover, while in office, judges are required by statute to continue living in the district of appointment.[4]

*   *   *

Because of the location of the courts in scattered districts Frankfurter and Landis regard localism, or the influence of those factors of the local environment, as a key characteristic of the federal district

4. *United States Code,* 28:134, 1958.

court system, the root conception of its organization.[5] And while they interpret localism essentially in organizational and administrative terms, it is clearly a factor in political behavior as well. Some political scientists suggest that local influences have a decisive impact on policy makers who represent and are elected from districts. In a sense federal judges represent the district to which they are appointed. They must live in the district, usually sit only in that district, and hear all the cases of proper jurisdiction occurring in the district. Demands for policy enactment which are judicable must be made before the constituents' district court, just as requests are made of one's district Congressman.

*   *   *

. . . A number of studies have indicated that a large percentage of Negroes in the population affects in an important way the policy processes in the South. In general those parts of the South with the least proportion of Negroes in the population have been most permissive in attitudes towards race relations while those sections with a large proportion have been less tolerant. One study which investigated the influence of a number of factors in the Southern environment on Negro registration levels found that Negro-white population balance was the most significant of all factors in affecting Southern policy.[6] Southern judicial districts differ widely among themselves with respect to the presence of this important factor, ranging from a low of 4.1 per cent in the East Tennessee district to a high of 51.1 per cent in the South Alabama district.

*   *   *

There is considerable variation in the way different judicial districts disposed of race relations cases, as described by Table 3. In dealing with similar political problems often stated in similar legal ways, Southern district courts evidenced quite wide differences in

5. Felix Frankfurter and James Landis, *The Business of the Supreme Court* (Macmillan and Co., 1927), pp. 218–19.
6. Donald Matthews and James Prothro, "State Political Systems and Negro Voter Registration in the South," unpublished article, p. 16.

their decisions. Given the differences among the districts in Negro-white population balance, we can find whether or not the two variables are related. A measure of relationship would provide one test of the proposition that courts are influenced by their social environment.

Table 3

DISPOSITION OF CASES BY JUDICIAL DISTRICTS

Percentage Favoring Negroes	Number of Districts
90–100	3
80–89	2
70–79	1
60–69	5
50–59	5
40–49	2
30–39	3
20–29	2
10–19	0
Below 10	5
	28

The coefficient of correlation between the two factors is R = −48. That is, the proportion of Negroes in the population of Southern judicial districts is negatively related to the percentage of cases decided in favor of Negroes in the district. The higher the proportion of Negroes in a district, the less apt, at least to the extent of R = −48, is the court to decide the cases in favor of Negroes.

*   *   *

THE DISTRICT JUDGES—INFLUENTIAL FACTORS

Among the 60 judges who sat in the Southern district courts on race relations cases from 1954–1962 there were . . . 37 judges who sat on 3 or more cases and among them these judges decided 267 cases. . . .

*   *   *

Ranked according to the disposition of cases for and against Negroes, the judges fall into three groups: the first group we may call the "Segregationists" and they decided in favor of Negroes in less than one-third of the cases; the second group who decided in favor of Negroes in 34–67 per cent of all cases handled, we call the "Moderates"; the third group whose record in favor of Negro claimants was better than 67 per cent of all cases, we call the "Integrationists." These terms are doubtless not an accurate description of the judicial philosophies of the respective groups, but they can serve as identifications for the three groups and as rough indicators of their roles in Southern politics.

*   *   *

The factor of Negro-white population balance, we have seen, has limited explanatory power in accounting for the differences in the disposition of cases within the various districts. For further information on the factors associated with the differential judicial behavior, we may turn to the judges themselves, their backgrounds and experiences. Some studies of judicial behavior in various courts have indicated that judicial behavior is related to the social backgrounds and political experiences of the judges.[7] The general thesis in all these studies is that social and political factors are related to judicial behavior in much the same fashion that social and political characteristics are related to the political behavior of voters and non-judicial policy makers.

*   *   *

. . . Historically, the Democratic party in the South has been identified with the maintenance of segregation and white supremacy, while the Southern Republican party has a tradition of a more permissive attitude in race relations. Consequently, we might wonder whether judicial behavior in the South is related to partisan affiliation.

7. See my "Political Functions of a State Supreme Court," *Tulane Studies in Political Science,* Vol. 8, pp. 51–75; and John Schmidhauser, "Judicial Behavior and the Sectional Crisis of 1837–1860," *Journal of Politics,* Vol. 23 (1961), pp. 615–641.

Table 4

PARTY AFFILIATIONS OF THREE GROUPS OF SOUTHERN JUDGES *

Affiliation	Segregationists	Moderates	Integrationists
Democratic	78.6%	50.0%	45.4
Republican	21.4	50.0	54.6
	100.0 (N = 14)	100.0 (N = 12)	100.0 (N = 11)

* X^2 indicates marginal significance at .08 level.

The figures in Table 4 indicate that the Republican judges are located disproportionately among the Moderates and Integrationists, half of whose members are Republicans. Only 3 out of 14, or 21.4 per cent, of the Segregationist judges are Republicans. Republican candidates in the South today are often as enthusiastically in favor of segregation and as racially demagogic as their Democratic opponents. Yet, there is some evidence here that the traditions of the Southern Republican party still have some impact upon political behavior. The relative isolation of Southern Republicans may also contribute to their more permissive attitude toward Negroes in race relations cases. Even if active and politically involved, Southern Republicans are apt to have fewer occasions to seek state political office, to attend regional political meetings, and publicly to defend Southern political values. The political roles which result in white supremacy among the Democratic office seekers and party workers are often lacking in the more restricted political lives of Southern Republicans. A further possible explanation may be found in the character of the Republican judges appointed by Eisenhower. Not restricted by senatorial courtesy, the President was able to appoint with relative freedom and his appointments include the "new" Republicans with urban backgrounds.

*   *   *

Religious affiliation, while it cannot be considered of great significance in itself, may provide a clue to the relationship of the judge to the Southern social structure. Very largely (except in quite restricted areas such as Southern Louisiana) Southern society is Protestant and orthodox. The Protestant church far from providing an exception to the structure of a segregated society, remains an almost totally segregated institution and must be regarded as one of the important institutional supports of traditional Southern values.

Table 5
RELIGIOUS AFFILIATION OF GROUPS OF SOUTHERN JUDGES *

Religious Affiliation	Segregationists	Moderates	Integrationists
Orthodox Protestant	71.4%	66.7%	36.4%
Catholic	0.0	0.0	18.2
None listed	21.4	25.0	45.4
Don't know	7.2	8.3	0.0
	100.0% (N = 14)	100.0% (N = 12)	100.0% (N = 11)

* X^2 indicates significance at .05 level.

The data in Table 5 indicate that there are significant differences among the groups of judges on the matter of religious affiliation. Only about one-third of the Integrationists list orthodox Protestant religions (36.4 per cent) while two-thirds or more of the Moderates (66.7 per cent) and the Segregationists (71.4 per cent) list such religion. The few Catholic judges are found among the Integrationists and almost half of the Integrationists (45.4 per cent) list no religion. We may speculate that the non-affiliation of the Integrationists with orthodox Protestant religions provides suggestive evidence that these judges are not closely related to the conventional social structure; this may be one of the sources of their unorthodox conduct of race relations cases.

The path to the district judiciary in the South, as Table 6 shows, has often involved holding public office. Experience in public office has been important in the careers of judges in all three groups, but there are some important differences in the types of experiences. No office, federal or state, judicial or non-judicial, has dominated the political experiences of all three groups with uniform frequency. While close to one-half of the Segregationists (57.1 per cent) and the Moderates (41.1 per cent) have held state office, only 9.1 per cent of the Integrationists have. Federal offices have been occupied by nearly half the Segregationists (42.9 per cent) and the Integrationists (45.5 per cent) but by only 8.4 per cent of the Moderates.

Table 6 *

PREVIOUS PUBLIC OFFICES HELD BY SOUTHERN JUDGES **

Public Office	Segregationists (N = 14)	Moderates (N = 12)	Integrationists (N = 11)
State political office	57.1%	41.7%	9.1%
Federal political office	42.9	8.4	45.5
State judicial office	50.0	33.3	9.1
Federal judicial office	28.6	8.4	45.5
State and local judgeship	35.7	33.3	0.0

* Columns do not add up to 100.0 per cent because some judges held more than one office.
** X² indicates significance at .01 level.

Looking at the variation in the types of offices held by the three groups we may advance some suggestions concerning the relationship between political experience on the way to the bench and judicial behavior. Since about half of both the Segregationists and the Integrationists held federal office before coming to the court, we may conclude that political experiences gained in the services of the federal government do not function as an educational experience for the judge steeped in the values of Southern society. As a district attorney or assistant district attorney, the judicial candidate prosecutes cases involving various national political values, meets numerous kinds of litigants and serves in many political situations. Such experiences might be expected to broaden the outlook of prospective judges inducing respect for national values when these conflict with regional ones. However, federal political experience is apparently not enough, by itself, to accomplish this.

Tenure in a state political position, on the other hand, could strengthen the identification of the judge with Southern norms. As a legislator, state administrator, or state judge, he is often called upon to enact or enforce policies which implement the Southern point of view and sometimes to defend these values against what is called federal encroachment. Moreover, in seeking office, regional symbols may be invoked, or at least, paid lip service. The difference between Segregationist and Integrationist judges here is striking. Well over half the Segregationists (57.1 per cent) have held state political office while only 9.1 per cent of the Integrationists or less than one-tenth have held state office.

The Segregationist group is clearly distinguished from the Integrationist group by pre-judicial experiences in state government. Both in policy making and campaigning the Southern state officeholder can rarely remain indifferent to the issues involving the political and social position of the Negro. The frequency with which Segregationist judges have held state office suggests that state political experience corroborates Southern values. Integrationists, on the other hand, have seldom held state political positions. When they have held public office, it has been a federal one and in all cases also a federal judicial office. Here the service of judicial candidates as federal attorneys, when not combined with officeholding in the state political structure, seems to have marked out many members of the Integrationist group for deviation from traditional Southern values. It is important that the future judge has not undergone commitment to the state political system. Not identified with the state political system the judge may be more sympathetic toward national values and less sympathetic toward Southern state efforts to resist federal policies.

*   *   *

The evidence points to the conclusion that Southern federal judges in district courts are influenced by their social and political environment. In this they join other Southern politicians, state legislators, Congressmen, and state executives, who also respond to local factors. To this extent, we can say that judges, though ostensibly "different," react to environmental factors like other policy makers. We do not exclude the possibility of the influence of the legal environment upon the behavior of judges, but suggest that if legalistic influences are operative they must be considered along with social and political factors.

Harris v. New York 401 U.S. 222 (1971)

Mr. Chief Justice BURGER delivered the opinion of the Court.

We granted the writ in this case to consider petitioner's claim that a statement made by him to police under circumstances rendering it inadmissible to establish the prosecution's case in chief under *Miranda v. Arizona* (1966), may not be used to impeach his credibility.

The State of New York charged petitioner in a two-count indictment with twice selling heroin to an undercover police officer. At a subsequent jury trial the officer was the State's chief witness, and he testified as to details of the two sales. A second officer verified collateral details of the sales, and a third offered testimony about the chemical analysis of the heroin.

Petitioner took the stand in his own defense. He admitted knowing the undercover police officer but denied a sale on January 4, 1966. He admitted making a sale of contents of a glassine bag to the officer on January 6 but claimed it was baking powder and part of a scheme to defraud the purchaser.

On cross-examination petitioner was asked seriatim whether he had made specified statements to the police immediately following his arrest on January 7—statements that partially contradicted petitioner's direct testimony at trial. In response to the cross-examination, petitioner testified that he could not remember virtually any of the questions or answers recited by the prosecutor. At the request of petitioner's counsel the written statement from which the prosecutor had read questions and answers in his impeaching process was placed in the record for possible use on appeal; the statement was not shown to the jury.

The trial judge instructed the jury that the statements attributed to petitioner by the prosecution could be considered only in passing on petitioner's credibility and not as evidence of guilt. In closing summations both counsel argued the substance of the impeaching statements. The jury then found petitioner guilty on the second count of the indictment.

At trial the prosecution made no effort in its case in chief to use the statements allegedly made by petitioner, conceding that they were inadmissible under *Miranda v. Arizona* (1966). The transcript of the interrogation used in the impeachment, but not given to the jury, shows that no warning of a right to appointed counsel was given before questions were put to petitioner when he was taken into custody. Petitioner makes no claim that the statements made to the police were coerced or involuntary.

Some comments in the *Miranda* opinion can indeed be read as indicating a bar to use of an uncounseled statement for any purpose, but discussion of that issue was not at all necessary to the Court's holding and cannot be regarded as controlling. *Miranda* barred the prosecution from making its case with statements of an accused made while in custody prior to having or effectively waiving counsel. It does not follow from *Miranda* that evidence inadmissible against an accused in the prosecution's case in chief is barred for all purposes, provided of course that the trustworthiness of the evidence satisfies legal standards.

In *Walder v. United States* (1954), the Court permitted physical evidence, inadmissible in the case in chief, to be used for impeachment purposes.

> It is one thing to say that the Government cannot make an affirmative use of evidence unlawfully obtained. It is quite another to say that the defendant can turn the illegal method by which evidence in the Government's possession was obtained to his own advantage, and provide himself with a shield against contradiction of his untruths. Such an extension of the *Weeks* doctrine would be a perversion of the Fourth Amendment.
>
> [T]here is hardly justification for letting the defendant affirmatively resort to perjurious testimony in reliance on the Government's disability to challenge his credibility."

It is true that Walder was impeached as to collateral matters included in his direct examination, whereas petitioner here was impeached as to testimony bearing more directly on the crimes charged. We are not persuaded that there is a difference in principle that warrants a result different from that reached by the Court in *Walder*. Petitioner's testimony in his own behalf concerning the events of January 7 contrasted sharply with what he told the police shortly after his arrest. The impeachment process here undoubtedly provided valuable aid to the jury in assessing petitioner's credibility, and the benefits of this process should not be lost, in our view, because of the speculative possibility that impermissible police conduct will be encouraged thereby. Assuming that the exclusionary rule has a deterrent effect on proscribed police conduct, sufficient deterrence flows when the evidence in question is made unavailable to the prosecution in its case in chief.

(1) Every criminal defendant is privileged to testify in his own defense, or to refuse to do so. But that privilege cannot be construed to include the right to commit perjury. See *United States v. Knox* (1969); cf. *Dennis v. United States*, (1966). Having voluntarily taken the stand, petitioner was under an obligation to speak truthfully and accurately, and the prosecution here did no more than utilize the traditional truth-testing devices of the adversary process. Had inconsistent statements been made by the accused to some third person, it could hardly be contended that the conflict could not be laid before the jury by way of cross-examination and impeachment.

(2) The shield provided by *Miranda* cannot be perverted into a license to use perjury by way of a defense, free from the risk of confrontation with prior inconsistent utterances. We hold, therefore, that petitioner's credibility was appropriately impeached by use of his earlier conflicting statements.

Affirmed.

Mr. Justice BLACK dissents.

Mr. Justice BRENNAN, with whom Mr. Justice DOUGLAS and Mr. Justice MARSHALL, join, dissenting.

It is conceded that the question-and-answer statement used to impeach petitioner's direct testimony was, under *Miranda v. Arizona* (1966), constitutionally inadmissible as part of the State's direct case against petitioner. I think that the Constitution also denied the State the use of the statement on cross-examination to impeach the credibility of petitioner's testimony given in his own defense. The decision in *Walder v. United States,* (1954), is not, as the Court today holds, dispositive to the contrary. Rather, that case supports my conclusion.

The State's case against *Harris* depended upon the jury's belief of the testimony of the undercover agent that petitioner "sold" the officer heroin on January 4 and again on January 6. Petitioner took the stand and flatly denied having sold anything to the officer on January 4. He countered the officer's testimony as to the January 6 sale with testimony that he had sold the officer two glassine bags containing what appeared to be heroin, but that actually the bags contained only baking powder intended to deceive the officer in order to obtain $12. The statement contradicted petitioner's direct testimony as to the events of both days. The statement's version of the events on January 4 was that the officer had used petitioner as a middleman to buy some heroin from a third person with money furnished by the officer. The version of the events on January 6 was that petitioner had again acted for the officer in buying two bags of heroin from a third person for which petitioner received $12 and a part of the heroin. Thus, it is clear that the statement was used to impeach petitioner's direct testimony not on collateral matters but on matters directly related to the crimes for which he was on trial.

Walder v. United States was not a case where tainted evidence was used to impeach an accused's direct testimony on matters directly related to the case against him. In *Walder* the evidence was used to impeach the accused's testimony on matters *collateral* to the crime charged. Walder had been indicted in 1950 for purchasing and possessing heroin. When his motion to suppress use of the narcotics as illegally seized was granted, the Government dismissed the prosecution. Two years later Walder was indicted for another narcotics violation completely unrelated to the 1950 one. Testifying in his own defense, he said on direct examination that he had never in his life possessed narcotics. On cross-examination he denied that law enforcement officers had seized narcotics from his home two years earlier. The Government was then permitted to introduce the testimony of one of the officers involved in the 1950 seizure, that when he had raided Walder's home at that time he had seized narcotics there. The Court held that on facts where "the defendant went beyond a mere denial of complicity in the crimes of which he was charged and made the sweeping claim that he had never dealt in or possessed any narcotics," the exclusionary rule of *Weeks v. United States* (1914), would not extend to bar the Government from rebutting this testimony with evidence, although tainted, that petitioner had in fact possessed narcotics two years before. The Court was careful, however, to distinguish the situation of an accused whose testimony, as in the instant case, was a "denial of complicity in the crimes of which he was charged," that is, where illegally obtained evidence was used to impeach the accused's direct testimony on matters directly related to the case against him. As to that situation, the Court said:

> Of course, the Constitution guarantees a defendant the fullest opportunity to meet the accusation against him. He must be free to deny all the elements of the case against him without thereby giving leave to the Government to introduce by way of rebuttal evidence illegally secured by it, and therefore not available for its case in chief.

From this recital of facts it is clear that the evidence used for impeachment in *Walder* was related to the earlier 1950 prosecution and had no direct bearing on "the elements of the case" being tried in 1952. The evidence tended solely to impeach the credibility of the defendant's direct testimony that he had never in his life possessed heroin. But that evidence was completely unrelated to the indictment on trial and did not in any way interfere with his freedom to deny all elements of that case against him. In contrast, here, the evidence used for impeachment, a statement concerning the details of the very sales alleged in the indictment, was directly related to the case against petitioner.

*   *   *

The objective of deterring improper police conduct is only part of the larger objective of safeguarding the integrity of our adversary system. The "essential mainstay" of that system, *Miranda v. Arizona,* is the privilege against self-incrimination, which for that reason has occupied a central place in our jurisprudence since before the Nation's birth. Moreover, "we may view the historical development of the privilege as one which groped for the proper scope of governmental power over the citizen. . . . All these policies point to one overriding thought: the constitutional foundation underlying the privilege is the respect a government . . . must accord to the dignity and integrity of its citizens." *Ibid*. These values are plainly jeopardized if an exception against admission of tainted statements is made for those used for impeachment purposes. Moreover, it is monstrous that courts should aid or abet the law-breaking police officer. It is abiding truth that "[n]othing can destroy a government more quickly than its failure to observe its own laws, or worse, its disregard of the charter of its own existence." *Mapp v. Ohio* (1961). Thus even to the extent that *Miranda* was aimed at deterring police practices in disregard of the Constitution, I fear that today's holding will seriously undermine the achievement of that objective. The Court today tells the police that they may freely interrogate an accused incommunicado and without counsel and know that although any statement they obtain in violation of *Miranda* cannot be used on the State's direct case, it may be introduced if the defendant has the temerity to testify in his own defense. This goes far toward undoing much of the progress made in conforming police methods to the Constitution. I dissent.

3   Impact on State and Local Government and Politics

In the past decade or so, the Supreme Court of the United States has rendered several decisions that, if fully implemented, would have wrought drastic modifications in American life. The target of these decisions was state and local officialdom and the message was that it should mend its ways. To the Supreme Court, law was being violated —and flagrantly; that is, many officials of state and local government were acting unconstitutionally with some knowledge of that fact. They were told to refrain from certain activities and to adopt new policies or methods of procedure. Some of these Supreme Court decisions have had penetrating, lasting, broad-gauge effects; some have already had spotty results; and some remain little more than words in a law book. A number of local officials have heard the Court speak and have complied diligently. Others have not bothered to listen. The visible pattern of compliance, evasion, and defiance is highly erratic.

The greatest amount of trickery and stubbornness at the grass roots in response to the Court's wishes has been triggered by the decisions requiring desegregation of educational facilities.[1] Researchers have made it their business to describe the panorama of village, town, city, county, and state reactions to the school desegregation decisions, but perhaps the finest cataloguing of the fruit of Southern ingenuity in outflanking the Court is one chapter in a book called *Desegregation*

1. The most celebrated one, of course, is *Brown v. Board of Education* 347 U.S. 483 (1954).

95

and the Law.[2] We have included portions of that in this section; the title of the chapter is—sadly—"Avoidance, Evasion and Delay."

Meanwhile, researchers have also tried their hand in describing and analyzing the local consequences of other Supreme Court decisions. One area of unusual magnetism for political scientists has been the Court's recent attempt to clarify the law on church-state relations. The Supreme Court has, in a long line of decisions, both validated and forbade special religious programs (e.g., validated some forms of released time for religious education and invalidated others; forbade official prayers, forbade Bible reading) in local public schools.[3] Where the Court legally damned a particular procedure, town reaction was for the most part hostile, for the "nine old men" were attacking God! Lawfully appointed men who considered themselves law-abiding citizens felt little compunction in openly flaunting a Supreme Court decision with which they disagreed morally. Ironically, the supreme law-maker of the land was breeding a new strain of outlaw. Actually, though, this account unfairly accentuates the negative and eliminates the positive, for there has been a good deal of obedience as well. This brings us to the main question: What factor or factors are chiefly responsible for whether a local school district rejects, avoids, or accepts the mandate of a Supreme Court decision?

Some modern political scientists have gone beyond mere speculation on this subject and have developed and applied skillful research designs. We have selected several studies to illustrate some of the techniques employed as well as the general run of theories tested. The reader will notice that in this work there is a heavy reliance on questionnaires, sociological data, interviews, and statistical analysis. The study by Robert Birkby is a sophisticated successor to Frank Sorauf's trail-blazing survey of released time decisions.[4]

2. Albert Blaustein and Clarence Ferguson, *Desegregation and the Law* (New Brunswick: Rutgers University Press, 1957). A far more exhaustive listing, though, can be found in Robert B. McKay, " 'With All Deliberate Speed': A Study of School Desegregation," *New York University Law Review* 31 (June 1956), pp. 991–1090.
3. See, *McCollum v. Board of Education* 333 U.S. 203 (1948); *Zorach v. Clauson* 343 U.S. 306 (1950); *Engel v. Vitale* 370 U.S. 421 (1962); *Abington School District v. Schempp* 374 U.S. 203 (1963).
4. Frank Sorauf, "*Zorach v. Clauson*: The Impact of a Supreme Court Decision," *American Political Science Review* 53 (Sept. 1959), pp. 777–91.

Birkby was interested in locating which factors, if any, linked with 121 Tennessee school district decisions either to notice or ignore the Court mandate against Bible reading. After tracing the pattern of impact, he tested to determine if any relationship existed with such standard factors as: urbanization, extent of religious pluralism in the community, and the socio-economic background of the members of the school board. His findings may astonish the reader.

The article by James P. Levine tries to explain the wide disparity found in twelve states in their implementing of the Supreme Court's definition of "obscenity" in *Roth v. United States*.[5] Of added interest in the Levine piece is his analysis of the tremendous range of opinion represented by the twelve state supreme courts on how to interpret *Roth* or, put another way, how the state courts reconciled the Supreme Court's intent in *Roth* with their own widely divergent prejudices.

A more difficult impact to assess than that of the school and obscenity decision is another line of recent Supreme Court opinions on the police and on law enforcement. The Court, in trying to outline and protect the rights of arrested citizens, has elicited vigorous protests from various police agencies and some legal circles. Also, it has spurred certain political sectors into action. The more popular discussion emphasizes that the police have been severely hampered in their efforts to make arrests, to get confessions and crucial evidence for convictions, and in general to do their job. The thesis of a 1966 Detroit symposium was: "Has the Supreme Court Handcuffed the Police?" The question could have been worded: "Has the Supreme Court Adequately Increased Citizen Protection Against Overzealous Police?" Issues are framed initially by those who are upset.

In a series of landmark cases, the Court set forth its great dissatisfaction with police procedures of search and seizure and with the treatment of arrestees in the police station.[6] The Court's foremost

---

Actually some consider the first judicial impact study in political science to be an offshoot of a dissertation by Gordon Patric. See his "The Impact of a Court Decision: Aftermath of the McCollum Case," *Journal of Public Law* 6 (Fall 1957), pp. 455–64.

5. *Roth v. United States* 354 U.S. 476 (1957).

6. *Mapp v. Ohio* 367 U.S. 643 (1961); *Escobedo v. Illinois* 378 U.S. 478 (1964); *Miranda v. Arizona* 384 U.S. 436 (1966).

objective in these cases was to thwart police tactics that brazenly trod upon the rights of citizens. Judges who sit on the Supreme Court find crime waves no more appealing than anyone else, and one can presume that the Justices were sufficiently sensitive to the police contention that their practices were necessary to check criminal behavior. By its decision the Court rejected this argument and said, in effect, that crime rates would not necessarily soar if policemen kept within constitutional bounds. Moreover, we can assume that even if the Justices did believe that there would be an increase in outlawry, they also believed that it would not be so great an evil as to outweigh the degree of harm inherent in continuing (or accelerating) the current degree of abuse of the constitutional rights of Americans by the police themselves. In any event, the decisions were made and several questions as to their impact have been raised: (1) To what extent have the police actually changed their practices? (2) To what extent has any change in police practices affected their ability to make arrests, get important evidence and obtain confessions? (3) To what extent has the crime rate been altered, if at all?

Reliable answers to the first question are hard to come by. One can assume that policemen, like cooks, do not like anyone to peer over their shoulder while they work. Nonetheless, there have been several studies that have secured some police co-operation in an attempt to get answers. In addition, there is available probably more objective evidence to help us find answers to the other questions. We are including two studies dealing with these questions: one conducted by a group of researchers at the Institute of Criminal Law and Procedure at Georgetown Law Center (Medalie and his associates), and one conducted by two law professors at the University of Pittsburgh School of Law (Seeburger and Wettick). Together they are reasonably representative of the entire run of findings to date on the effects of the Supreme Court decisions on police procedures. In addition the reader is invited to glance again at our excerpts from the Nixon Court's opinion in *Harris v. New York* which is a more recent and different type of response to the Warren Court's rulings in *Miranda* and *Escabedo*.

Some observers believe, though, that the most important cases— in terms of actual or potential impact on local (and national) politics—are the famous (or notorious) "One man one vote" reapportionment decisions.[7] These decisions threatened to thin the ranks of, if not rout, traditionally dominant political coalitions in many state legislatures as well as in Congress. But ten years after the celebrated decision of *Baker v. Carr* and after reapportionment by virtually all fifty of the states, no panacea for the ills of state and local governments seems to have been produced. Roger Hanson and Robert Crew point out how the impact of reapportionment has been more limited than initially suspected. On the other hand, they do show how it has resulted in some substantial changes in at least some areas.

Still another legal swamp into which the Warren Court plunged head-long was the uncharted area of juvenile justice. In the unusually sweeping ruling of *In re Gault,*[8] the Court strongly implied that juveniles possess the same constitutional rights and guarantees as do adult defendants, and the same procedural safeguards for adults must equally apply to juveniles. This ruling directly challenged the principle of *in loco parentis,* the philosophy of paternalism upon which the entire American system of juvenile justice is built. More particularly, the *Gault* case required juvenile court judges to affirm the privilege against self-incrimination and the rights to notice of charges, counsel, confrontation, and cross examination. In other words, the Warren Court felt that juvenile hearings were trials and that juveniles, like adults, were citizens with all attendant civil rights. This view has not met with wild enthusiasm from many juvenile authorities, men and women steeped in the paternalistic legal and judicial philosophy of traditional juvenile law. Needless to say, compliance with the letter and spirit of *Gault* has been less than total. The article by Lefstein and his associates has begun the task of identifying and attempting to account for the different rates of compliance in various cities.

7. *Reynolds v. Sims* 377 U.S. 533 (1964). Glendon Schubert has amassed an excellent collection of articles and materials on this topic. See his *Reapportionment* (New York: Charles Schribner and Sons 1965). The case followed the more widely known *Baker v. Carr* 369 U.S. 186 (1962), which opened the whole question of reapportionment to the courts. Cf. Robert G. Dixon, Jr., *Democratic Representation: Reapportionment in Law and Politics* (New York: Oxford University Press, 1968).

8. 387 U.S. 1 (1967).

ALBERT P. BLAUSTEIN
CLARENCE C. FERGUSON, JR.

Avoidance, Evasion and Delay

Southern opposition to desegregation has led directly to legal measures admittedly designed to circumvent the mandate of *Brown v. Board of Education*. But while the avowed purpose of those legal devices is to frustrate the Supreme Court determinations of May 17, 1954, and May 31, 1955, that fact alone does not necessarily make them unconstitutional. Southern lawyers have entered upon a concerted program to find doctrine and precedent which will permit the continued existence of racial segregation and still somehow survive the scrutiny of judicial review. Should they succeed in their quest, those pro-segregation measures which do survive will have met the test of constitutional "legality." Other governmental measures (meaning other governmental actions under color of law) obviously will not survive the requirements of "constitutional" or "legal."

Every legislative enactment, executive order or court decision which conforms to constitutional procedures is a "legal" measure in the sense that it is a manifestation of state action under color of law. And any measure which would be effective in avoiding desegregation would be "legal" in the sense that it had been held valid and binding.

In analyzing the legality of any measure designed to circumvent the operation of an announced rule of law, the courts make an important distinction between "avoidance" and "evasion." There are no

From *Desegregation and the Law* by Albert P. Blaustein and Clarence C. Ferguson, Jr. Copyright © 1957 by Rutgers University Press. Pp. 240–42, 245, 247–50, 252–55, 257–60, 262, 265–68. Reprinted by permission of the publisher and the authors.

Albert P. Blaustein is President of Rutgers, The State University. Clarence C. Ferguson, Jr., is Dean of the School of Law at Howard University.

constitutional limitations to measures of "avoidance." It is perfectly proper—at least as far as the courts are concerned—for an individual or a state full of individuals to attempt to "avoid" the consequences of desegregation. "Evasion," on the other hand, is against the law. Individuals who attempt to evade the mandate of *Brown* v. *Board of Education* would be subject to punishment; and governmental measures designed to evade the Supreme Court's conclusions would be struck down as unconstitutional.

Whether an attempt to circumvent a rule of law is "illegal" because it involves "evasion," or whether an attempt at circumvention is labeled "evasion" because it is "illegal" is immaterial. Solution to this problem necessitates an excursion into the realm of legal dialectics which sheds no light on the enforcement problems involved in racial desegregation. The important fact is that circumvention measures in the field of desegregation *may* be "legal," just as they may be "illegal."

An amendment to the Constitution specifically authorizing the states to enact segregation laws would obviously be a legal method of "avoiding" the effects of *Brown* v. *Board of Education*. Legislative re-enactment of the laws which the Supreme Court declared unconstitutional on May 17, 1954, would just as obviously be struck down as an attempt to "evade" the law.

It is inconceivable that a constitutional amendment could be passed in mid-century America authorizing racial segregation, and just as incongruous to think in terms of re-enacting legislation already declared unconstitutional. What the South is really doing lies somewhere between such extremes of "avoidance" and "evasion."

The various legal attempts to avoid the consequences of desegregation fall into . . . [several] categories. Many of the Southern states have reintroduced into the legal scene one or more of the multiple variations of the pre-Civil War doctrines of interposition and nullification. Other states have entered upon a course of legislative action designed to disqualify potential plaintiffs and the NAACP from bringing court actions to end segregation. Still other states have sought to retain separate school systems by changing the theoretical basis of the separation from a classification explicitly based upon race to a classification based upon such factors as "scholastic aptitude," "psychological aptitude" and "free choice." . . .

INTERPOSITION AND NULLIFICATION

Derived from constitutional doctrines first advanced by Jefferson and Madison, the concepts of interposition and nullification have long provided the theoretical basis of the states' rights philosophy. This is the view that the central government is nothing more than a compact between and among the several sovereign states, and that each state has the right to determine the constitutionality of any act of federal authority. In declaring a federal act unconstitutional, a state would be interposing its sovereignty between the central government and the state's own citizens—hence the term interposition.

*   *   *

Virtually dormant for more than eighty years, these theories have been revived as one aspect of the legal struggle to circumvent the consequences of *Brown* v. *Board of Education*. It started in Virginia. On January 11, 1956, an interposition act was introduced in the Virginia General Assembly [1] asserting the "right" of the state to maintain a segregated school system. Making obvious reference to *Brown* v. *Board of Education*, the proposed act declared that the "commonwealth is under no obligation to accept supinely an unlawful decree of the Supreme Court of the United States based upon an authority which is not found in the Constitution of the United States nor any amendment thereto." [2] Three weeks later, the General Assembly restated the compact theory in passing a joint resolution "interposing the sovereignty of Virginia against encroachment upon the reserved powers of this state." [3]

But the resolution meant little more than an expression of dissent —even in Virginia. The state attorney general delivered an opinion as to the "scope, effect, and legal efficacy" of the resolution on February 14, 1956, and admitted its lack of legal validity. While he characterized the legislative action as "far more than a 'stern protest and

1. See 1 RACE REL. L. REP. 252 (1956).
2. *Id.*, at 253.
3. Senate Joint Resolution No. 3, General Assembly of Virginia, Feb. 1, 1956. See 1 RACE REL. L. REP. 445 (1956).

a memorial,' " he was forced to give negative answers to the two important legal questions submitted for his opinion:

"6. Is it within the powers of (a) the General Assembly of Virginia by resolution, or (b) the people of Virginia in convention assembled by ordinance, to legally nullify, in whole or in part, the said [*Brown* v. *Board of Education*] decision, or to thereby suspend for any period of time its enforcement in Virginia?"

The response of Virginia's attorney general was simply: "a (No), b (No)." [4]

* * *

DISQUALIFYING POTENTIAL LITIGANTS

In the second broad classification of Southern legal action are the various enactments designed to forestall judicial enforcement of the decree of May 31, 1955. The lower federal courts, charged by the Supreme Court with the responsibility for implementation, are powerless to act unless a desegregation suit is in litigation before them. The South is trying to take advantage of this situation by creating legal barriers which would preclude potential plaintiffs' seeking judicial remedies.

Litigation is expensive. Few Southern Negroes could possibly afford to bring suit against school boards in order to obtain admission to all-white elementary and high schools. And, as no governmental agency had taken the initiative in bringing legal proceedings, the task of instituting litigation fell by default to the National Association for the Advancement of Colored People. Where proceedings have been begun in the name of individual Negro school children, it is common knowledge that the NAACP has usually been behind the suit. Consequently, an important part of the Southern legal strategy has been to prevent the NAACP from operating in the deep South.

Three devices have been used to gain this end. The first involved court actions brought by state attorneys general seeking to enjoin the NAACP from any activities within the state. . . .

4. Opinion of the Attorney General, State of Virginia, Feb. 14, 1956. See 1 RACE REL. L. REP. 462, 464 (1956).

A second method of undermining the NAACP is through its members. South Carolina has taken the lead in this area, enacting legislation [5] prohibiting the employment of any NAACP member by a state agency. The statute also provides for a fine against any person hiring a NAACP member for a public post.

Criminal sanctions, obviously directed against the NAACP, represent the third line of attack. . . .

In addition to their campaign against the NAACP, the Southern states have taken legislative action to harass others who would assist potential plaintiffs—as well as the potential plaintiffs themselves. One of the many Virginia plans [6] to circumvent the Supreme Court's determination requires each plaintiff in a state court desegregation proceeding to prepare a long and complicated statement, listing the organizations and individuals who have provided advice or contributed funds in the suit. Failure to reveal the names of those assisting in the litigation—and even failure to comply completely with the vaguely worded statutory requirements—may subject the would-be plaintiffs to judicial punishment. Even where a potential plaintiff is able to comply with the rules, he may be reluctant to do so. . . .

*　　*　　*

SEPARATION—BUT NOT BY RACE

The third general approach to avoiding the consequences of *Brown* v. *Board of Education* is an attempt to find some method of classification ostensibly devoid of racial overtones—which will still result in the continued separation of the races in the Southern school systems. Many of the Southern states believe that they have found the desired classification factor.

One of the reasons given for the decision of May 17, 1954, was that separate schools "deprive the children of the minority group of equal educational opportunities." Segregated education is more than

5. Act No. 920, General Assembly of South Carolina, 1956. See 1 RACE REL. L. REP. 600 (1956); Act No. 741, General Assembly of South Carolina, 1956. See 1 RACE REL. L. REP. 751 (1956).
6. Act 670 of 1956. 22 VA. CODE § 22-10.1.

a century old, and in the absence of equal educational opportunities, most Negro pupils are considerably less advanced than white children of the same age and school grade. By setting up a classification factor based upon scholastic achievement, the Southern states would be creating a dividing line which would separate white and Negro school children in by far the majority of cases.

This method of classification has been supplemented by the amorphous test of "aptitude." . . .

*   *   *

Mississippi and Virginia have also enacted legislation setting up classification tests which appear to be nonracial in character.

While the Mississippi statute makes reference to "the educational needs and welfare of the child involved," it puts primary emphasis on "health and moral factors." [7] In order to provide a moral basis which would justify racial segregation, the Mississippi legislature passed another statute which takes advantage of the prevalent disregard for marriage licenses in large parts of the state. Deeply religious, many of the people of rural Mississippi are married by a duly ordained minister of the gospel, but few ever register such marriages with the office of the county clerk. In the eyes of governmental authority, such marriages are deemed common law marriages—both recognized and respected until 1956. Now the State of Mississippi has abolished common law marriages and has declared "any children born as a result thereof illegitimate." [8] This statute applies to the whites as well as to the Negroes of the "Bible Belt," but it is unlikely that it will result in any investigation of the marriage contract of the parents of the white children who apply for admission to the schools.

The test of "aptitude" also appears in the legislation proposed in 1955 by the Gray Commission in Virginia. Giving local school boards all pupil assignment responsibilities, the statute authorizes these boards "to take into consideration such factors as availability of facil-

7. Sec. 6334-02, MISSISSIPPI CODE ANN. (1942).
8. House Bill No. 13, Mississippi Legislature, Regular Session, 1956. See 1 RACE REL. L. REP. 434 (1956).

ities, health, aptitude of the child and the availability of transportation." [9]

All these plans are constitutionally valid—if they are literally enforced without regard to race or color. And whether or not any of these statutes will be held constitutional must depend upon a factual determination. The key is not whether race is omitted as a classification factor, but whether race is truly disregarded in the process of enforcement.

*   *   *

Recognizing the constitutional infirmities of these classification schemes, Virginia's Gray Commission recommended a final statutory provision, "that no child be required to attend an integrated school." [10] Virginia seeks to implement this policy by either of two methods.

Under one aspect of the Virginia plan, any child who objects to his assignment to a nonsegregated school has a "free choice" to attend a segregated school. Theoretically, this would result in the maintenance of three separate school systems: white, Negro and mixed. As a practical matter, however, since adherence to the Virginia "way of life" would result in objections by substantially all the white children assigned to integrated schools, the state would continue to run the same sort of segregated school organization as it operated prior to *Brown* v. *Board of Education.* The fact that the Virginia plan really provides for the continuation of the traditional Negro-white school separation is further evidenced by resolutions passed by various county school boards in 1956. These boards have provided that no public revenue will be used for the support of "public schools in said count[ies] wherein white and colored children are taught together under any plan or arrangement whatsoever." [11]

9. Report of Commission on Public Education (Gray Commission), Virginia, Aug. 30, 1954. See 1 RACE REL. L. REP. 241, 242 (1956).

10. *Supra,* note 9, 1 RACE REL. L. REP. 241, 243.

11. Resolution of Board of Supervisors, Prince Edward County, Virginia, May 3, 1956. See 1 RACE REL. L. REP. 780 (1956). Resolution of Board of Supervisors, Loudoun County, Virginia, Aug. 6, 1956. See 1 RACE REL. L. REP. 940 (1956).

As a second means of effectuating the Virginia policy, provision has been made for the payment of tuition grants to those children who object to attending an integrated school and who are unable to find a segregated public school in the local area. This would have the effect of creating a state-wide system of new "private-public" schools such as has been proposed by many of the Southern states as a means of avoiding desegregation.

The decision of May 17, 1954, was directed only against state action which required or permitted racial discrimination. Nothing was said—or could be said—about all-white or all-Negro private schools. Southern lawyers thus hope to avoid desegregation through the device of separating the schools from the states. It is their view that constitutionally they can do indirectly what they cannot do directly: that is, give Southern children segregated education by appropriating state funds to be given to the pupils for tuition rather than appropriating those same funds to maintain the public schools.

*   *   *

If South Carolina *completely* abandons its public school system and makes no provision for any alternate system of education, it will have effectively avoided the consequences of *Brown* v. *Board of Education*. If, on the other hand, South Carolina pursues its present plan of closing a public school whenever a court orders the admission of a Negro to a particular school, the whole scheme will probably be held unconstitutional. At such time as the state would have closed down some schools and would still be operating others, it obviously would be denying some of its school children—both white and colored—the equal protection of the laws.

*   *   *

Under the Virginia plan, on the other hand, the schools which would educate the children who had received state tuition grants would be schools which had always been private in character. And whether or not racial segregation would be constitutionally valid in those private schools would depend upon whether the Supreme

Court held that the receipt of the tuition grants from the states by those institutions transformed them into state agencies for the purposes of the Fourteenth Amendment.

*   *   *

It is probable that the Supreme Court will go even further in extending the application of the present meaning of state action. Language indicating this trend was used by Chief Justice Warren and Justices Black and Douglas in a dissenting opinion during the summer of 1956. "[T]he courts may not be implicated in . . . a discriminatory scheme," wrote the dissenters. "Once the courts put their imprimatur on such a contract, government, speaking through the judicial branch, acts. . . . And it is governmental action that the Constitution controls." [12] This represents an extremely broad reading of the restrictive covenant case of *Shelley* v. *Kraemer* where the Supreme Court declared that the state could not enforce private discriminations. For in the Warren-Black-Douglas view, any slight participation by any state instrumentality in a discriminatory scheme —no matter how limited that "participation"—is unconstitutional state action.

The rule of law that state-imposed racial discrimination is unconstitutional may well result in decisions of future Supreme Courts declaring the invalidity of the racial discrimination now practiced legally by privately operated schools, privately operated businesses and privately operated clubs. This can be done in one of two ways: either by applying the existing law to new factual situations, or by changing the present legal meaning of state action.

*   *   *

It was not until the Supreme Court issued its implementation decree of May 31, 1955, that even the most astute of lawyers became aware of the far-reaching implications of the *School Segregation Cases*. It was only by studying the 1955 determination that the 1954 decision could be understood. And it was not until 1956 that it be-

12. Black v. Cutter Laboratories, 351 U.S. 292, 302, 76 Sup. Ct. 824, 829, 100 L. Ed. 681, 688 Adv. (1956).

came obvious that all state-imposed racial discrimination had been declared unconstitutional *per se*.

But a real understanding of what the nine men said and did on May 17, 1954, goes far beyond the issue of school segregation and far beyond its attendant legal implications. Regardless of personal feelings about racial segregation and regardless of social attitudes toward the Supreme Court's approach and conclusion, *Brown* v. *Board of Education* must be acknowledged as an important, existing fact. While no attempt has been made within these pages to arrive at sociological judgments as to the rights and wrongs of segregation, there is no discounting the fact that the Supreme Court has spoken and that the law has been determined. Whatever may be done in the future to advance or delay the course of desegregation must be accomplished within the legal framework of this decision. *Brown* v. *Board of Education* must stand as the most significant civil rights decision ever rendered by an American court and as the symbol of the social revolution which marks mid-twentieth-century America.

ROBERT H. BIRKBY

The Supreme Court and the Bible Belt: Tennessee Reaction to the "Schempp" Decision

* * *

If the *Schempp* decision had any effect in Tennessee it should be noticeable in the policies adopted and enforced at the school district level. The State Commissioner of Education was reported as saying that it was permissible to read the Bible in public schools despite *Schempp* but he left the final decision to local school officials.[1] The school boards were left free to continue the practice required by state law or to comply with the Court's ruling. This study was undertaken to determine what the school boards did and, if possible, why. Even though it was expected that, in Gordon Patric's words, the "decision was put into effect in diverse ways and 'obeyed' to varying degrees," [2] board action in response to *Schempp* was classified as changing or not changing policy. All districts reporting a departure from the pre-*Schempp* provisions of state law were considered changing districts. It was believed that one of several factors could be used to explain the differences between changing and non-changing districts. These were degree of urbanization, extent of religious pluralism, articulate opposition within the district to devotional exercises, or

1. *Nashville Tennessean*, August 23, 1963, p. 1. In an interview October 16, 1964, the Commissioner confirmed that he had left the decision to local officials. He said at that time that he had taken no official position on the issue.
2. Gordon Patric, "The Impact of a Court Decision: Aftermath of the McCollum Case," 6 *Journal of Public Law*, 455 (1957).

From the *Midwest Journal of Political Science*, 10 (Aug. 1966), pp. 304–15. Reprinted by permission of the Wayne State University Press and the author.

Robert H. Birkby is Associate Professor of Political Science at Vanderbilt University.

differences in the socio-economic composition of the school boards.[3]

To test these suppositions three questionnaires were prepared and sent out in late 1964 and early 1965. One was mailed to each of the 152 superintendents of schools in the state. The second was mailed to the chairman and two other randomly selected members of each school board. The third was sent to the remaining school board members in those districts from which responses were obtained to either or both of the first two questionnaires. The superintendents were asked what the policy on Bible reading and devotional exercises had been in their district before June, 1963, and what it currently was. They were asked to identify any factors inducing change and to describe, in each time period, the policy-making role of the board, superintendent, principals, teachers, parents, religious groups, and any other participants. The first group of board members was asked about current (post 1963) policy, how it differed from that of the past, what groups or persons made policy suggestions to the board, and what groups or persons were consulted by the board. The second group of board members was simply asked to supply information on age, occupation, education, income, religious affiliation, length of service on the board, and length of residence in the school district of its members. Response to the first and third questionnaires was good. . . .

Of the 121 districts, 70 were reported to be still following the requirements of state law. The other 51 districts were reported to have made some changes in their policy but only one of these completely eliminated all Bible reading and devotional exercises. The other 50 merely made student participation voluntary and left the decision whether to have devotional exercises to the discretion of the classroom teacher. Thus 42 percent of the reporting school districts no longer adhere strictly to the provisions of state law even though all but one could have some form of classroom devotional exercise.

The most reasonable explanation for these differences in response to *Schempp* seemed to lie in the extent of urbanization. Table 1 shows the distribution of changing and non-changing districts according to this factor.

3. Daniel F. Boles, *The Bible, Religion and the Public Schools*, 3rd ed. (Ames: Iowa State University Press, 1965). The author suggests (p. 340) the urbanization and religious pluralism explanations.

Table 1

RELATIONSHIP OF URBANIZATION AND SCHOOL RELIGIOUS EXERCISE
POLICY CHANGE

% of District Population Urbanized *	Number of Districts	
	Changing	Not Changing
90–100	17	19
80–89	1	0
70–79	0	0
60–69	0	0
50–59	1	0
40–49	3	1
30–39	2	0
20–29	5	9
10–19	3	4
0–9	19	37
Totals	51	70

* On the basis of 1960 census data.

Using the point bi-serial correlation [4] the relationship between urbanization and tendency toward partial compliance with *Schempp* was found to be practically non-existent ($r_{pb} = -0.08$). Thus, on the basis of questionnaire responses, school boards and superintendents in urban areas showed no greater tendency to change Bible reading and devotional exercise policy than the respondents from rural areas.

The possibility that increasing religious pluralism may account for objections to religion in the schools must remain largely in the realm of speculation since accurate figures on denominational membership by school district or even county do not exist. The National Council of Churches has issued a rough compilation by counties and in lieu of anything else these figures were used to test this possibility. Only those counties with a single area-wide school district (no city districts) and those counties in which the county district and the city district took the same position could be used. This distorts the results somewhat but was made necessary by the impossibility of breaking county religious affiliation figures down into smaller units. On this rough test there is only slight correlation between religious pluralism and tendency to change ($r_{pb} = 0.02$). The pattern of change classified

4. Allen L. Edwards, *Statistical Methods for the Behavioral Sciences* (New York: Rinehart & Company, 1954), pp. 182–85.

by total population of the district was also checked on the theory that heavily populated districts would be more likely to be religiously heterogeneous; again only a slight correlation was found ($r_{pb} = 0.24$).

The other two possibilities advanced above are equally ineffective in explaining the pattern of change. From only one of the eighty-four districts represented by responses from the first group of board members was there a report that the board had been approached by an individual who objected to a continuation of the Bible reading and devotional exercises. In this instance the protester's efforts were in vain since that district still complies with state law. Either there was no significant opposition to devotional exercise or else no board member wanted to admit that there had been any.

Using the chi square test and rejecting the null hypothesis at the 0.01 level of significance, tabulation of the responses of the second group of board members produced no significant differences in socio-economic characteristics between changing and non-changing boards. . . .

In each instance the null hypothesis must be accepted.

Thus far this paper has presented only negative results. Partial compliance with *Schempp* is not explained by degree of urbanization. There are no significant differences in the socio-economic characteristics of changing and non-changing board members. In the changing districts the board members did not report any overt pressure for compliance. And, by a rough test, the extent of religious pluralism in the district had no effect. These findings are significant and justify reporting. It may well be that the population of the State of Tennessee is too homogeneous—socially, religiously, and economically—for any of these tests to be significant. In some other state with greater diversity, urbanization and religious pluralism might be more important. Even so, Tennessee reaction would remain unexplained.

The reported response by Tennessee school districts to *Schempp* might be explained by one other hypothesis. There is in the questionnaires some support for it but not enough to make it possible to assert that it is correct. What follows then is largely speculative. The line of reasoning starts with a distinction between procedural and substantive change in policy. Policy change in any situation may take the form of (1) altering procedure without altering the policy goal, (2) changing procedure to reach a new policy goal without, however, making the new goal explicit, or (3) changing the policy goal with or without a change in procedure. Although we cannot be sure, it seems fairly safe to say that in the fifty school districts which overtly changed their policy on Bible reading and delegated the decision to the teachers there has been little change in fact. That is, it is suspected that the classroom teachers are "voluntarily" conducting Bible reading and devotional exercises just as they did before *Schempp*.[5] One might go a step further and assert, without being able to prove it, that the school boards were aware that this would probably happen. I am suggesting that the board members acted consciously either to save the substance of the program or to avoid upsetting the community status quo by making slight procedural changes. In the language of Sayre and Kaufman, the contestants who had the prizes of the game were able to keep them by responding to a rules change with a rules change of their own.[6] A comment by a lawyer on the board of a changing district indicates the compromise nature of the policy adopted:

> My personal conviction is that the Supreme Court decisions are correct, and I so told the Board and Superintendent; but I saw no reason to create controversy. If the Board had made public a decision abolishing devotional exercises, there would have been public outcry. I believe all staff members understand that the continuance of devotional exercises in their schools and in their rooms is entirely voluntary and subject to discontinuance upon objection of any individual or minority group.

There are other reasons that a board might adopt this strategy of procedural change. It could be used to reduce disagreement within the board itself. It could be suggested by an individual as a means of reducing his own tensions between a desire to comply with the Court's decision and a desire to retain perceived advantages of devotional exercises. Finally, change in procedure without change in

5. This suspicion is based on unsystematic conversations with classroom teachers from two or three districts which made this formal change and on the questionnaire responses of a few superintendents who indicated doubt that any actual change had occurred.

6. Wallace S. Sayre and Herbert Kaufman, *Governing New York City* (New York: Russell Sage Foundation, 1960).

substance might be made to forestall demands for even greater change. There is nothing in the questionnaire responses to indicate which of these alternatives is correct and it is possible that all were present to some extent. If any or all of these suppositions are correct, a desire to retain the program rather than religious pluralism and urbanization would be responsible for the formal change. To this point the hypothesis does not provide an answer to the question of why the form was changed in some districts and not in others. It does emphasize that the answer must be sought in psychological rather than in demographic or socio-economic factors.

The question being asked in any impact study is why the Court's decision is not self-executing. In a different context Richard Neustadt has concluded that a self-executing order must have five characteristics: (1) the issuer of the order must be unambiguously involved in making the decision, (2) the order must be unambiguously worded, (3) the order must receive wide publicity, (4) those receiving the order must have control of the means of implementation, and (5) there must be no doubt of the individual's authority to issue the order.[7] Neustadt was speaking of orders issued by the President but there is no reason that the same analysis cannot be applied to Court decisions. In this instance, there was no doubt that the Court did in fact make the decision though one school board member suggested that the Court was "controlled by small pressure groups." When applied to the Tennessee statute the wording of the order, although negative in content, was clear enough.[8] There was wide publicity. The members of the boards of education had control of the means of implementation. However, the fifth factor was not so obviously present.

There was some confusion about the Court's decision. It was clear enough that required devotional exercises were forbidden but the Court did not commit itself on the status of voluntary programs such

7. Richard E. Neustadt, *Presidential Power* (New York: John Wiley and Sons, 1960), p. 19.

8. In some instances this criterion will not be met by a decision. The best examples are the confusion resulting from the "with all deliberate speed" formula in school desegregation and general ambiguity in the majority opinion in *Zorach v. Clauson*, 343 U.S. 306 (1952). See Jack W. Peltason, *Fifty-Eight Lonely Men* (New York: Harcourt, Brace & World, 1961), and Frank J. Sorauf, "*Zorach v. Clauson*: The Impact of a Supreme Court Decision," 53 *American Political Science Review*, 777 (1959).

as those adopted by the fifty changing districts in Tennessee. This ambiguity caused one superintendent to assert confidently "we believe our policy [voluntary participation] is in accordance with the ruling of the Supreme Court and in accord with the desires of the people in this community."

More important is the question of the Court's authority to issue the order. The policy maker's reaction to a judicial decision will be conditioned by his perception of the Court's role in general, his beliefs concerning the importance of the challenged activity or program, his perception of the attitudes of his reference groups and constituents on the issue, and his perception of his role. The differences in policy position may be the result of a general attitude toward the Court and its role in the American system of government.[9] The following comments are typical in content and intensity.

> *Changing Districts*
> *A Surgeon:* We must conform with Federal law. If we are to teach our children to obey laws we must set an example.
> *A Farmer:* We did not want to violate any federal law.
> *A Superintendent:* I think the Supreme Court is correct. Very few people understand the religious issue, less seem to understand what is meant by religious freedom, and relatively few seem to understand the Supreme Court's role in our government.
> *A Farmer:* We are commanded by the Bible to be subject to civil powers as long as their laws do not conflict with laws of God.
>
> *Non-Changing Districts*
> *A Superintendent:* Impeach Earl Warren.
> *A Housewife:* The decision of the Supreme Court seemed senseless and I could see no advantage in making changes.

9. Speaking to the American Philosophical Society in 1952, Justice Felix Frankfurter observed that "broadly speaking, the chief reliance of law in a democracy is the habit of popular respect for law. Especially true is it that law as promulgated by the Supreme Court ultimately depends upon confidence of the people in the Supreme Court as an institution." Frankfurter, *Of Law and Men* (New York: Harcourt, Brace & Co., 1956), p. 31. Brehm and Cohen report an experiment demonstrating that the more credible the source of a communication the greater the change in the recipient's attitude even when there was wide discrepancy between the recipient's initial attitude and the content of the communication. Jack W. Brehm and Arthur R. Cohen, *Explorations in Cognitive Dissonance* (New York: John Wiley and Sons, 1962), pp. 247–48.

A College Professor: The Supreme Court decision didn't mean a damn.

A Banker: The general public in this country do not have the respect for the U. S. Supreme Court as they once did. They think it is packed, so to speak, and doubt very much if all are qualified and unbiased and listen to the whims of the President that gave them the appointment. The standards are on a lower level than back several years ago.

A Superintendent: I am at a loss to understand the necessity for this survey. I am of the opinion that 99% of the people in the United States feel as I do about the Supreme Court's decision— that it was an outrage and that Congress should have it amended. The remaining 1% do not belong in this free world.

A Lawyer: We felt that in the absence of some good specific objection, there was no compelling reason to change previous policy.

If one had these comments without information on the policy adopted, it would not be too difficult to predict the position taken by each of these school boards.

The Court-attitude is only one of the variables affecting the impact of a judicial decision. The other major variable is the policy maker's assessment of and commitment to the challenged program or activity. . . .

*   *   *

Perceptions of the attitudes of constituents or clientele are important but seem to be secondary. They play the role of reinforcing or modifying the Court-attitude and/or the program-attitude. A dentist on the board of a changing district observed that "we thought public opinion would want us to comply with Federal Law," while a chairman of a non-changing board (who did not indicate his occupation) said that the most important factor influencing him was that "we would have had complaints if we did not have Bible reading." Both of these board members were reacting to their perception of constituent attitude. . . .

*   *   *

On the basis of the information available, it is impossible to weigh the value of the perceptions that went into the making of the policies.

But one might hazard a guess that in the changing districts a perception of the Court as an authoritative body exercising legitimate power was strong enough to override any commitment to devotional exercises. The reverse, of course, would hold true in non-changing districts. The weight given to reference group attitudes and the direction of those attitudes probably, though not necessarily, varied in the same direction as the final policy decision and served to reinforce attitudes toward the Court or beliefs in the value of devotionals. That is, public opinion in changing districts probably was perceived by the board as favoring or at least not opposing compliance with *Schempp* and strengthened the board's desire to comply.

One warning is in order. It is not asserted that procedural change to save substance and intensity of attitude explains what took place in Tennessee. All that is claimed here is that with the failure of the initial hypotheses in this study this additional explanation is possible and is supported to some extent by the response to the questionnaires.

*   *   *

JAMES P. LEVINE

Constitutional Law and Obscene Literature:
An Investigation of Bookseller Censorship Practices *

Because individual freedoms are central to democratic theory and ideology, it is surprising to discover the paucity of systematic research concerned with conditions supportive of civil liberties. There have been few studies treating the behavioral fact of freedom as a dependent variable, the existence or absence of which is to be explained by politico-legal, sociological, or psychological factors.[1] This study is an exploration of some determinants of one kind of freedom—the freedom to acquire literature dealing with sexual behavior.

Sexual speech was selected as a testing ground for hypotheses

* The author is indebted to the Russell Sage Program in Law and the Social Sciences at Northwestern University for its generous support during all phases of this study. Victor G. Rosenblum deserves special thanks for his useful suggestions and his never-ending encouragement.

1. Exceptions are: Marjorie Fiske, *Book Selection and Censorship* (Berkeley: University of California Press, 1959); Marie Jahoda and Stuart Cook, "Security Measures and Freedom of Thought: An Exploratory Study of the Impact of Loyalty and Security Programs," *Yale Law Journal*, 61 (March 1952), 295–333. Many survey studies of public attitudes toward freedom have accumulated, among which are: Samuel Stouffer, *Communism, Conformity, and Civil Liberties* (New York: Doubleday, 1955); James Prothro and Charles Gregg, "Fundamental Principles of Democracy: Bases of Agreement and Disagreement," *Journal of Politics*, 22 (May 1960), 276–294. Major works dealing with the social determinants of extremist voting behavior are: William Kornhauser, *The Politics of Mass Society* (New York: The Free Press, 1959); Seymour Lipset, *Political Man* (New York: Doubleday, 1963).

This article is based on Mr. Levine's unpublished Ph.D. dissertation, "The Bookseller and the Law of Obscenity: Toward an Empirical Theory of Free Expression" (Northwestern University, 1967) and was written expressly for this volume.

James P. Levine is an Associate Professor of Political Science at The City University of New York–Brooklyn College.

about civil liberties because of the relevance of sex to so many facets of life. The subject of sex is not only an integral part of aesthetic expression (especially in so much of contemporary fiction and drama), but allusions to sex abound in the fields of advertising, entertainment, psychoanalysis, and even religion. We are a highly sex-conscious society.

Bookseller self-censorship practices were used as an index of freedom of sexual speech prevailing in a community. This measure was chosen because books are an important medium of public communications and the retail bookseller plays a vital role in their dissemination. Furthermore, casual observation suggested that variance in the amount of censorship exercised by bookstores was considerable—ranging from ultra-restrictive "Bible shops" that weed out all books making reference to sex to the ultra-permissive "smut shops" which specialize in "pulp" literature focusing on sexual deviance. This variation allows the researcher to observe, measure, and chart, if only imprecisely, the scope of freedom in a society.

A THEORY OF FREE SPEECH

Although our knowledge about the efficacy of law as an instrument of social control is slight, it is frequently urged that constitutional checks on political power, enforced vigorously by judicial institutions, provide the best defense of individual liberties. As early as 1835, Alexis de Tocqueville contended that the American judiciary, with its power of judicial review, was "one of the most powerful barriers which has ever been devised" to prevent mass tyranny.[2] Similarly, implicit in much legal writing of today is the thesis that courts are the major protectors of freedom. Charles Black states this position forthrightly:

> The judicial power is one of the accredited means by which our nation seeks its goals, including the prime goal . . . of self-limitation. Intellectual freedom, freedom from irrational discrimination,

2. Alexis de Tocqueville, *Democracy in America,* trans. Phillips Bradley (New York: Vintage Books, 1954), I, 102–109.

immunity from unfair administration of the law—these (and others similar) are the constitutional interests which the Court can protect on ample doctrinal grounds. They often cannot win protection in rough-and-tumble politics. The Supreme Court is more and more finding its highest institutional role is the guarding of such interests.[3]

Given the multivariate nature of most social scientific explanations, it is likely that notions of judicial omnipotence suffer from oversimplification.[4] Consequently, the perspective taken here is that judicial policy-making is only one of a host of independent variables which relate to the phenomenon of social freedom.

The theory may be stated briefly in propositional form. If appellate courts are permissive in establishing the boundaries of constitutionally protected speech, political elites will be prevented from invoking legal sanctions to suppress speech. If a community is urban and its population is wealthy, educated, mobile, and young, it is likely to have a tolerant climate of public opinion which nullifies customary restraints on speech.

Alternatively, booksellers' personal attitudes toward sexual speech may insulate them from the effects of both law and custom. If the bookseller is tolerant of deviant expression, he will adopt permissive practices, marketing all kinds of books freely; contrariwise, intolerance will lead to restrictive sales policies. This is really a "safety-valve" hypothesis: if the data fail to confirm primary hypotheses about the effects of appellate court behavior and community structure, a high correlation between attitudes of booksellers and censorial practices may help to account for these negative findings.

3. Charles Black, *Perspectives on Constitutional Law* (Englewood Cliffs, New Jersey: Prentice-Hall, 1963), p. 5.
4. Equally implausible are contentions that courts are completely impotent, such as the following assertion made by Judge Learned Hand:

. . . this much I think I do know—that a society so riven that the spirit of moderation is gone, no court *can* save; that a society where that spirit flourishes no court *need* save; that in a society which evades its responsibility by thrusting upon the courts the nurture of that spirit, that spirit in the end will perish.

The Spirit of Liberty (New York: Vintage Books, 1959), p. 125.

THE ROLE OF THE COURTS

Modern obscenity law was born in 1957 when the United States Supreme Court upheld the constitutionality of federal and state obscenity laws in *Roth v. United States*.[5] The Court side-stepped the delicate problems of the "clear-and-present-danger" test by devising a "two-level free-speech theory." [6] The first step asks whether a communication has any social utility; if the answer is negative, the second step, an evaluation of the clarity, proximity, and gravity of the danger, need not be taken. In the Court's own words:

> All ideas having even the slightest redeeming social importance —unorthodox ideas, controversial ideas, even ideas hateful to the prevailing climate of opinion—have the full protection of the guarantees, unless excludable because they encroach upon the limited areas of more important interests. But implicit in the history of the First Amendment is the rejection of obscenity as utterly without redeeming social importance.[7]

By engaging in some intricate historiography, the Court establishes to its satisfaction that obscenity is, and always has been, outside the coverage of the First Amendment.

Although the constitutionality of restrictions on speech about sex thus hinged on the definition and applicability of the concept of obscenity, the Court was elusive in describing the kind of material falling within this category. Criteria used in thirteen lower court cases were approved, as was the norm advocated by the American Law Institute in its *Model Penal Code*. The proper test of obscenity was said to be:

> whether to the average person, applying contemporary community standards, the dominant theme of the material taken as a whole appeals to prurient interest.[8]

Expertise in constitutional law is not required to recognize the ineffable quality of the terms of this "standard." The Court failed to

5. 354 U.S. 476 (1957).
6. Harry Kalven, "The Metaphysics of the Law of Obscenity," *The Supreme Court Review*, 1960, p. 8.
7. 354 U.S. 476, 484 (1957).
8. 354 U.S. 476, 489 (1957).

provide a neat "pigeon-hole" into which obscene speech could be sorted with any degree of objectivity. In short, the *Roth* opinion avoided grappling with the concrete limits of permissible sexual speech.[9]

However, in a series of subsequent cases, the Court relied on *Roth* to reveal its anti-puritanical posture. From 1957 to 1965, several lower court findings of obscenity were reversed in *per curiam* decisions without opinions. The following specimens of sexual speech were legitimated: (1) imported "art" magazines containing photographs of nude females;[10] (2) *The Game of Love,* a foreign "art" film;[11] (3) homosexual magazines with pictures of scantily-clad males;[12] (4) nudist magazines;[13] (5) *Pleasure Is My Business,* a pocket-book detailing the adventures of a nymphomaniac;[14] (6) Henry Miller's *Tropic of Cancer;*[15] and (7) *A Stranger Knocks,* a Danish film containing implied scenes of sexual intercourse.[16] The terribly abstract verbiage of *Roth* proved to be sufficiently flexible to limit severely the sphere of expression which could be constitutionally banned by the state.

The Supreme Court's post-*Roth* decisions also were permissive. The prohibition of "ideological" or "thematic" obscenity was held unconstitutional in *Kingsley International Pictures v. Regents*[17] in which the Court overturned a censorship board's denial of a license to exhibit the film *Lady Chatterley's Lover* because it depicts adultery in an approving manner. In *Manual Enterprises v. Day*[18] the additional criterion of "patent offensiveness" was tacked on to the requirements of *Roth;* it was held that a magazine including photographs of nude males does not go "beyond the pale of contemporary

---

9. The Court did, however, create two constitutional requisites which loosened legal restraints on sexual speech: (1) findings of obscenity must be based on the effects of the disputed work on the average adult rather than the most susceptible elements of society; (2) material must be judged as a whole and isolated words and passages cannot be singled out for independent evaluation.
10. *Mounce v. United States,* 355 U.S. 180 (1957).
11. *Times Film Corp. v. Chicago,* 355 U.S. 35 (1957).
12. *One, Inc. v. Oleson,* 355 U.S. 371 (1958).
13. *Sunshine Book Co. v. Summerfield,* 355 U.S. 372 (1958).
14. *Tralins v. Gerstein,* 378 U.S. 576 (1964).
15. *Grove Press v. Gerstein,* 378 U.S. 577 (1964).
16. *Trans-Lux Distributing Corp. v. Regents,* 380 U.S. 259 (1965).
17. 360 U.S. 384 (1959).
18. 370 U.S. 348 (1962).

notions of rudimentary decency" and therefore cannot be excluded from the mails. In 1964, the Court reversed a conviction for exhibiting *Les Amants,* a French film in which an explicit love scene is portrayed, holding that national standards must be used in applying state obscenity statutes.[19] Finally, in 1966, John Cleland's *Memoirs of a Woman of Pleasure,* an example *par excellence* of "erotic realism," [20] was declared non-obscene on the grounds that material must be "utterly without redeeming social importance" to be constitutionally proscribable.[21]

The development of the procedural law of obscenity paralleled the liberal tendency of the Supreme Court's substantive decisions. The use of injunctive remedies to prevent further distribution of materials adjudicated obscene has been sustained,[22] but the Court has used the due process clause to restrict searches and seizures of *allegedly* obscene publications.[23] Similarly, the abstract principle of administrative censorship of motion pictures prior to exhibition has been upheld,[24] but the Court has severely curtailed the discretion of the administrator,[25] thereby pulling the teeth out of many censorship operations.

In 1966, in the case of *Ginzburg v. United States,*[26] the Court reversed directions when it affirmed a conviction for sending erotica through the mails on the ground that the defendant was exploiting the sexual content of the publications and pandering to the sexual instincts of his audience. In a companion case, the Court was also restrictive, holding that the prurient appeal of literature dealing with abnormal sexuality was to be assessed in terms of the sexual interests of its intended and probable primary recipient group, rather than the sexual interests of the average member of the community.[27]

19. *Jacobellis v. Ohio,* 378 U.S. 184 (1964).
20. Eberhard Kronhausen and Phyllis Kronhausen, *Pornography and the Law* (New York: Ballantine Books, 1964), pp. 303–324.
21. *Memoirs v. Massachusetts,* 383 U.S. 413 (1966).
22. *Kingsley Books v. Brown,* 354 U.S. 436 (1957).
23. *Marcus v. Search Warrants of Property,* 367 U.S. 717 (1961); *A Quantity of Books v. Kansas,* 378 U.S. 205 (1964).
24. *Times Film Corp. v. Chicago,* 365 U.S. 43 (1961).
25. *Freedman v. Maryland,* 380 U.S. 51 (1965).
26. 383 U.S. 463 (1966).
27. *Mishkin v. New York,* 383 U.S. 502 (1966).

These two cases, however, represent an aberration in the long-term trend toward liberalization of the restrictions on sexual expression. Not once in the years prior to 1966 had the Supreme Court declared a specific work to be obscene; for all practical purposes, judicial policy-making had been a one-way street.

Although the thrust of the Court's decisions is manifest, the norms and concepts which emerged are broad and ambiguous. The Court has done little to refine substantive doctrines (e.g., what *kind* of social value is redeeming?) nor has it provided common-sense translations of its amorphous terminology (e.g., what *is* prurience?). Even if it is assumed that the Court subscribes to the theory under which "hard-core pornography" exhausts the category of the constitutionally obscene,[28] much doubt lingers about the sum and substance of this class of materials. If obscenity embraces *more* than the kind of speech connoted by the hard-core, then, *a fortiori*, the problems of applying the Supreme Court's doctrines to specific cases are exacerbated.

A significant implication of this ambiguity is the enormous discretion which has devolved on state appellate courts as they apply the constitutional guidelines furnished by the High Court. Acting consistently with their subordinate status within the federal system, the state courts have been relatively free to create public policy and infuse their own values into the law. Indeed, the generally accepted duty of rendering independent judgement on the constitutionality of disputed publications has impelled the courts in many states to declare themselves on the issue of sex expression.

A brief comparison of two appellate courts at opposite ends of the policy spectrum illustrates the variance in judicial approaches to obscenity cases. The Maryland Court of Appeals, by ruling in favor of sexual speech in ten out of twelve obscenity cases handled in the last decade, has seriously obstructed the state's motion picture censorship operation. Among the films approved are: *This Picture Is*

---

28. This interpretation was advanced by the Supreme Court's oblique equation in *Redrup v. New York*, 386 U.S. 767, 770 (1967), of the hard-core standard with the "not dissimilar" three-sided test articulated by the Court in *Memoirs v. Massachusetts*, 383 U.S. 413 (1966). The "three sides" are prurient interest, patent offensiveness, and social value.

Censored, consisting of "provocative" clips from banned films; [29] *Dirty Girls;* [30] and *Lorna,* which contains implied scenes of sexual intercourse.[31] Other media have also fared well in the "Free State": convictions for the sale of *Tropic of Cancer* were upset prior to the book's legitimation by the United States Supreme Court; [32] packets of photographs comprising sequential strip tease acts have been sanctioned.[33] The doctrines accompanying these decisions have also been permissive; for example, the Court ruled in *Yudkin v. State* [34] that the trial court is required to admit expert evidence when deciding issues of contemporary community standards and social value.

The *modus operandus* of the Maryland Court of Appeals is antithetical to the behavior of the Florida appellate courts which have endorsed lower court findings of obscenity in six out of eight cases decided in recent years. Among the works condemned by the highest tribunals in Florida have been *Tropic of Cancer,*[35] *Pleasure Is My Business,*[36] several "girlie" magazines including *Shape, Sizzle,* and *Harem,*[37] and *Miami Life,* a newspaper in which sexual relations between Negroes and whites are described.[38] In *Rachleff v. Mahon,* the hard-core pornography theory was explicitly rejected and obscenity was said to cover any "presentation and exploitation of illicit sex . . . passion, depravity, or immorality." [39]

If lower courts actually do adhere to the directives of superordinate

29. *Hewitt v. Maryland Board of Censors,* 241 Md. 283, 216 A.2d 557 (1966). The Maryland Court's stoic orientation toward obscenity is manifested in its assessment of *This Picture Is Censored:*

> While there is a most generous display of the female epidermis, both fore and aft, the whole thing is about as titillating and exciting as a ton of coal.

216 A.2d 557 (1966).
30. *Leighton v. Maryland Board of Censors,* 242 Md. 705, 218 A.2d 179 (1966).
31. *Dunn v. Maryland Board of Censors,* 240 Md. 249, 213 A.2d 751 (1965).
32. *Yudkin v. State,* 229 Md. 223, 182 A.2d 798 (1962).
33. *Monfred v. State,* 226 Md. 312, 173 A.2d 173 (1961).
34. 229 Md. 223, 182 A.2d 798 (1962).
35. *Grove Press v. Gerstein,* Fla., 151 So.2d 19 (1963), rev'd 378 U.S. 577 (1964).
36. *Tralins v. Gerstein,* Fla., 151 So.2d 19 (1963), rev'd 378 U.S. 576 (1964).
37. *Rachleff v. Mahon,* Fla., 124 So.2d 878 (1960).
38. *State v. Clein,* Fla., 93 So.2d. 876 (1957).
39. Fla., 124 So.2d 878, 882 (1960).

courts and if local elites (e.g., mayors, prosecutors, police chiefs) do pay heed to judicial policies, then booksellers located in states in which appellate courts have been permissive in their handling of obscenity cases should be more permissive in stocking, promoting, and selling sex literature than booksellers situated in states where higher court have been restrictive. Where the courts have fluctuated in their decision-making, bookseller behavior should fall midway on the self-censorship continuum.

THE EFFECT OF PUBLIC OPINION

Social pressures to conform to accepted norms can deter free expression just as rigorously as politico-legal restraints. Large-scale mass intolerance can overwhelm the palliative checking actions of courts, while public permissiveness can turn the anti-libertarian efforts of zealous officials into futile gestures ignored by society. Notwithstanding the oft-noted disparity between public opinion and social behavior, the public can set the gross limits of permissible expression. Furthermore, given the persistent and pervasive populist tendency in American social life,[40] "vox populi, vox Dei" is a force not to be ignored in an examination of censorship in the United States.

Public opinion can be conceptualized as the aggregate of individual attitudes on an issue of social policy. If a community is composed largely of persons with permissive attitudes toward sexual speech, the thresholds of public tolerance for sexual candor and crudity should be higher and social restraints imposed on booksellers should be fewer. Since an individual's attitudes on civil liberties issues are apparently related to his objective social characteristics,[41] the general

40. Daniel Bell, "The Dispossessed—1962," in Daniel Bell (ed.), *The Radical Right* (New York: Doubleday, 1963), p. 31.
41. The author analyzed two sets of data to show that well-established social determinants of intolerance are somewhat related to the issue of sex censorship. Urbanism, wealth, and education are statistically related to county voting behavior on the California anti-obscenity initiative of 1966 ("Proposition 16") while individual attitudes toward restrictions on sexual speech, as inferred from national survey data, are affected by urbanism, age, and physical mobility. See James Levine, "The Bookseller and the Law of Obscenity: Toward an Empirical Theory of Free Expression" (Unpublished Ph.D. dissertation, Department of Political Science, Northwestern University, 1968), chap. 4.

parameters of public opinion can be estimated by analyzing the demographic composition of a community.

In particular, the diversity of people, behavior, ideas, and values found in urban areas should be conducive to an atmosphere of public tolerance and sophistication, while the simplicity of small-town social structures and the homogeneity of rural populations should have the opposite effect of fostering intense negative public reactions to deviant expression. Also, public intolerance and bookseller self-censorship should be directly related to aggregate age levels within communities and inversely related to composite measures of education, wealth, and physical mobility.

THE BOOKSELLER SURVEY: METHODOLOGY AND FINDINGS

The data on self-censorship was obtained from a mail questionnaire returned by 63 per cent of a random sample of 250 booksellers in 12 states. Three categories of appellate court treatment of obscenity were represented as follows:

> permissive policies: California, Maryland, Oregon, and Pennsylvania
> fluctuating policies: Connecticut, Illinois, Massachusetts, Wisconsin
> restrictive policies: Florida, Missouri, New York, Ohio

The classification was made on the basis of a systematic scrutiny and analysis of all discoverable obscenity decisions of the highest courts of all fifty states over the last twenty years.[42]

By comparing the way in which different species of sex expression (e.g., "girlie" magazines, "art" films, sado-masochistic novels) were treated by different courts, it was possible to attain a reasonably detached and unbiased impression of the approach courts were taking in handling obscenity cases. Indeed, certain works, such as Henry Miller's *Tropic of Cancer* and John Cleland's *Fanny Hill*, were adjudicated in several jurisdictions prior to their appraisal by the United States Supreme Court. These decisions were particularly

42. Several categories of the "key" system of case indexing prepared by the West Publishing Company were searched to derive a complete list of obscenity cases, but it is entirely conceivable that some cases went unnoticed because they were catalogued in a legal rubric not scanned by this researcher.

useful in classifying courts, because they enabled us to observe variance in judicial output while controlling for the facts at issue.[43]

The criteria utilized to rank courts were twofold: (1) what the courts *said*, i.e., the severity or laxity of the rules of law enunciated, and (2) what the courts *did*, i.e., how frequently they ruled for or against sexual speech on trial. So that policies on obscenity could be isolated from judicial orientations toward other civil liberties questions, cases were weighted less heavily where the court refrained from evaluating the contents of specific works and grounded its judgement on issues of law enforcement procedure or the constitutionality of a statute on its face.

For both theoretical and practical reasons, the survey was restricted to dealers who are presumably "reputable," i.e., those who are making a *bona fide* effort to stay within the confines of the law of obscenity. Booksellers were randomly selected from the 1965 edition of the biennially revised *American Book Trade Directory* [44] which was the most authoritative source of active book dealers.

The questionnaire was intended to find the openness of the routine, day-to-day retail trade in books. A self-censorship scale was constructed by summating the responses to a series of "forced-choice" questions concerning book selection, sales, and promotion procedures. The following are a sample of the items incorporated into the scale:

> If a book has a reputation for being "controversial" due to its "realistic" or "shocking" portrait of sex, do you make a special effort to acquaint yourself with its contents?
> If a book contains frequent use of vulgar and profane language, does this in itself ever deter you from selecting the book for your store?
> Does your store generally refrain from selling books in which the central themes center on sexual perversion of one sort or another?
> Would you refrain from stocking a book that has a sexually seductive or erotic cover (e.g., a picture of a barely clad woman), even if you are certain that the contents of the book are not obscene?

43. No attempts were made to control for differences in statutory language among the twelve states. It was assumed that verbal variation in obscenity laws are inconsequential when courts are faced with the chore of deciding the constitutionality of suppressing particular works.
44. Eleanor Steiner-Prag, *American Book Trade Directory*, (New York: R. R. Bowker Co.; 17th ed., 1965).

Also included in the self-censorship scale were a series of items asking whether respondents stocked ten "sex books," ranging from the literary classic *Catcher in the Rye* (in which the word "fuck" is used incidentally) to *Fanny Hill*, which John Ciardi of the *Saturday Review* has called unmistakable pornography.[45]

At the permissive end of the scale fell booksellers who refrained from censorship and made available, candidly and unabashedly, a wide variety of publications dealing with sexual behavior or using profane language. At the other extreme, book dealers who systematically exclude sexually oriented materials from their inventories were considered to be restrictive.

The survey is inconclusive about the impact of legal norms of obscenity on bookseller behavior. Only 3 per cent of all respondents seek legal advice about the sale of books about sex on more than isolated occasions. More than half (57 per cent) acknowledged that they were unfamiliar with the specific provisions of local statutes and ordinances. Of even more significance is Table 1 which shows that only a small minority of booksellers are enlightened about the supposedly momentous decisions of the United States Supreme Court.

The wide abyss between judicial pronouncements and social responses can be observed by examining the short-run effects of *Ginzburg v. United States*,[46] the restrictive obscenity decision of 1966. Despite the extensive publicity and commentary which the case received in both mass media and professional journals, it failed to live up to its expectation as a harbinger of ill tidings for the retail bookseller. Although almost a full year had elapsed between the decision and the study, only 5 per cent of the entire sample consciously instigated any changes in their policies and practices as a direct result of *Ginzburg* and none of the modifications that were reported seemed to be major in scope. The Supreme Court may have donated a wealth of raw materials for the benefit of legal scholars, but its influence on the dissemination of sex literature in the general bookstore has been miniscule.

The hypothesis concerning the impact of state appellate courts was not confirmed by the data. Although Table 2 indicates that book-

45. John Ciardi, "What Is Pornography?" *Saturday Review*, July 13, 1963, p. 20.
46. 383 U.S. 463 (1966).

Table 1

BOOKSELLERS' KNOWLEDGE OF SUPREME COURT DECISIONS

Booksellers' General Awareness of Supreme Court Decisions [a]		Booksellers' Knowledge of *Roth v. United States* [b]	
I follow them very carefully.	15%	I am very familiar with the doctrines.	10%
I try to note the general trend in the law which they represent.	60	I know the major points made by the Court.	16
I don't follow them very much.	25	I have heard of the case, but don't know many details.	32
	100%	I am not familiar with the case.	42
Number of Cases	144		100%
		Number of Cases	144

[a] Item: How closely do you follow the decisions and opinions of the United States Supreme Court in the field of obscenity?
[b] Item: How familiar are you with the constitutional doctrines expressed by the United States Supreme Court in *Roth v. United States,* an obscenity case handed down in 1957?

Table 2

RELATION OF STATE APPELLATE COURT POLICY-MAKING TO NUMBER OF SEX BOOKS STOCKED [a] AND BOOKSELLER SELF-CENSORSHIP PRACTICES [b]

Number of Sex Books Stocked	Judicial Policy-Making			Self-Censorship Practices	Judicial Policy-Making		
	Restrictive	Fluctuating	Permissive		Restrictive	Fluctuating	Permissive
0–3	25%	35%	17%	Restrictive	34%	54%	25%
4–7	22	40	21	Moderate	32	27	31
8–10	53	25	61	Permissive	34	19	44
	100%	100%	99% [c]		100%	100%	100%
Number of Cases	55	40	47	Number of Cases	56	41	58

[a] Gamma = .10, not significant.
[b] Gamma = .10, not significant.
[c] Does not sum to 100 per cent because of rounding.

stores in permissive jurisdictions are slightly more lenient about peddling sex books than those in restrictive states, the percentage differences are so small that they could easily have resulted from mere chance. Booksellers governed by fluctuating courts, instead of exercising moderate censorship, turn out to be most restrictive of all. Because states in the "middle-of-the-road" category of judicial policy-making are out of expected alignment and the distributions of the two "extreme" classes of states do not differ radically, the rank-order correlations between judicial behavior and bookseller behavior are statistically insignificant.

It is conceivable that the anarchic patterns of Table 2 are artifacts of a faulty research methodology. The original respondent selection process may be responsible: if the three classes of states were not "matched" according to essential characteristics (such as the distribution of types of communities), the effects of judicial behavior are "contaminated" by extraneous variance. Also, the coding of appellate courts may have been unreliable, with the final court classification being more a figment of the researcher's imagination than a product of real differences.

On the other hand, theoretical conceptions may have been erroneous. The lines of communications connecting appellate courts, trial courts, political elites and booksellers may be so tenuous and haphazard that policy messages emanating from state capitols either become garbled or peter out entirely before reaching the local bookstall. Even if judicial dictates are successfully transmitted, they may be disregarded by local judges, police, prosecutors and merchants.

Whatever the reason, most respondents appeared to be unaffected by the policy-making of the state courts. Although 70 per cent of the sample answered affirmatively when asked if they usually find out about state and local court rulings on obscenity, these decisions are probably misunderstood or ignored.[47] From an academic point of view, the state judiciary plays a major role in the development and articulation of obscenity law, but the effect of the state courts on the censorship practices of the general bookseller is yet to be established.

47. The percentage probably overstates the extent of bookseller enlightenment because many of the responses may have been colored by a desire to appear knowledgeable and sophisticated. Others who claimed that they were aware of most judicial rulings may have been honestly mistaken.

Community characteristics also fail to explain a large part of the variance in bookseller behavior. The most powerful predictor is urbanism, and Table 3 indicates that aggregate population is indeed related to differences in censorship activity. It is quite clear that the bookstores located in large cities stock more "sex books" than their counterparts in smaller cities. However, the relationship between city size and self-censorship practices, barely significant statistically at the .10 level, is considerably weaker.

Table 3

RELATION OF COMMUNITY POPULATION TO NUMBER OF SEX BOOKS
STOCKED [a] AND BOOKSELLER SELF-CENSORSHIP PRACTICES [b]

Number of Sex Books Stocked	Population [c]			Self-Censorship Practices	Population [c]		
	Under 25,000	25,000–249,999	250,000 and Over		Under 25,000	25,000–249,999	250,000 and Over
0–3	31%	28%	16%	Restrictive	37%	44%	25%
4–7	33	27	21	Moderate	37	20	39
8–10	36	45	63	Permissive	25	36	36
	100%	100%	100%		99% [d]	100%	100%
Number of cases	39	60	43	Number of cases	40	61	44

[a] Gamma = .27, significant at the .01 level (one-tailed).
[b] Gamma = .14, significant at the .10 level (one-tailed).
[c] Population data are taken from the 1960 census.

In order to rebut the urbanism hypothesis, one might contend that more sex books are stocked in large cities *only because* of greater consumer demand. According to this argument, the low correlation between population and self-censorship practices is *more* significant in that it is based on questions about activities intended to be censorial in nature. Acts of commission would be deemed more important than acts of omission.

A rejoinder is available. First, booksellers can actively manipulate demand curves through their merchandising policies, and the reader's freedom is really dependent on the willingness of retailers to expose customers to a broad range of literary matter. Second, responses to questions about specific books may be a more reliable indicator of self-censorship because booksellers have an identical frame of reference and little room is left for subjective interpretation. Finally, because a book is either stocked or not stocked, unless a bookseller lies outright, it is more difficult for him to falsify his position in an attempt to project either a Comstockian or libertarian image.

Population density, another component of urbanism, is more strongly correlated with marketing practices, as is evidenced by Table 4. This tends to confirm the hypothesis suggested by Louis

Table 4

RELATION OF POPULATION DENSITY OF COMMUNITIES TO NUMBER OF
SEX BOOKS STOCKED [a] AND BOOKSELLER SELF-CENSORSHIP PRACTICES [b]

Number of Sex Books Stocked	Population Density [c]			Self-Censorship Practices	Population Density [c]		
	Low	Medium	High		Low	Medium	High
0–3	36%	21%	17%	Restrictive	56%	36%	25%
4–7	23	29	22	Moderate	17	31	32
8–10	41	50	60	Permissive	26	32	42
	100%	100%	99% [d]		99% [d]	99% [d]	99% [d]
Number of cases	22	38	40	Number of cases	23	39	40

[a] Gamma = .24, significant at the .05 level (one-tailed).
[b] Gamma = .29, significant at the .05 level (one-tailed).
[c] Population density is taken from the 1960 census and is measured in terms of population per square mile.
[d] Does not sum to 100 per cent due to rounding.

Wirth that density "reinforces the effects of numbers by diversifying men and their activities and increasing the complexity of the social structure." [48] Concentration of large numbers of people into relatively small physical spaces such as apartment buildings apparently conduces public tolerance by increasing exposure to variegated stimuli and necessitating, in the interest of social harmony, an "each-to-his-own" attitude among residents.

48. Louis Wirth, "Urbanism as a Way of Life," in Albert Reiss (ed.), *On Cities and Social Life* (Chicago: University of Chicago Press, 1964), p. 73.

Many respondents in small communities explained and defended their restrictiveness by referring to the necessity of respecting community mores so as to maintain a good reputation among the public. The remarks of a Maryland bookseller reveal the powerful regulative effects of social custom in settings involving relatively limited numbers of people:

> We are a modest store in a moderately sized city. Many of our customers are, or have become, friends. We have tried to build a store which would reflect ourselves as persons, through the atmosphere of the store, our personnel, and the kind of services we offer, as well as the books we sell. We do our own censoring, but primarily we take our standards from those of the community. This policy has worked very well for us.

Nevertheless, when the low correlations between urbanism and bookseller behavior are taken in conjunction with the even smaller relationships detected between self-censorship and other demographic variables, there is ample cause for skepticism about the supposed connection between public sentiment toward freedom and actual curtailment of civil liberties. Of course, it is possible that gross census data on community structure (e.g., median income) is too broad-gauged of a measure to permit inferences about community opinion. It may have been erroneous or misleading to use entire cities as relevant communities (as was done in the present study) when public opinion within smaller social units, such as the neighborhood, may have a greater effect on bookseller behavior. However, the null hypothesis may be correct: what the public thinks, feels, fears, and dislikes may have little bearing on the kinds of literature available in the open market.

The meager findings reported above are in stark contrast to the strong positive relationship between booksellers' personal attitudes toward obscenity and their self-censorship practices. Booksellers' attitudes were determined from a series of questions about the desirability of sex censorship, and Table 5 convincingly demonstrates that variance in censorship behavior is explicable in terms of respondents' psychological predispositions on this social issue.

The rank-order correlations of .80 and .78 practically speak for themselves, and the almost symmetrical matrices of Table 5 attest to

Table 5

RELATION OF BOOKSELLERS' ATTITUDES TOWARD SEXUAL SPEECH TO
NUMBER OF SEX BOOKS STOCKED [a] AND SELF-CENSORSHIP PRACTICES [b]

	Booksellers' Attitudes				Booksellers' Attitudes		
Number of Sex Books Stocked	Restrictive	Moderate	Permissive	Self-Censorship Practices	Restrictive	Moderate	Permissive
0–3	52%	24%	0%	Restrictive	72%	29%	4%
4–7	36	31	12	Moderate	18	48	29
8–10	11	45	88	Permissive	9	24	67
	99% [c]	100%	100%			99% [c]	101% [c]	100%
Number of cases	52	42	49	Number of cases	54	42	49

[a] Gamma = .80, significant at the .001 level (one-tailed).
[b] Gamma = .78, significant at the .001 level (one-tailed).
[c] Does not sum to 100 per cent due to rounding.

a convergence of attitudes and behavior. Booksellers who find coarse or detailed discussions of sex personally repugnant are likely to avoid handling this kind of merchandise, restricting their inventory to books which are reticent about sex. Conversely, dealers who welcome, or at least condone, explicit portrayals of sexual conduct are more willing to carry books about sex which are shocking and repulsive to large segments of the society.

Although legitimate questions could be raised about the validity of the attitude measure, the quantitative analysis is complemented by the written remarks offered by booksellers. A fascinating consistency can be discovered between the degree of censorship exercised and the "temper" and emphasis of respondents' discourses on the subjects of censorship and obscenity. For example, a permissive Wisconsin bookseller replied as follows:

> Obscenity . . . is not a large problem today. After all, we have minds and can pick and choose what we wish to put into them. The so-called blunt or obscene language used in many books are in all cases tame compared to the vocabulary of most people, whether "high or low born." So personally, I cannot find reason to condemn a book on that basis. Keep them from children, yes, but adults should be able to pick and choose as they will. After all, who wants

to be their "brother's keeper" all the time or even is capable of the task.

A quite different tone is conveyed by the words of a Pennsylvania respondent who imposes rigorous censorship controls:

> They tell me *The Arrangement* which shocked me isn't any worse than the *Valley of the Dolls*. I didn't even read the first pages of that, but since it held the bestseller top place so long it probably was sexy. I wouldn't know—a good *clean* murder story for me!

The role perceptions of booksellers also affect their marketing practices. Where booksellers visualized their social positions as civic leaders, protectors of children, or guardians of public morals, it is not surprising to discover that they eschew "racy" literature. Contrariwise, booksellers who perceive themselves as merchants, pure and simple, often suppress their personal feelings about obscenity because of their preoccupation with the attainment of financial profits. The words of a Massachusetts respondent bespeak a businessman's plea more than a libertarian's credo:

> I run a bookstore; it's my only living. I sell only what the public buys. In my store, you can buy a crossword puzzle book, a Bible, Shakespeare, *Fanny Hill, Candy*, etc. If outsiders want to run my store, I'll give them the key and they can send me my pay and sell whatever they want. Remember, you can only sell what people want to buy.

The data compellingly intimate that *internal psychological forces* impinging on booksellers, be they attitudes or role perceptions, are primary causes of freedom and censorship in the general bookstore. This was surmised over a decade ago by Eric Larrabee:

> Of all the forms of sex censorship, that of the individual psyche —which sees to it that some things cannot be said, even to oneself— is undoubtedly the most effective.[49]

To a great extent, public access to books about sex is dependent upon the open-mindedness and the moral irresponsibility of individuals who comprise the bookselling profession.

49. Eric Larrabee, "The Cultural Context of Sex Censorship," *Law and Contemporary Problems*, 20 (Autumn 1955), p. 673.

CONCLUSION

In the domain of sex censorship, "what is obscene?" has been called the "core constitutional question," [50] and in the literary realm of communications, it is the bookseller, rather than the courts or the masses, who provides the most definitive and relevant answer. This suggests that individuals who occupy social positions enabling them to screen public speech may possess considerable autonomy in controlling the range of freedom permitted in a society. Since judicial behavior and community demography were poor predictors of censorship in the bookstore and since booksellers' attitudes correlated highly with their censorship behavior, it may well be that neither legal nor social forces can easily pierce the inner shell of personal prejudices, preferences, and inhibitions which seem to motivate those who function as "gatekeepers" of public speech. The courts may command and the public may opine, but the bookseller is, by and large, the master of his own fate.

If these limited findings can be extrapolated to other social situations having civil liberties dimensions, then some of our *a priori* notions about the empirical roots of freedom may need overhauling. The external forces of constitutional law and public opinion may actually be less significant and influential than the internal moralities and attitude structures of the corps of elites and sub-elites who, like the bookseller, allocate freedom to the society.

50. William Lockhart and Robert McClure, "Obscenity Censorship: The Core Constitutional Question—What Is Obscene?" *Utah Law Review,* 7 (Spring 1961), p. 289.

RICHARD J. MEDALIE, LEONARD ZEITZ,
AND PAUL ALEXANDER

Custodial Police Interrogation in Our Nation's Capital: The Attempt To Implement Miranda

The Miranda Premises

In *Miranda*, the Court's aim was to devise proper safeguards which would preclude custodial police interrogation practices designed to impair a defendant's capacity to remain silent. Once a suspect in custody was to be questioned by police, he would have to be "adequately and effectively apprised of his rights" and assured of "a continuous opportunity to exercise them." To this end, the police were to warn the suspect "in clear and unequivocal terms"
—that he had the right to remain silent;
—that anything said "can and will" be used against the individual in court;
—that he had not only the right to consult with counsel prior to questioning, but also the right to have counsel present at the interrogation;
—that if he could not afford an attorney, one would be appointed for him prior to any questioning if the defendant so desired.

At least three related premises seemed to underlie the Court's decision: (1) that the police will give adequate and effective warnings of legal rights and will honor the accused's exercise of those rights; (2) that the defendant will understand the meaning of the warnings and their significance in application to himself and that he

From the *Michigan Law Review*, 66, no. 7 (May 1968), pp. 1347–1422. Reprinted by permission of the publisher and the authors.

Richard D. Medalie is the Director of the Institute of Criminal Law and Procedure at the Georgetown Law Center, Washington, D.C.

will thereby have sufficient basis to decide in his own best interest whether or not to remain silent and whether or not to request counsel; and (3) that the presence of an attorney in the police station will protect the accused's fifth amendment privilege.

The Nature of the Present Study

In order to test these premises, the Institute of Criminal Law and Procedure of the Georgetown University Law Center [1] undertook an empirical study of the attempt to implement *Miranda* in the District of Columbia.[2] In contrast to other studies which have concentrated on the police and law enforcement,[3] the Institute concerned itself

1. The Institute of Criminal Law and Procedure was established in October 1965 under a grant from the Ford Foundation, at the Georgetown University Law Center. The staff of the Institute is composed of attorneys and research associates from other disciplines, including sociology, psychiatry, psychology, social work, forensic science, history, and political science. The primary aim of the Institute is to engage in systematic studies of the criminal law process from police investigation practices to appellate and post-conviction procedures. The research for this article was conducted in a project of the Institute of Criminal Law and Procedure, under a grant from the Ford Foundation. The authors are greatly indebted to Samuel Dash, Director of the Institute, who provided helpful guidance and direction to the research throughout the course of the project and who contributed many useful suggestions during the writing of this article.
2. See Dash, *Foreword*, in R. MEDALIE, FROM ESCOBEDO TO MIRANDA: THE ANATOMY OF A SUPREME COURT DECISION xix (1966).
3. These studies analyzed police interrogation procedures in the following cities: (1) Boston, Chicago and Washington, D.C.: Reiss & Black, *Interrogation and the Criminal Process*, ANNALS OF THE AM. ACAD. OF POL. & SOC. SCI., Nov. 1967, at 47; see also Black & Reiss, *Patterns of Behavior in Police and Citizen Transactions*, in 2 PRESIDENT'S COMMISSION ON LAW ENFORCEMENT AND ADMINISTRATION OF JUSTICE FIELD SURVEY III—STUDIES IN CRIME AND LAW ENFORCEMENT IN MAJOR METROPOLITAN AREAS 1 (Reiss ed. 1967). (2) Detroit: V. Piersante, Confession in Felony Prosecutions for the Year of 1961 as Compared to Jan. 20, 1965, through Dec. 31, 1965 (unpublished manuscript, July 27, 1965); see N.Y. Times, Feb. 28, 1966, at 18, col. 1. (3) Los Angeles: E. Younger, Results of Survey Conducted in the District Attorney's Office of Los Angeles County Regarding the Effects of the *Dorado* and *Miranda* Decisions upon the Prosecution of Felony Cases, Aug. 4, 1966. See also Younger, *Interrogation of Criminal Defendants—Some Views on Miranda v. Arizona*, 35 FORDHAM L. REV. 255 (1966). (4) New Haven: *Interrogation in New Haven: The Impact of Miranda*, 76 YALE L.J. 1519 (1967). See also Griffiths & Ayres, *A Postscript to the Miranda Project: Inter-*

primarily with the effect of *Miranda* on the role played by defense counsel at the stationhouse and on the defendant's perception of his legal rights. Moreover, unlike other studies which obtained data by stationing observers with the police,[4] the Institute obtained its data primarily through questionnaires administered to attorneys who had volunteered their time to service defendants at the stationhouse in a year-long "Precinct Representation Project," and through interviews with defendants in the Institute's Defendant Interview Study. To the extent permitted by the available data obtained from the attorneys and defendants, police warning and interrogation practices were also analyzed.

The Defendant Interview Study

To assess the impact of *Miranda* on the defendant directly, the Institute devised its Defendant Interview Study. The Institute staff conducted interviews with 260 persons who had been subjected to arrest procedures in the District of Columbia during 1965 and 1966.

The interview schedule was designed to gather a wide variety of data concerning (1) the defendant's reaction to actual and hypothetical arrest situations; (2) his attitudes toward the adversary system, the assistance of counsel, and police investigative practices; (3) his perception of constitutional and other legal rights coincident to arrest and initial presentment; (4) his awareness of judicial decisions defining those rights; and (5) his knowledge and understanding of the criminal law process itself.

---

rogation of Draft Protestors, 77 YALE L.J. 300 (1967). (5) New York: Sobel, *The Exclusionary Rules in the Law of Confessions: A Legal Perspective— A Practical Perspective*, 154 N.Y.L.J. 1 (1965). *See also* N. SOBEL, THE NEW CONFESSION STANDARDS 136–39 (1966). (6) Pittsburgh: Seeburger & Wettick, *Miranda in* PITTSBURGH—A STATISTICAL STUDY, 29 U. PITT. L. REV. 1 (1967).

4. *See, e.g.*, Reiss & Black, *supra* note 3, at 51–52; *Interrogation in New Haven*, *supra* note 3, at 1527–28, 1637–38. Although we attempted to conduct a similar observation study of the police in the District of Columbia, we were unable to work out satisfactory arrangements with the Metropolitan Police Department.

The Central Findings

Two central findings stand out in our study. First, approximately 40 per cent of the defendants in our study who were arrested in the post-*Miranda* period stated that they had given statements [5] to the police.[6] Second, an astonishingly small number of defendants—1,262 —requested counsel from the Precinct Representation Project, even though volunteer attorneys were readily available around the clock, seven days a week.[7] This number represented only 7 per cent of the 15,430 persons arrested for felonies and serious misdemeanors in the District of Columbia during fiscal 1967.

These central findings bring into question the three basic premises of *Miranda*. To assess their significance, we shall . . . explore the reaction of the defendants to the *Miranda* warnings—their understanding of the warnings, their attitudes toward the warnings, and their reasons for deciding whether or not to obtain counsel and whether or not to cooperate with the police. . . ." [A long statement of methodology follows. —ed.]

THE DEFENDANTS' REACTION TO THE MIRANDA WARNINGS

The Court's Reasons for Requiring the Warnings

James Mill in his *Essay on Government* propounded the view that a proper knowledge of one's self-interest would lead one to act in

5. As in *Miranda*, the term "statements" includes for purposes of the present study "statements which are direct confessions . . . statements which amount to 'admissions' of part or all of an offense . . . inculpatory statements and statements alleged to be merely 'exculpatory.'" Miranda v. Arizona, 384 U.S. 436, 467–77 (1966). In addition, for the sake of completeness, unrelated and uncharacterized statements are included in the definition and will be noted, where relevant.
6. A slightly higher percentage of defendants in our study who were arrested before *Miranda* also gave statements to the police. . . .
7. After the first month of operation of the Project, Julian Dugas, then head of the NLSP found it "incredible" that his attorneys had received so few calls. As he observed, "[S]ince the free legal service was organized . . . only 78 defendants have taken advantage of it. It seems extraordinary—in fact, it seems incredible—in light of the number of serious offenses committed each day in Washington." Washington Post, July 20, 1966, at C-1, col. 1.

accordance with that interest.[8] According to Mill's son, John Stuart, so complete was his father's "reliance on the influence of reason over the minds of mankind . . . that he felt as if all would be gained if the whole population were taught to read." [9] James Mill's "fundamental doctrine," said his son, "was the . . . unlimited possibility of improving the moral and intellectual condition of mankind by education." [10]

The underlying philosophy of the Court's decision in *Miranda* is closely akin to Mill's eighteenth century Utilitarian views. Implicit throughout the opinion is the assumption that once the defendant is properly warned of his legal rights he will be in a position to act in accordance with his interest in remaining silent and requesting a lawyer.

The Court's philosophical position may be most clearly seen in its characterization of the right-to-silence warning. The warning is needed, the Court avowed, in order to make the accused "aware" of the right.[11] In effect, the silence warning is "the threshold requirement for an intelligent decision as to its exercise." [12] It "insure[s] that the individual knows he is free to exercise the privilege at that point in time" [13] and shows the individual "that his interrogators are prepared to recognize his privilege should he choose to exercise it." [14] In like manner, the Court maintained, the warning that anything said can and will be used against the accused makes him aware "not only of the privilege but also of the consequences of foregoing it." [15] This awareness assures a "real understanding and intelligent exercise of the privilege" and serves to make the accused "more accurately aware that he is faced with a phase of the adversary system—that he

8. "[I]f the parties who act contrary to their interest had a proper knowledge of that interest, they would act well. What is necessary, then, is knowledge." J. Mill, *An Essay on Government,* in THE ENGLISH PHILOSOPHERS FROM BACON TO MILL 885 (1939).
9. J. MILL, AUTOBIOGRAPHY 89 (World Classics ed. 1931).
10. *Id.* at 91; *see also* J. PENNOCK, LIBERAL DEMOCRACY: ITS MERITS AND PROSPECTS 17 (1950).
11. 384 U.S. at 468.
12. 384 U.S. at 468.
13. 384 U.S. at 469.
14. 384 U.S. at 468.
15. 384 U.S. at 469.

is not in the presence of persons acting solely in his interest." [16]

Unfortunately, the Court's vision of how *Miranda* would operate has become somewhat blurred in practice, as our statistics of interrogation and confession demonstrate. We must therefore ask what did the *Miranda* warnings mean to the defendants and to what extent were they helped by the recital of warnings.

The Defendant's Behavior Following the Warnings

A definite relationship existed between the giving of the warning of the right to stationhouse counsel [17] and the "post-*Miranda* defendants'" decision to obtain counsel: close to two-thirds of these defendants who reported receiving this warning did request counsel. Yet the fact remains that over one-third of these defendants receiving the warning did not request counsel. Moreover, when no warnings were given or when warnings other than the right to stationhouse counsel were given, the overwhelming response of well over three-quarters of the remaining "post-*Miranda* defendants" was not to request counsel. The results are set forth in Table 1.

16. 384 U.S. at 469. The Court continued in this vein for the other warnings as well. Thus, concerning the right to the presence of an attorney, it said: "Only through such warning is there ascertainable assurance that the accused was aware of this right." 384 U.S. at 472. Concerning the right to an appointed counsel, the Court added:

> Without this additional warning, the admonition of the right to consult with counsel would often be understood as meaning only that he can consult with a lawyer if he has one or has the funds to obtain one. The warning of a right to counsel would be hollow if not couched in terms that would convey to the indigent—the person most often subjected to interrogation—the knowledge that he too has a right to have counsel present. As with the warnings of the right to remain silent and the general right to counsel, only by effective and express explanation to the indigent of this right can there be assurance that he was truly in a position to exercise it. [U.S. at 473]

17. The warnings we used were as follows:

> You have been placed under arrest. You are not required to say anything to us at any time or to answer any questions. Anything you say may be used against you as evidence in Court.
>
> Your lawyer may be present here during the police interrogation and you may consult with him.
>
> If you cannot afford to retain a lawyer privately, you have the right to have a lawyer appointed to represent you free of charge at the police station.

Table 1

RESULTS OF SPECIFIC WARNINGS OF POST-MIRANDA DEFENDANTS [a]
BY WHETHER COUNSEL REQUESTED [b]

Warnings of Rights	Counsel Requested		Counsel Not Requested	
	No.	%	No.	%
Non-stationhouse Counsel	2	17	10	83
Stationhouse Counsel	21	64	12	36
Silence Alone	3	23	10	77
Neither Counsel nor Silence [c]	3	12	21	88
Undetermined			3	* [d]
Total	29		56	

[a] Only 2 of the 175 pre-Miranda defendants requested counsel.
[b] Data source: Defendant Interview Schedules.
[c] Includes warnings of phone and/or bond, as well as no warning.
[d] Irrelevant or insignificant percentage.

Similarly, a parallel relationship existed between the warning of the right to silence and the "post-Miranda defendants'" refusal to give statements to the police: 60 per cent of these defendants who said they were given the warning gave no statements; the other 40 per cent, however, did give statements despite the warning. At the same time, when no silence or other warnings were said to have been given, over half of the remaining "post-Miranda defendants" gave statements to the police. . . .

The Defendant's Understanding of the Warnings

In order to test their cognitive understanding, we gave full Miranda-type warnings one at a time to the defendants, and, after each, asked what the warning meant to them.[18] The defendants' answers

18. Our interviewers gave these warnings to the defendants interviewed in as neutral a manner as possible. To be sure, this procedure could not duplicate the atmosphere at arrest or at the stationhouse, where the possible anxiety of the defendant and the possible partisan manner of the police (see Interrogation in New Haven, at 1552) would probably lead to greater misunderstanding and confusion as to the meaning of the warnings than was registered by the defendants in our interviews. Consequently, if anything, our results understate the defendants' rate of misunderstanding of the warnings.

were then rated as signifying either "understanding" or "misunderstanding." [19] The ratings indicated that 15 per cent of the eighty-five "post-*Miranda* defendants" failed to understand the right to silence warning, 18 per cent failed to understand the warning of the right to the presence of counsel, and 24 per cent failed to understand the warning of the right to appointed counsel.

We were able to derive an added insight into the defendants' understanding of the warnings by obtaining their verbatim comments of what they felt about the way the police told them of their rights. A number were cynical about the procedure, and believed the warnings to be "merely a formality" given to them only because the police "had to." Thus, one defendant complained that the police "didn't seem to care whether we understood or not," and another noted that the police officer giving the warnings "was as ignorant of my rights as I was myself. He was only reading a statement."

On the other hand, several other defendants accepted the warnings from the police at their face value. As one remarked, "They were helpful. [The police] . . . explained . . . [the warnings] very clearly, which is more than they used to do." Others remarked that "[t]hey talked like they meant it"; "they made a big thing about it"; "they wanted it to be known they had about eight people watching as witnesses."

There were many misconceptions as to the meaning of the right to stationhouse counsel. The following were typical misinterpretations of the warning by the defendants:

—The police "had some lawyer of their own who was working with them."

—It means that "I would have to pay for a lawyer."

—They planned to "appoint someone at court."

19. "Understanding" included both complete and partial understanding. Complete understanding was indicated either by an explanation which signified understanding or a definitional statement as to the specified right. A number of respondents answered by saying that the right "means just what it says." This response was considered to be a partial understanding. Our interviewers reported that the somewhat more educated or aggressive persons gave this response and resented any attempt at clarification. "Misunderstanding" included both complete and partial misunderstanding. Complete misunderstanding included the response, "I don't know." Partial misunderstanding included such responses as "That would mean I'm in trouble"; "That wouldn't mean anything to me since I'm innocent"; or "That would mean a lot to me."

—"I just have to write for one and wait for him to answer."

—"I don't know why one would need a lawyer in a stationhouse; it's never done."

—The warning "means I would answer [questions by the police] if a lawyer is present."

Other defendants were not even able to get to the point of interpreting the warning. For example, one was shown the police card with the warnings on it, but failed to read it, and another was so wrought up that his "mind wasn't functioning." "I couldn't think," he reported.

Some defendants had comparable misconceptions about the right to silence warning. Several understood it to mean that they had the right to talk. Some had the opposite impression that the police either did not want them to talk or would not let them talk. Others perceived a garbled version. As one said, it means that "I should have the right to say something so they can use it in evidence in court," and another added that it meant that "[I]f I . . . like try to bribe them, they would use it against me in court." Still others propounded more involved interpretations. "If I'm innocent," said one, "I should tell the truth." Another recognized the dilemma presented: [t]he warning means "that if I said anything false it would go hard on me; if I tell the truth, then trouble."

The Relationship of the Defendant's Understanding to His Behavior

More significant than the defendant's understanding of the warnings is the relationship of this understanding (or misunderstanding) to the decisions each defendant made concerning the right to counsel and the right to silence. . . . 66 per cent of those who understood the stationhouse counsel warning given by the police requested counsel, and approximately sixty per cent of those who understood the silence warning did not give statements.

The Inverse Relationship of Defendant's Understanding to His Behavior

A . . . question raised . . . is why the 34 per cent of the "post-*Miranda* defendants" who understood the counsel warnings did not request counsel and why the 41 per cent who understood the silence warning did not remain silent.

Several commentators have attempted explanation. Elsen and Rosett have observed:

> To predict how a suspect's insistence on his rights will affect his chances of avoiding prosecution requires an intimate knowledge of the system which cannot be conveyed by a warning, however improved. . . . The suspect . . . does not know if his request for counsel will annoy the police, the prosecutor or a jury. The fact that he has been warned as required by *Miranda* may have little bearing on his decision whether counsel should be waived. . . . A suspect may well choose not to be a "wise guy" who will land in jail as a reward for his insistence on his rights.[20]

And Wald and his fellow editors of the *Yale Law Journal* have noted:

> The suspect arrested and brought downtown for questioning is in a crisis-laden situation. The stakes for him are high—often his freedom for a few or many years—and his prospects hinge on decisions that must be quickly made: To cooperate and hope for leniency, to try and talk his way out, to stand adamantly on his rights . . . The likely consequences of the alternatives open to him are unclear —how much leniency cooperation may earn, how likely fast talk is to succeed, how much a steadfast refusal to talk may contribute to a decision by the police, prosecutor or judge to "throw the book" at him.[21]

Thus, while these defendants may have had a cognitive understanding of their rights, they had no appreciation of them and lacked the ability to apply them to their "crisis-laden" situations. This is borne out by many of the statements of the defendants we obtained in our interviews. Although these statements could not be quantitatively analyzed, they did afford us an opportunity to gain an insight into the reasons for rejection of counsel and for talking to the police.

Concerning the right to stationhouse counsel, one defendant did not believe he could really obtain a lawyer at the station. Another did not trust a lawyer furnished by the police. "I don't dig those jail-

20. Elsen & Rosett. *Protections for the Suspect under Miranda* 67 COLUM. L. REV. 645, 658 (1967).
21. *Interrogation in New Haven, supra,* at 1613–14.

house deals," he said. "The police have their own lawyer. I wouldn't be interested." And another added, "I only wanted to talk to people I could trust who would let me know what I was up against." Other defendants were too preoccupied with other concerns to recognize the value of a lawyer. Thus, one noted, "I wasn't thinking about anything but calling my mother and wife," and another's "main concern was bond." Still others believed that they themselves knew the system too well to risk having a lawyer. As one "sophisticated" defendant observed, "I wouldn't want one. That's the *worst* place to have a lawyer because the police play it straight then. I wanted them to make a mistake."

As for the right to silence, some feared being hit or beaten up by the police. Several maintained they had been threatened by the police or tricked. Another answered questions only because they did not relate to the charge against him. Still others wanted to convince police of their innocence. In this regard, a general response was that "I saw no harm in it," or that "I had nothing to hide," or that "I thought I was not at fault so I talked." One defendant insisted that there is always a tendency for a person to want to cooperate. And others explained that they would get lenient treatment if they cooperated. As a defendant said, "I figured I could straighten out the whole thing right there." Finally, there were those who just felt compelled to talk. As one explained, "I did it. I knew why the police wanted me, and they had me cold."

* * *

In light of the foregoing data on police practices under *Miranda* and the defendants' response, even in an optimum system of precinct representation, with well-trained counsel at the police station available as soon as a defendant is brought in, the odds against even beginning to approach the model established by the Court in *Miranda* would have been exceedingly high.

RICHARD H. SEEBURGER
AND R. STANTON WETTICK, JR.

Miranda *in Pittsburgh—A statistical study*

The purpose of this statistical study is to determine the extent to which the *Miranda*[1] decision has impaired the ability of Pittsburgh's law enforcement agencies to apprehend and convict the criminal and has created a backlog in the Allegheny County criminal courts. We have collected data showing, *inter alia*, the change in the confession rate following *Miranda*; the percentage of cases in which a confession probably was or would have been necessary in order to obtain a conviction; the change in Pittsburgh's clearance rate following *Miranda*; and the percentage of criminal cases in Allegheny County disposed of through a guilty plea before and after *Miranda*.

SOURCE OF DATA

Most of the data for this Study was obtained from the files of the Detective Branch of the Pittsburgh Police Bureau. This Branch is the investigative arm of the Pittsburgh Police Bureau. It conducts investigations of every homicide committed within the city and most serious felonies other than those immediately solved by the uniformed policemen from the precincts for which no investigative assistance is needed to build the case.[2]

1. Miranda v. Arizona, 384 U.S. at 441.
2. In 1966 the Detective Branch made 54% of the robbery arrests in Pittsburgh; 44% of the burglary arrests; 26% of the auto theft arrests and 57% of the forceful rape arrests. Pittsburgh Police Department Service Defense Annual Report 1966, p. 15.

Richard H. Seeburger is Associate Professor of Law, University of Pittsburgh. R. Stanton Wettick, Jr. is Assistant Professor of Law, University of Pittsburgh.

From The University of Pittsburgh Law Review, 29:1 (October, 1967), pp. 2 and 5–12. Reprinted by permission of the publisher and the authors.

The Detective Branch makes a file for each case which it clears.[3] Such files contain all the written information which the Branch has on the case.[4] Such information usually includes a description of the crime, the suspects, the case against the suspects and any statements (oral or written) made by the suspects.

For this study we examined the entire contents of each file of the Detective Branch for each case, starting in 1964, which has been tried or dropped and involves the following types of crime: homicide, forceful sex, robbery, burglary (including receiving stolen goods) and auto larceny.

POLICE PROCEDURE

For almost every file which we examined, the Detective Branch attempted to obtain a confession from all the suspects involved. It is standard practice for the Branch to question every suspect in all cases in which it makes an arrest.

Even before the *Miranda* decision, the Detective Branch met many of the requirements imposed by *Miranda*. For at least 10 and probably 25 years before the *Miranda* decision, it has been the procedure of the Detective Branch to advise suspects of their right to remain silent, and shortly after the *Escobedo* decision, the Detective Branch began to advise suspects of their right to counsel.[5] This advice, however, did not include an offer to provide counsel free of charge to those who could not afford counsel. Moreover, this advice was not given clearly and unequivocally at the beginning of the interrogation, but rather was woven into the conversation between

3. A case is "cleared" when the Detective Branch considers the case solved regardless of the outcome of any prosecution.
4. In most instances this is the only written information which the law enforcement agencies have on the case. The office of the Allegheny County District Attorney keeps no independent files for Pittsburgh crimes other than homicide.
5. Throughout Pennsylvania all police departments should have begun advising suspects of their rights to remain silent and to counsel by the end of 1965. On September 29, 1965 in Commonwealth v. Negri, 419 Pa. 117, 213 A.2d 670 (1965) (overruled by Commonwealth v. Schmidt, 423 Pa. 432, 224 A.2d 625 (1966) the Pennsylvania Supreme Court, following United States *ex rel* Russo v. New Jersey, 351 F.2d 429 (3d Cir. 1965), held that under the fourteenth amendment a confession from a suspect in custody who has not been warned of his rights to counsel and to remain silent is inadmissible.

the suspect and the detective. Furthermore, the detectives would attempt to persuade the suspect who indicated that he wanted to remain silent or to be assisted by counsel to change his mind and make a statement.

Within one week after the *Miranda* decision the Detective Branch began complying with the additional requirements imposed by *Miranda* that the indigent suspect be offered counsel at no cost, that the suspect be advised of his right to remain silent and to the assistance of council in clear and unequivocal terms at the beginning of the questioning, and that all questioning cease if the suspect indicates that he wishes to remain silent or to be assisted by counsel.[6]

Miranda has not been accompanied by any significant changes in Pittsburgh's other investigative procedures. There has been no significant increase in expenditures for additional investigators. In fact since June, 1966 there has been approximately a 10% reduction in the manpower of the Detective Branch, as a result of the transfer of the vice and narcotics enforcement functions from the Branch.

To determine the impact of *Miranda* on the police's ability to obtain confessions, we compared the percentage of cases involving confessions in which the arrest was made prior to the Detective Branch's compliance with the *Miranda* requirements with the percentage of cases involving confessions in which the arrest was made after the Detective Branch's compliance with the *Miranda* requirements.

Our criteria for classifying statements made to the police were to include as confessions all admissions (oral or written) to police officers which were self-incriminating and contained no self-serving declarations which would substantially lessen the offense and all admissions which were helpful to the police's case even if they contained such self-serving declarations. On the other hand, we did not include as confessions any statements which contained certain self-incriminating statements but were primarily self-serving in nature and of little value to the police and any statements which did not

6. The post-*Miranda* procedures of the Detective Branch include orally advising a suspect in custody at the beginning of the interrogation of his constitutional rights to remain silent and to the assistance of counsel which will be furnished free of charge if the suspect can't afford counsel and of the fact that anything which the suspect says can be used against him. The suspect is then asked whether he wishes to waive these rights and make a statement. If the suspect answers negatively, there is no further interrogation.

directly incriminate the suspect even though they could be helpful to the police (for example an alibi which the police found to be a lie).

For purposes of this comparison we chose June 21, 1966 as the time at which the Detective Branch began complying with the *Miranda* requirements.

Even though the Detective Branch, as we have mentioned, advised suspects of their rights to remain silent and to be assisted by counsel prior to the *Miranda* decision, the giving of such advice, according to Assistant Superintendent Coon, did not impair the police's opportunity for effective interrogation. The significant requirements imposed by *Miranda*, according to Assistant Superintendent Coon, are that a suspect in custody be *clearly* advised of his rights to be assisted by counsel and to remain silent *before* any questioning and that all questioning cease once the suspect advises the police that he wishes to remain silent or wants the assistance of counsel. These are the requirements that prevent effective interrogation. Accordingly, for purposes of our comparison we used the time at which the Detective Branch began complying with these requirements.

The comparison of the percentage of cases involving confessions before and after compliance with the *Miranda* requirements is contained in Table 1.[7] For purposes of these figures one case consists of the commission of one or a series of crimes by the same suspects. Figures relating to cases instead of suspects probably give a more accurate picture of the extent to which *Miranda* has hampered the police because frequently crimes are committed by more than one person and one confession is sufficient to solve the case and to pro-

---

7. The figures in the various tables, including Table 1, do not include cases after the *Miranda* decision involving only persons under 18 who were turned over to Juvenile Court because in these cases the Detective Bureau did not comply with the *Miranda* requirements before the decision of In re Gault 387 U.S. 1 (1967).

In addition the figures in these tables do not include files in which it was not clear whether a suspect had confessed, files indicating that the suspect was probably innocent, and files involving matters in the nature of a family or neighborhood squabble rather than a crime. These latter exclusions involve less than 10% of the files for all types of crime other than forcible sex. We excluded more than 100 forcible sex files in which the existence of force seemed to us fairly disputable.

vide evidence for the conviction of all participants in the crime. A second or third confession is of limited benefit to the police.[8]

Table 1

CONFESSION RATE—CASES

Type of Crime		No. of Cases with Confessions	No. of Cases without Confessions	% of Cases with Confessions
Homicide				
	Pre-Miranda	51	36	58.6
	Post-Miranda	5	11	31.3
Robbery				
	Pre-Miranda	108	65	62.4
	Post-Miranda	22	38	36.7
Burglary (including RSG)	Pre-Miranda	123	92	57.2
	Post-Miranda	30	39	43.5
Auto Larceny				
	Pre-Miranda	55	46	54.5
	Post-Miranda	3	6	33.3
Sex (forceable)	Pre-Miranda	16	57	21.9
	Post-Miranda	3	11	21.4
Total				
	Pre-Miranda	353	296	54.4
	Post-Miranda	63	105	37.5

These figures show that before compliance with the *Miranda* requirements the Detective Branch obtained confessions in 54.4% of the cases and after compliance in only 37.5% of the cases. If the comparison is limited to robbery and burglary—the crimes with which most of the post-*Miranda* cases are involved—the decline in the confession rate is even greater. Before *Miranda* the Detective Branch obtained confessions in 59.9% of the burglary and robbery cases and after *Miranda* this percentage dropped to 40.3% of the cases. The most significant decline was in robbery—more than 25%. Burglary, on the other hand, fell only 14%.

8. The primary benefit from obtaining confessions from all participants in the crime is to avoid the hearsay rule which excludes the use of one defendant's confession against the other defendants. But since the defendant who confessed will probably be convicted on the basis of his confession, it will usually be to his advantage to cooperate by testifying against the other defendants.

ROGER HANSON
AND ROBERT CREW

The Effects of Reapportionment on State Public Policy Out-Puts

I. INTRODUCTION

Prior to 1962, positions in state assemblies generally were assigned to counties. In some houses of some state legislatures, a limited number of additional seats were given to the most populated constituencies. However, state legislatures seldom used only population either as the basis for constructing districts or as a criterion for determining the number of seats for given districts. With the development of the social force of urbanization, a limited number of counties became the residence of a majority of the citizens. Since state governments continued to operate with counties as the fundamental unit of legislative apportionment, significant differences in the size (population) of districts were created. Individuals residing in most populated districts constructed the legal argument that the design of legislative districts on the basis of non-population factors violated the U.S. Constitution. They claimed that the value of their votes was less than the weight of the voter preferences in sparsely populated areas. By measuring the value of a vote in terms of its theoretical probability of affecting an *election outcome,* these individuals demonstrated that the size of representational districts determined the worth of a vote. Each citizen's vote is some fraction of the total possible number of votes in a district. As the magnitude of a dis-

A slightly different version of this article appeared in the *Law and Society Review,* Vol. VIII (February 1973). Reprinted by permission of the publisher and the authors.

Roger Hanson is Assistant Professor of Political Science at the University of Wisconsin-Milwaukee. Robert Crew is the Executive Director of the Minnesota Crime Commission.

trict's population increases, that fraction decreases. Consequently, as the size of a district expands, the probability of a voter electing a candidate is reduced and the value of the person's vote diminishes. Moreover, since collective choices about office seekers are the summation of individual voter preferences, the proportion of a state's population living in a district is an index of the value of all of the citizen's votes in that district. This means that different sized proportions imply that entire constituencies are more influential in electing candidates to public office. Persons who resided in larger sized districts regarded their votes as having been diluted by the existing apportionment arrangements. They took action to remedy this situation and sought relief in the federal courts. They focused the issue of what criteria should govern the distribution of seats upon the 14th Amendment's "equal protection of the law" clause. On the basis of that provision, they reasoned that the disparities in the size of districts and the resultant inequalities in the value of the votes of citizens in different sized constituencies were discrimatory practices. They believed that residency should not be a basis for the unequal weighting of voter preferences.

Until 1962, the U.S. Supreme Court and the lower federal courts chose not to directly adjudicate the disputes concerning the legality of non-population based methods of apportionment.[1] The U.S. Supreme Court declined to intervene in the challenges of the existing modes of apportionment on the grounds that such matters involved "political, nonjusticiable questions." However, in a series of decisions beginning in 1962, the U.S. Supreme Court has altered this position and vigorously acted to establish population as the defining characteristic of legislative districts and to require that the ratio of

---

1. The U.S. Supreme Court initially chose not to adjudicate a dispute over Illinois' allocation of Congressional seats because it involved "political, nonjusticiable questions." See *Colegrove v. Green* 328 U.S. 599 (1946). It subsequently dismissed for want of a federal question challenges to Illinois' state legislative apportionment. See *Colegrove v. Barrett* 304 U.S. 804 (1947). With these background decisions, the Court dismissed future cases in which citizens objected to legislative apportionment arrangements. See *Remmy v. Smith* 342 U.S. 916 (1952) and *Kidd v. McCanless* 352 U.S. 920 (1956). In another instance, it affirmed a lower court's refusal to hear such petitions from citizens. See *Radford v. Gary* 352 U.S. 991 (1957).

legislative seats assigned to a district *to* the size of the constituency be the same for all districts.[2]

Without necessarily accepting the content of the arguments behind the reapportionment decisions, what knowledge can legal scholars and political scientists offer about the probable impact of this nationwide reapportionment of major governmental institutions? The law reviews contain innumerable essays concerning major court decisions relevant to the question of legislative apportionment. The content of many of these analyses can be classified under the following general headings: constitutional histories of legislative apportionment,[3] descriptions of the political context surrounding legislative apportionment,[4] difficulties confronting the courts in specifying judicial standards in adjudicating disputes about legislative apportionment,[5] and problems of techniques for measuring inequalities in district size.[6] In some studies, the writers raised questions about the

2. *Baker v. Carr* 369 U.S. 186 (1962); *Gray v. Sanders* 372 U.S. (1963); *Wesberry v. Sanders* 376 U.S. 1 (1964); *Reynolds v. Sims* 377 U.S. 533 (1964); *Lucas v. the Forty-fourth General Assembly of the State of Colorado* 377 U.S. 733 (1964).

3. Robert G. Dixon, "Legislative Apportionment and the Federal Constitution," *Law and Contemporary Problems*, Vol. 27 (Summer 1962) No. 3, pp. 329–89. Robert G. McCloskey, "Foreword: The Reapportionment Case," *Harvard Law Review*, Vol. 76 (November, 1962), No. 1, pp. 54–74.

4. Gus Tyler, "Court Versus Legislature," *Law and Contemporary Problems*, Vol. 27 (Summer 1962) No. 3, pp. 390–407; Ruth C. Silva, "Legislative Representation with Special References to New York," *Law and Contemporary Problems*, Vol. 27 (Summer 1962), No. 3, pp. 408–33.

5. Charles L. Black, "Inequities in Districting for Congress: *Baker v. Carr* and *Colegrove v. Green*," *Yale Law Journal*, Vol. 72 (November 1962), No. 1, pp. 13–22; Alexander M. Bickel, "The Durability of *Colegrove v. Green*," *Yale Law Journal*, Vol. 72 (November 1962), No. 1, pp. 39–45. Thomas I. Emerson, "Malapportionment and Judicial Power," *Yale Law Journal*, Vol. 72 (November 1962), No. 1, pp. 81–89. Robert B. McKay, "Political Thickets and Crazy Quilts," *Michigan Law Review* (February 1963), Vol. 61, No. 4, pp. 645–710. Jo Desha Lucas, "Legislative Apportionment and Representative Government," *Michigan Law Review* (February 1963), Vol. 61, No. 4, pp. 711–804.

6. Arthur Goldberg, "The Statistics of Malapportionment," *Yale Law Journal*, Vol. 72 (November 1962), No. 1, pp. 90–107. James B. Weaver and Sidney W. Hess, "A Procedure for Non-partisan Districting," *Yale Law Journal*, Vol. 73 (November 1963), No. 1, pp. 288–308. Jerold Israel, "On Charting a Course Through the Mathematical Quagmire," *Michigan Law Review*, Vol. 61 (November 1962), No. 1, pp. 107–46. For related literature in political

policy impact of the change in the mode of apportionment.[7] However, these pieces were written without the benefit of systematic data. The conclusions suggest hypotheses about the policy consequences of judicial decisions, but the authors do not test any empirical generalizations in this regard.

In addition some political scientists and politicians responded to the Court's decisions in *Baker v. Carr* and the cases following with great enthusiasm and high expectations. A striking example of these reactions is Martin Landau's view that the reapportionment cases have the causal potency of first "urbanizing" the state legislatures and then shifting the political party system to the "urban-national side as against the state local side."[8] While Landau's projection remains untested, available evidence does not suggest that the short-run effects of reapportionment are dramatic shifts in the partisan composition of legislative bodies.[9]

Other observers of state politics have also perceived definite connections between reapportionment and policy issues. *They linked the probability of a voter affecting the selection of a candidate with the ability of a legislator to affect policy choices.* It was thought that the limited number of urban legislators emasculated most of their capacity to affect the outcomes of public policy. On the other hand, a coalition of nonurban legislators was described as acting in concert to withhold programs that could benefit urban constituencies. With reapportionment, this influence of nonurban legislators was believed to have been reduced, and as a result, major policy changes in the

---

science consult the following: Alan L. Clem, "Measuring Legislative Malapportionment," *Midwest Journal of Political Science,* VII (May 1963), pp. 125–44. Glendon Schubert and Charles Press, "Measuring Malapportionment," *American Political Science Review,* LVII (June 1964), pp. 302–27.
7. E. E. Schattschneider, "Urbanization and Reapportionment," *Yale Law Journal* (November 1962), No. 1, pp. 7–12. Allan P. Sindler, "*Baker v. Carr:* How To Sear the Conscience of Legislators," *Yale Law Journal,* Vol. 72 (November 1962), No. 1, pp. 23–38.
8. Martin Landau, "*Baker v. Carr* and the Ghost of Federalism," in *Reapportionment* (ed.). Glendon Schubert (New York: Charles Scribner's Sons, 1965), pp. 241–48.
9. A comprehensive before and after study of the partisan impact of reapportionment has been completed. See Robert S. Erikson, "The Partisan Impact of Reapportionment," *Midwest Journal of Political Science,* XV (February 1971), pp. 57–71.

specific areas of taxation, welfare, education, and transportation were forecasted.[10]

Like the articles in the law reviews, such prognostications were the product of insight, experience, and shrewd observation, with little in the way of "hard data" to support them. Furthermore such observations have been seriously questioned by a second wave of literature in political science journals, which has found few, if any, connections between malapportionment and public policy. Based upon empirical analysis, these writings encouraged the expectation that reapportionment would not produce widespread changes in state policies.[11] Since the publication of this body of findings, other empirical studies have maintained that malapportionment is related to particular types of state governmental policies.[12] Consequently, until evidence is obtained about possible shifts in policy allocations after reapportionment, scholars can remain committed to the belief that reapportionment is likely to produce cataclysmic changes while other individuals do not anticipate even mild tremors.

10. Charles R. Adrian, State and Local Government (New York: McGraw-Hill, 1960), pp. 304–09. Daniel R. Grant and H. C. Nixon, State and Local Government in America (Boston: Allyn and Bacon, 1963), pp. 202–19. V. O. Key Jr., American State Politics (New York: Alfred A. Knopf, 1956), pp. 64–67. Duane Lockhard, New England State Politics (Princeton: Princeton University Press, 1969), pp. 322–23. George Blair, American Legislatures (New York: Harper and Row, 1967), p. 108. Malcolm Jewell (ed.), The Politics of Reapportionment (New York: Atherton Press, 1962), pp. 17–21; "The Political Setting," in State Legislatures in American Politics (ed.), Alexander Heard (Englewood Cliffs: Prentice-Hall, 1966), pp. 71–73. Gordon Baker, The Reapportionment Revolution (New York: Random House, 1966).
11. Richard Hoffebert, "The Relation Between Public Policy and Some Structural and Environmental Variables in the American States," American Political Science Review, Vol. LX (March 1966), pp. 73–82. Thomas Dye, "Malapportionment and Public Policy in the States," Journal of Politics, Vol. 27 (August 1965), pp. 586–601; Politics, Economics, and the Public (Chicago: Rand McNally, 1966), pp. 294–95. "State Legislative Politics," in Politics in the American States, edited by Herbert Jacob and Kenneth Vines (Chicago: Rand McNally, 1965), pp. 157–65. Herbert Jacob, "The Consequences of Malapportionment: A Note of Caution," Social Forces Vol. 43 (December, 1964), pp. 256–61. David Brady and Douglas Edmonds, "One Man, One Vote—So What," Trans-action, IV (March 1967), pp. 41–46.
12. Allan G. Pulsipher and James Weatherby, Jr., "Malapportionment, Party Competition, and the Functional Distribution of Governmental Expenditures," American Political Science Review, Vol. LXII (December 1963), pp. 1207–19. Jack L. Walker, "The Diffusion of Innovations Among the American States," American Political Science Review, Vol. LXII (September 1969), pp. 880–886.

The inference of our research reported here is that reapportionment is associated with important policy changes in at least some areas of policy out-puts. By means of a longitudinal analysis, we have gathered evidence which shows that reapportionment *preceded and constituted changes* in the pattern of policy outputs. While the results of reapportionment are not found to be either uniform in every state or very dramatic in any state, they do suggest that legislative apportionment is one important component in explaining changes in state policies during the late 1960's.

II. RESEARCH DESIGN

The methodological framework selected for the purpose of examining the causal efficacy of reapportionment within the boundaries of the individual states is a before and after test. In this context, reapportionment is conceptualized as an event which occurs within the broader time frame of the on-going process of policy formation. The *before* period includes observations about the policy outcomes prior to the date of the application of a reapportionment plan. The *after* period takes in measurable decisional outcomes which happen subsequent to the implementation of the structural reform. The first task of the empirical analysis is to ascertain whether any significant changes in authoritative policies are visible after reapportionment is introduced into a state political system. The second job is to ascertain whether it is reapportionment or some other antecedent condition which is the source of any discernible policy change. In order to attempt to satisfy these research goals, the data sets employed in this paper are analyzed in a manner approximating the standards of logical and statistical inference for quasi-experimental designs.[13]

Forty-eight states (Hawaii and Alaska are excluded) are the subjects for comparisons of intra-unit variations in public policies. By looking at 48 units, this research effort complements the scope of prior analyses of the impact of reapportionment which tend to be

13. For a description of methodological requisites of quasi-experimental designs applied to longitudinal data, a relevant reference is a study by Donald T. Campbell. See Donald T. Campbell and H. Laurence Ross, "The Connecticut Crackdown on Speeding," *Law and Society Review*, Vol. III (August 1968), pp. 33–53.

close examinations of legislative roll call voting and legislative committee occupancy in a single state.[14] Each state is examined for the temporal location of the *first* state election that is held under the guidelines of an enacted reapportionment plan. Because reapportionment plans are not necessarily adopted for both houses of a state assembly simultaneously, a change in *one* house is sufficient for a state to be considered reapportioned. Since state expenditures are adopted as the indicators of public policies, the *fiscal year* budgets that are the result of legislative activity prior to reapportionment are part of the data set of the before period. Those fiscal year expenditures which are the policy product of legislators elected under the reapportioned districts form the data base of the after period.

	BEFORE	AFTER
New York	1958–66	1967–69
Massachusetts	1958–63	1964–68
Oregon	1958–63	1964–68
South Carolina	1958–63	1964–68
Kentucky	1959–64	1965–68
Delaware	1959–64	1965–68
Georgia	1958–63	1964–68
Mississippi	1959–64	1965–68
Virginia	1959–66	1967–69
Kansas	1958–66	1967–69
West Virginia	1958–65	1966–69
Wisconsin	1958–66	1967–69
Michigan	1958–65	1966–69
Wyoming	1958–65	1966–69
Oklahoma	1958–66	1967–69

In order to undertake appropriate quantitative analysis, there must be a sufficient number of observations of public policy during both periods. This requirement eliminates most states from being classified as reapportioned because many did not hold an election under a reapportionment plan until 1968. After the election of 1968, there

14. Brett Hawkins and Cheryl Welchel, "Reapportionment and Urban Representation in Legislative Influence Positions," *Urban Affairs Quarterly*, III (March 1968), pp. 68–70. Ira Sharkansky, "Reapportionment and Roll Call Voting," *Social Science Quarterly*, Vol. 51 (June 1970), pp. 129–37.

are, at the time that this study is completed, data for only two fiscal years. Thus, all of the units classified as reapportionment underwent the treatment of reapportionment in a state election before 1966. In spite of this common feature, not all of these states received the same dosage of reapportionment. Some states were treated to major shifts in district boundaries and the number of urban legislators increased significantly while other units felt only minor rearrangements. In future studies of the effects of reapportionment it will be important to estimate the association between the degrees of structural modification and the variation in governmental outlays. However, in this exploratory study attention is not given to this problem. The units which are *reapportioned* to some degree are listed with the fiscal years in the respective time periods.[15]

The non-reapportioned states are those states in which a reapportioned legislature is not elected during the first five years of the 1960's. Any state legislature elected in 1966 under a reapportionment plan would consider allocations for fiscal year 1968. Since fiscal 1969 is the last year for which data are available, the paucity of observations obviated classifying such a state as "reapportioned." Instead, states which did not elect a reapportioned legislature before 1965 are utilized as a control group. Since the states are not randomly assigned to the control category, it is not possible to assume that all features of state political systems other than the date of reapportionment are purely randomly distributed among all the states. The lack of random assignment introduces some impurity into such an assumption about the variables, nevertheless the policy decisions of the states in the imperfect control category are analyzed in order to determine if the patterns of policy development without the intervention of reapportionment are similar to, or different from, the configurations exhibited in a reapportioned state. The non-reapportioned states are divided artifically into before and after periods. These available control units can be scrutinized for policy changes between the two time segments. If events other than reapportionment are the

15. This category of reapportioned states is obtained from a listing of states that allegedly have reapportionment plans in operation. This listing is found in *Congressional Quarterly*, Vol. XXIV (June 17, 1966), pp. 1285–1306. Letters were then written to the Secretary of State in those enumerated legislatures who had been elected under a recent reapportionment plan in order to verify the listing in the C.Q.

foundation for state policy changes, then such events would be nearly as equiprobable in both reapportioned and non-reapportioned states. (The assumption of exact equi-probability cannot be made because of the non-randomization of items into the control set). Since events other than reapportionment, e.g. a sudden influx of federal aid or a social commitment by a governor to a new program area, can occur in between the pre-test and post-test periods, the existence of any policy changes in a reapportioned state cannot be immediately attributed to reapportionment. If similar changes are found in non-reapportioned states, then there is no justification for rejecting the rival hypothesis which claims that policy changes follow from non-reapportionment factors.

The states that are included in the *nonreapportioned* category include Alabama, Arizona, Arkansas, California, Colorado, Connecticut, Florida,[16] Idaho, Illinois, Indiana, Iowa, Louisiana, Maine, Maryland, Minnesota, Missouri, Montana, Nebraska, Nevada, New Hampshire, New Jersey, New Mexico, North Dakota, North Carolina, Ohio, Pennsylvania, Rhode Island, South Dakota, Tennessee, Texas, Utah, Vermont, and Washington. The before period for all of these states is 1958–63, and the after period is 1964–67. By using 1967 as the end point, there is no state in which a fiscal year expenditure which is the product of a legislature reapportioned after 1965.

The canons of inference used in before and after tests stipulate that the possible policy effects of social and economic processes not be attributed to legislative reapportionments. Economic growth and cultural transformations could be the foundation of adjustments in a state government's budgetary priorities. Again, the control group of non-reapportioned states functions as a means of detecting policy changes that are induced by variables other than reapportionment. While it cannot be assumed that there is perfect randomization of social and economic attributes across all 48 states, if increases in

16. Florida is classified as a nonreapportioned state even though a reapportioned legislature was elected in 1964. The reason for excluding Florida is because it remained very malapportioned after the plan was adopted and only meager changes could be expected. Second, Florida was reapportioned again for the 1966 election and retained very little malapportionment. Thus, it seems reasonable to look for the effects of reapportionment in Florida after the 1966 election.

urbanization, industrialization, or wealth can cause changes in policy allocations, such activities are apt to occur in both reapportioned and nonreapportioned states. If that is the case, then a policy change in non-reapportioned would prevent reapportionment from invalidly being inferred to be the basis of policy changes. Although this design incorporates no explicit controls on intraunit variation in social and economic conditions other than the non-random control group, it is possible to know if there are systematic differences in the social system attributes of the states. The similarity of the reapportioned states with the non-reapportioned states is measureable. Any such statistical comparison is not a substitute for knowledge about intra-unit variation in key environmental components. However, a test of the differences in the levels of the two groups of states is relevant to the assumption of near randomization of social and economic variables. If the difference between the two sets of states are not statistically significant, the assumption is strengthened and, the existence of significant differences counters the assumption.

The environmental conditions which are examined are those included in many other state policy studies. They are: urbanization, wealth, and industrialization, and are operationalized as the percentage of residents living in urban areas, per capita income, and the labor force in manufacturing, respectively.[17] Data are collected for the years 1960 and 1966. The statistical technique used is the difference of means test. The null hypothesis is that the average numerical value (mean) for each of the two categories of states at a given date are the same. The results of the tests are that there are no significant differences in these key variables in either of the two time periods. (1960 and 1966). The t-values (which is a measure of the comparison of the two separate mean scores) are $-.690$ and $-.673$ (urbanization), $.958$ and 1.325 (wealth), and -0.872 and $-.646$ (industrialization). None of them is significant at the .05 or .01 level of significance with 46 degrees of freedom. Since the null hypothesis is not rejected, the assumption of near randomization is supported.

17. The data sources for urbanization, wealth, and industrialization are U.S. Bureau of the Census, *City, County, Data Book,* 1967. (Washington: U.S. Government Printing Office and U.S. Bureau of the Census, 1967) *Statistical Abstract* (Washington: U.S. Government Printing Office).

Some words are in order about the confirmatory-bases for the hypotheses. There are two sets of data to be used as the basis for tests of verification of the hypotheses. The first group consists of state governmental expenditures for various areas of public policy. These data represent the total amount of spending that a state government produces in a given fiscal year for some specified function. The item selected are the following per capita spending categories: higher education, inter-governmental expenditures for education (local schools), highways, public welfare, and hospitals.[18]

There are at least two reasons for operationalizing public policy to mean state spending. First, some advocates of reapportionment have argued that reapportionment would result in more extensive social welfare programs.[19] Since some of these programs would require state government financing, the level of state spending is a measure of such policies. Second, the conclusions drawn from extensive analyses of state expenditures are that levels of spending do not readily change over time. Incremental budgeting is inferred to be a method of decision-making which results in only marginal increases in spending levels.[20] Thus, if there are changes in spending after reapportionment, the findings are not unimpressive. The justification for selecting these particular spending categories is twofold. First, if reapportionment has had an impact upon public policy in the way its advocates have asserted, then these spending categories should reflect this impact. Second, to allow for some comparability of the current findings with prior research, spending categories are used. There is a limitation on duplicating all of the measures used in preceding studies because some of the indicators either are not available on an annual basis or include both local and state spending.

The second set of data is the amount of money that state governments allocate to municipal corporations. This set of data probably provides a more valid measure of the impact of reapportionment than the first batch. Since the major effect of reapportionment is alleged to make the state legislature more responsive to urban needs and demands, we have sought to determine if, *in fact*, the level of state

18. The data source is the U.S. Bureau of Census Compendium of *State Government Finances* (Washington: U.S. Government Printing Office).
19. See Gordon Baker, *Rural versus Urban Power*, (New York: Random House, 1965), pp. 23–26, 32–39.
20. Ira Sharkansky, *Spending in the States* (Chicago: Rand McNally, 1968).

resources being committed to major cities in the states has increased. This is particularly important since all prior research using spending categories as measures of public policies does not include any indicator of state to city allocations. To fill that gap, changes in the total revenue that municipal corporations over 100,000 in population receive from the state government is analyzed to measure any changes.[21] The years included in the anlaysis for all of the municipal corporations' revenue in the nonreapportioned states are 1959–64 for the before period and 1965–68 as the after period. For the reapportioned states, the time periods are identical to the other group of data.

There are definite limitations in the use of either of these data bases. First, it is not certain that either total state spending or the state allocation to cities is a valid measure of the state assistance to urban areas since our indicators do not measure *where* the money is being spent. An increase in either category does not necessarily mean that urban problems of housing, welfare, transportation, or education are being tackled with more well-financed programs. A second limitation is the small number of observations. There are very few fiscal years in either category of states for either period. This problem is further aggravated by the failure of some state legislatures to hold annual sessions. If they were to make their budgetary allocations for two fiscal years at a single sitting, the number of observations would be reduced even further. Substantively, the legislatures of 11 of the 15 reapportioned states meet annually, and 16 out of 33 non-reapportioned states meet each year. On the basis of contact with legislatures, where the legislature meets only once every two years, the budgets for each fiscal year are not determined by the same decision. However, from a statistical perspective, in spite of the small number of data points, there is a substantial basis for assuming the *validity* of the regression equations since the amount of variance explained (or the r^2) is generally .8 or higher for every regression equation. Furthermore the reliability of the measures can be inferred by looking at the pattern of the results. As an inspection of the data indicates, the configuration of spending is quite similar within each of the two respective categories of states.

21. The data source is the U.S. Bureau of the Census, *Compendium of City Government Finances* (Washington: U.S. Government Printing Office). Given this data source, cities must be at least 100,000 in population as of 1950.

Some mention needs to be made about the meaning of the term "policy change." For both sets of data, *if the trend of yearly budgetary allocation increases, a policy change occurs.* Generally, the level of public spending rises in an absolute amount year after year. Given that basic fact, important changes in expenditure patterns are evident by the *rate of increases or decreases* in levels of spending. Since the spending levels before and after a particular point in time are being compared, it is necessary to compute the trend of annual growth for the fiscal years in each period. It is not appropriate to compare rates of change for each year because there is only one breaking point (reapportionment).

III. MEASUREMENT TECHNIQUE

The measurement technique used to determine the presence of before and after policy changes is the comparison of linear regression coefficients. To ascertain the intra-state impact of reapportionment, regression equations are computed for each state. For every state the independent variable is the set of fiscal years included within the respective periods. As an illustration, with a six year time period, the values of the observations of the independent variable are . . . 1,2,3,4,5,6. The expenditure categories and the allocations to the cities are the dependent variables. By regressing each separate spending variable on fiscal years, the rate of the annual growth in spending can be obtained. The particular trend in growth for each state's before and after period is found by computing regression coefficients for each period. As an illustration, see Appendix I. For Massachusetts, there are two comparable regression coefficients each time a different dependent variable is regressed on fiscal years. In the case of the first set of data, there are five comparable pairs of regression coefficients because there are five dependent variables. Looking at one dependent variable, higher education expenditures, the rate of total spending in this area before reapportionment is represented by a coefficient of .492, and after reapportionment the rate is indicated by a coefficient of 3.647. In order to determine whether or not this difference of coefficients is significant, *a test is made of the statistical null hypothesis that $b_1 = b_2$, where b_1 is the regression coefficient of the before period and b_2 is the regression coefficient of the after* *period.* This procedure generates a t-value, which is a measure of the statistical difference between the two coefficients.[22]

The statistical null hypothesis is as follows: H.O. For every state, the trend of state spending in the before period is equal to the rate of state spending in the after period. This hypothesis is similar to the claim that only minimal policy changes will accompany reapportionment. If the t-value generated by the analysis is not statistically significant with a two tailed test level of significance, H.O. can not be rejected. In that case, the forecast of Dye, Hoffebert, Jacob, Brady, and Edmonds is confirmed. On the other hand those individuals who maintain that reapportionment can induce increases in budgetary allocations suggest an alternative hypothesis. Their hunch is as follows: H.I. For every state, the trend of state spending in the after period is a positive increase over the previous trend. With this relationship the regression coefficients are predicted to be different and the difference is a change in a particular direction. If the t-value obtained from the calculations is negative and statistically significant with a one tailed test, then H.I. can be provisionally accepted. (For example, in the case of Massachusetts the regression coefficients are .492 and 3.647 and yield a t-value of -15.626, significant at the .01 level.) On the basis of the high negative t-value, an important policy change is inferred.

There is a reason for employing this technique rather than others. Since the level of spending is likely to increase over time in every state, it is vital to work with a measure that will take this factor into account while still measuring the difference in the rate of spending. A difference of means test applied to these data would not consider the natural increase of expenditures and would only indicate that there are significant absolute differences in spending which is not very illuminating. With the comparison of regression coefficients, however, the general increase in expenditures is taken into consideration, and the rate of intercept in the regression model affects neither the computation of the regression coefficients nor the t-values. Hence, the absolute levels of spending in one period can be significantly different from the levels in the other period, which a difference of

22. The procedure for comparing regression coefficients is outlined in Wilfrid J. Dixon and Frank J. Massey, Jr., *Introduction to Statistical Analysis,* (New York: McGraw-Hill, 1969), pp. 193–210.

means test could show, but such a difference does *not* imply that there are differences in the rate of the total amount of spending, which is measured by the t-value. Unfortunately, given the limited number of observations, it is not possible to employ a test of significance which overcomes the problems of proximal autocorrelation among data points.[23] It is possible that the t-test used in this research indicates significant t-values because of the bias introduced with autocorrelation. The only means of minimizing this problem is by looking for unexpected significant t-values in the nonreapportioned states. If many do not appear, then perhaps there is only slight autocorrelation among the observations in both the non-reapportioned and the reapportioned units.

IV. FINDINGS

A blunt manner of interpreting the results of the regression analyses is to calculate the relative frequency of policy changes across all of the units within each of the two categories of states. The operational meaning of the term "policy change" refers to a negative t-value that is statistically significant. Such a t-value which is predicted by hypothesis 1 indicates that there is an upswing in a state's annual budgetary growth pattern when compared with the trend in public spending during a preceding period of time. These quantitative measures of policy differences are summarized in the Appendices.

Appendices I and II are based on the calculated t-values from operations performed on the five state expenditure variables for reapportioned and non-reapportioned states, respectively. H.1 is supported in 39 of the 75 possible instances for the reapportioned group. (See Appendix I) The 52 per cent level of corroboration of hypothesis 1 suggests that reapportionment accounts for changes in the direction of public expenditures. The occurrence of policy changes in the non-reapportioned states is not as frequent. On the basis of the figures displayed in Appendix I, policy changes occurred in 62 of the 165 possible instances. The relative frequency of policy changes

23. For a description of a test of significance which circumvents the effects of autocorrelation, consult Gene V. Glass, "Analysis of Data on the Connecticut Speeding Crackdown as a Time-Series Quasi-Experiment," *Law and Society Review,* Vol. III (August 1968), pp. 55–75.

among all of the nonreapportioned states is 37 per cent. A comparison of the two sets of states reveals that the percentage of changes in the reapportioned states is nearly one and a half times greater than in the non-reapportioned units. While a higher proportion of policy changes exists in the reapportioned states, it is clear that reapportionment is not a necessary condition for reallocations of governmental priorities. The fact that a higher proportion of policy changes takes place in states that are reapportioned than occur in non-reapportionment states offers the possibility that reapportionment is a sufficient condition for increases in budgetary allocation. However, the evidence outlined in Appendix III casts some doubts on this interpretation. Appendix III is a summary of the regression coefficients and t-values based on the data analysis of state assistance to municipal corporations. Statistics for cities in reapportioned states and those in non-reapportioned states are found in Appendix III. The proportion of communities experiencing an increase in revenue from the states which fall into the reapportioned category is 9/29 or 31 per cent. The incidence of policy changes in the nonreapportioned group of states and respective cities is 17/73 or 22 per cent. The margin of difference between the percentage of policy changes in the two states is not very striking. From the gross level of the two categories of states, it does not appear that reapportionment is inducing a much richer flow of financial blood into the body politic of the cities.

This finding is perhaps consistent with the viewpoint that reapportionment does not serve to strengthen the central cities politically, but it does increase the number of legislative seats allocated to suburban areas. Because inner cities are losing population while the suburbs are growing more rapidly than any other part of the states, reapportionment shifts legislative position from meager-sized districts to suburban-based constituencies. Even if a state is reapportioned according to this interpretation, the control over public policy is not going to be in the grips of city legislators. And reapportionment, consequently, will not produce increased policy benefits for the cities because of more central city districts. Under these circumstances, any increase in state governmental assistance to municipal corporations is likely to reflect the desires of the citizens who live outside the boundaries of the city's "core." The validity of the measure of state aid to municipal corporations is questionable because it fails to specify the functional areas of city spending to which the state monies are directed. However, it is possible to observe which policy areas of direct state expenditure are subject to change. This brings the cynosure of the study back to Appendices I and II.

By collapsing all of the states into the general categories of reapportioned and non-reapportioned, the percentage of policy changes by policy area can be determined. The information about such proportions is gathered and summarized in the table below.

An interesting aspect of the tabulations is the dissimilar percentages of policy changes that are included in the fields of highways and public welfare. In the reapportioned states, the functional

POLICY CHANGES BY POLICY AREA

	Higher Education	Local Schools	Highways	Welfare	Hospitals	
Reapportioned States	.18	.18	.26	.10	.28	n = 39
Non-reapportioned States	.34	.27	.06	.18	.15	n = 62

area of highways absorbs a quarter of the total number of policy changes (.26), and the smallest proportion is contained in the category of welfare (.10). A contrasting picture develops in the non-reapportioned states where a meager amount of the policy changes occurs in the field of highway spending (.06), and the per cent of change in welfare assistance (.18) is considerably higher. There is no obvious empirical explanation for these comparative findings. Nevertheless, these general results raise the question of the extent to which "urban-oriented programs" are defined in terms of the wants of non-central city dwellers. Problems of inconvenience for residents living outside of central cities are often given high priority as matters requiring social amelioration. (This point of view is an essential thesis of Edward Banfield's *The Unheavenly City*.) Thus, when governmental action is taken to satisfy citizen demands for solutions to the urban crisis, the collective decisions are likely to improve the transportation linkage *across* urban communities to the advantage of suburbanites. Fundamental problems of inner city poverty which require expensive and imaginative policies are less likely to receive attention. As a result, on-going welfare programs are expanded in increments and the likelihood of policy change is not very great. If it is the case that reapportionment actually enlarges the number of *metropolitan* representatives and not just central city legislators, then increases in financial commitments for urban centers would be more frequent in areas such as highways than in welfare. Although this is an intriguing line of inquiry, the absence of finer measures of policy impact prevents further discussion at this time. An obvious need in future studies is a set of indicators which, more acutely reflect the distribution of policy benefits.

V. CONCLUSION

Using a before-and-after test to determine the nature and rate of change in public expenditures, we found that the rate of increase was significantly greater in reapportioned than in non-reapportioned states. There were, however, a considerable number of exceptions to this pattern. In addition, we specifically sought to examine the frequently made assertion that reapportionment would produce a dramatic increase of state interest (and money) in the central cities. Contrary to popular opinion, we found little difference between the reapportioned and non-reapportioned states in this respect. Coupling these two sets of findings together and then examining the expenditure increases within several different issue-areas, we concluded that any increases due to reapportionment were more likely to have benefited suburban interests than the central cities. At present this is only an indirect inference, and more research on the impact of reapportionment is in order.

Appendix 1

RELATIVE FREQUENCY OF SIGNIFICANT INCREASES IN
ANNUAL BUDGETARY GROWTH IN REAPPORTIONED
AND NONREAPPORTIONED STATES

POLICY AREAS

States	Higher Education		Local Schools		High-ways		Public Welfare		Hos-pitals		Number of Cases
	no.	%	no.	%	no.	%	no.	%	no.	%	
Reapportioned	7	47	7	47	10	75	4	27	11	73	15
Non-reapportioned	21	63	17	52	3	9	10	30	9	27	33

Appendix 2

THE DISTRIBUTION OF SIGNIFICANT INCREASES IN
ANNUAL BUDGETARY GROWTH IN REAPPORTIONED
AND NONREAPPORTIONED STATES

NUMBER OF SIGNIFICANT INCREASES

States	0	%	1	%	2	%	3	%	4	%	5	%	No. of Cases
Reapportioned	0	—	5	33	2	13	3	20	4	26	1	7	15
Non-reapportioned	5	16	5	16	15	46	5	16	3	9	0	—	33
Totals	5	11	10	21	17	35	8	17	7	14	1	2	48

Appendix 3

THE RELATIVE FREQUENCY OF INCREASES IN STATE ALLOCATIONS TO CITIES

	Significant Increases		Not Significant Increases		No. of* Cities
	no.	%	no.	%	
Reapportioned States	9	31	20	69	15
Non-reapportioned States	17	22	56	78	73

THE DISTRIBUTION OF CITIES WITH SIGNIFICANT INCREASES IN REAPPORTIONED STATES

State	Number of Cities*	No. of Cities with Significant Increases
Delaware	1	0
Georgia	2	2
Kansas	2	1
Kentucky	1	1
Massachusetts	7	2
Michigan	3	2
New York	7	0
Oklahoma	2	0
Oregon	1	1
Virginia	2	0
Wisconsin	1	0
Totals	29	9

* Includes only those cities with populations over 100,000 as reported in the 1950 census.

NORMAN LEFSTEIN, VAUGHAN STAPLETON
AND LEE TEITELBAUM

In Search of Juvenile Justice
Gault *and Its Implementation**

I. INTRODUCTION

On May 15, 1967, the United States Supreme Court rendered, in
In re Gault[1] its first decision in the area of juvenile delinquency
procedure. Commentators have repeatedly construed the rulings in
Gault as requiring juvenile courts to adopt new and more liberal
practices. The privilege against self-incrimination, and the rights to
notice of charges, counsel, confrontation, and cross-examination were
heretofore primarily regarded as the cornerstones of an adversary
system of justice. The extension of these rights to juvenile courts
would have seemed to require an overnight transformation of the
court procedures.

* The material for this article was gathered during a research and demonstration project made possible by a Ford Foundation grant to the National
Council of Juvenile Court Judges. The opportunity to complete this article is
made possible through the Russell Sage Program in Law and Social Science
at the Yale Law School. Until the project's termination in the summer of 1968,
Norman Lefstein and Vaughan Stapleton shared responsibility for the project's administration. Lee Teitelbaum served as a staff attorney representing
indigent juveniles in one of the project cities.

1. 387 U.S. 1 (1967).

From *Law and Society Review*, Volume III, Number 4 (May 1969),
pp. 491–562. Reprinted by permission of the publisher and the author. Foot-
notes have been renumbered.

At the time they wrote this piece, Norman Lefstein was with the Wash-
ington, D.C., Legal Aid Agency, Vaughan Stapleton was associated with Yale
Law School, and Lee Teitelbaum was teaching at the University of North
Dakota School of Law.

This article examines the response of three urban juvenile courts—referred to as Metro, Gotham and Zenith[2]—to the *Gault* decision. The data presented here—drawn from numerous observations of court hearings—provide some indication of the extent of the changes in juvenile proceedings. Particular attention is paid to what the Supreme Court seems to have required in *Gault*, to what juvenile courts should now be expected to do under that decision, and to what was actually done in the observed courts.

* * *

It is likely that trial and appellate tribunals will increasingly be called upon to define how *Gault's* constitutional protections must be administered by juvenile courts. To do so without information would be necessarily speculative; it is hoped that this analysis will assist in pointing the direction for other such projects, and in furthering clarification, change and improvement in the system of juvenile justice.

II. CHARACTERISTICS OF COURTS AND SAMPLE STUDIED

The juvenile court in each of the three cities serves a heavily populated area. The population of the county served by the court in Zenith is by far the largest, slightly in excess of five million; Metro's is between one and two million; Gotham's county population is just under a million.

* * *

In the three juvenile courts, observers were present and took notes on 188 different court hearings, involving a total of 268 youths. Nevertheless, for purposes of analyzing compliance with the *Gault* decision, the final sample of court hearings and juveniles detailed in this article is substantially smaller. Using the Supreme Court's opinion in *Gault* as a guide, we determined that the sample should only include individuals, charged with delinquency, who were sub-

2. The decision to use fictional names for the three project cities was encouraged by the project's Advisory Board.

ject to commitment to an institution,[3] and not represented by an attorney.[4] Thus, we excluded cases where the petition's sole charge was a violation of probation, even if probation revocation could have resulted in institutionalization. Similarly, if the data related solely to a dispositional hearing, or if the observed hearing was a continuance from a previous court date, at which time the judge might have informed the parties fully of their rights under *Gault,* the case was excluded in our final sample. By far the greatest number of exclusions consisted of hearings where *all* juveniles before the court were represented by counsel. In cases where *some* youths had an attorney and others did not, and the criteria for inclusion in our final sample were otherwise met, the individuals without counsel were retained in the sample.

*   *   *

The number of court hearings and individual juveniles reported on in this article are summarized in Table 1.

Analysis of compliance with *Gault's* requirements is based on how individuals, rather than entire cases, were treated. This approach was necessary because we found that in some cases with more than one

3. We conclude that the Due Process Clause of the Fourteenth Amendment requires that in respect of *proceedings to determine delinquency which may result in commitment to an institution* in which the juvenile's freedom is curtailed, the child and his parents must be notified of the child's right to be represented by counsel retained by them, or if they are unable to afford counsel, that counsel will be appointed to represent the child.

In re Gault, *supra* note 1, at 41 (emphasis added). Under the statute that governs Metro's juvenile procedures, referees have the power to make findings and recommendations that must be submitted to a juvenile court judge for approval. Despite the absence of the power of referees to commit juveniles directly to an institution, cases of nine youths heard before Metro's two referees are included in our final sample. *See* Table 3, *infra.* It was found that the action of the referees, in actual practice, is rarely reversed by one of the juvenile court judges, and thus the referee's decision may very well "result in commitment to an institution."

4. For this analysis we have accepted the hypothesis that the presence of counsel insures implementation of the other rights in Gault—or at the very least, that these rights were relinquished upon legal advice. Nevertheless, this is an empirical question that remains to be investigated. Data bearing on this problem are currently being analyzed.

Table 1

NUMBER OF YOUTHS AND COURT HEARINGS ANALYZED

	Gotham	Metro	Zenith	Total
Number of Youths Reported on in this Article	59	71	18	148
Total Number of Different Court Hearings	39	40	12	91
Court Hearings Involving a Single Youth	24	26	6	56
Court Hearings Involving More Than One Youth	15	14	6	35

respondent, not all youths and their parents received precisely the same information regarding their constitutional rights.

* * *

III. METHODOLOGY

Although the data were gathered after the *Gault* decision, field-workers had been active in the Gotham, Metro, and Zenith courts since early 1966. At this time, their main objectives were to observe and take notes on delinquency cases, in an effort to collect qualitative data on the impact of counsel. With the *Gault* decision in May 1967, a unique opportunity was presented, within the context of the major research program, to study the day-to-day response of juvenile courts to the Supreme Court's landmark decision. As a result, special emphasis was placed on observing the degree of compliance with *Gault's* requirements in the courts.

* * *

IV. RIGHT TO COUNSEL

In General

In discussing the right to counsel, the Supreme Court in *Gault* commented:

> A proceeding where the issue is whether the child will be found to be "delinquent" and subjected to the loss of his liberty for years

is comparable in seriousness to a felony prosecution. The juvenile needs the assistance of counsel to cope with problems of law, to make skilled inquiry into the facts, to insist upon regularity of the proceedings, and to ascertain whether he has a defense and to prepare and submit it. *The child "requires the guiding hand of counsel at every step in the proceedings against him."* [5]

The court then directed its attention toward ensuring that this right, established in principle, would be meaningful in operation. Rejecting the view of some courts that even if a youth does have the right to counsel there is no requirement that he be so informed, the majority opinion expressly required that the juvenile and his parent be told of the child's right, and further that they be instructed that if they could not afford an attorney, one would be appointed for them. [6] The opinion also imported to the juvenile courts the concept of waiver; henceforth, counsel could be withheld from the parties only if they validly waived their rights to a lawyer.

In the delinquency cases reported in this study, compliance with the right to counsel was determined from the initial court hearings where juveniles and their parents appeared without counsel. However, two of the courts sent to the accused's parents, in advance of the first hearing, a notice which included reference to the right to counsel. In Metro, a form entitled *Notice: Legal Rights and Privileges* was delivered by a probation officer to the minor's parents, and the parents were asked to sign a return indicating their receipt of the notice. The part of the form relevant to the right to counsel reads as follows:

> You and/or your child have the right to be represented by a lawyer who will advise you as to the law and present your case in Court. If you wish to have a lawyer but are financially unable to employ one, we suggest that you contact the Legal Aid Defender's Office [giving address and phone number] or consult the yellow pages of the telephone book under "attorneys" for a listing of the Legal Aid Society Office nearest your home.

The Gotham juvenile court at the time of this study sent a summons by regular mail to the respondent and his parents containing the following information: "PARENTS, GUARDIAN or CUSTODIAN, of

5. 387 U.S. 1, 36 (emphasis added).
6. 387 U.S. 1, 41.

the juvenile and the juvenile _____, have the right to retain and be represented by counsel at every stage of the proceedings."

Neither notice complies satisfactorily with the right to counsel requirement imposed by *Gault*. The first carefully avoids mentioning the court's duty to appoint a lawyer for the minor, if for financial reasons one cannot be retained; the latter simply makes no mention at all of that duty. But even if the notices were complete, it is doubtful that the court's responsibility to inform the parents and juvenile of the right to counsel would be reduced. In federal criminal cases, the judge bears the responsibility of ascertaining that the defendant in fact knows of, and adequately understands, this right.

*   *   *

While it may be argued that the states are not bound to exercise all the precautions of federal criminal practice,[7] it would seem clear that the accused juvenile must be offered the right to counsel before it can be said that he has knowingly and intelligently waived it,[8] and that every presumption against such waiver must be indulged.[9] Similarly, it would seem that juvenile courts must insure that the minor and parents knew of their right to counsel, and that they understood its significance.[10] Indeed, particular care is necessary in cases involving minors in order to be assured that the youth knows he is entitled to a lawyer; in criminal prosecutions involving juveniles, it has frequently been held that the trial judge must so inform the defendant, or a subsequent waiver is invalid.[11] Since minors in

7. See Comment, *Waiver of the Right to Counsel in State Court Cases: The Effect of* Gideon v. Wainwright, 31 U. Chi. L. Rev. 591, 594–95 (1964).
8. See Carnley v. Cochran, 369 U.S. 506 (1962).
9. *Id.*; Johnson v. Zerbst, 304 U.S. 458 (1938).
10. See Von Moltke v. Gillies, 332 U.S. 708, 723–24 (1948) (plurality opinion by Black, J.); Cherrie v. United States, *supra* note 30; Snell v. United States, 174 F.2d 580 (10th Cir. 1949); People v. Hardin, 207 Cal. App. 2d 336, 24 Cal. Rptr. 563 (Dist. Ct. App. 1962).
11. See Uverges v. Pennsylvania, 335 U.S. 437 (1948) (17 years old); People v. Devanish, 285 App. Div. 826, 136 N.Y.S.2d 759 (1955) (16 years old); *In re* Gooding, 338 P.2d 114 (Okla. Crim. 1959) (18 years old). *Accord* United States *ex rel.* Brown v. Fay, 242 F. Supp. 273 (S.D.N.Y. 1965) (16 years old); People v. Byroads, 24 App. Div.2d 732, 263 N.Y.S.2d 401 (1965) (17 years old) (mem.); United States *ex rel.* Slebodnik v. Pennsylvania, 343 F.2d 605 (3rd Cir. 1965) (applying Pennsylvania law to a 17-year-old).

delinquency proceedings are almost always younger than those prosecuted criminally, the need for a careful appraisal of rights is, if anything, more pronounced. Further support for this proposition may be found where, as in most delinquency cases, the respondent and his parents are indigent. Reliance upon written notification presupposes that the recipient can read and understand the notice, that he does so if he can, and that, if it is the parent who is given notice, the parent conveys the information in an intelligible manner to the child. These assumptions, when applied to the population typically appearing before juvenile courts, are most dubious.

Degree of Compliance

"Full advice" has been used to describe those cases where the respondent and his parents were fully informed of the child's right to retained or appointed counsel. The following colloquy from a case in Zenith illustrates full advice:

> The judge, "You understand this is a serious charge, don't you?" "Yes." [This is response by father.] Now speaking to both the father and the boy, he continued, "I want you to know that you have the right to a private attorney, I'll appoint a public defender for you."

This case may be taken as an exemplar: the advice of rights is directed to both the parent and the youth, and it is made clear that the judge will appoint an attorney if the respondent is indigent. Although every warning should be as straightforward and complete as this one, instances where compliance was not so satisfactory have been treated as "full" for purposes of this article. For example, it is certainly not sufficient to tell only the parent that he has a right to counsel; the right to be informed runs equally to the child. Thus, if the judge specifically addresses only the parent in rendering advice of counsel, the requirements of *Gault* have not fully been met. On the other hand, if full advice was given and no person singled out, full compliance was assumed, even though only the parent responded and even though it was unclear that the child comprehended in any real sense that the right was *his*.

The judge also must clearly state that the respondent and his par-

ent not only have the right to retained counsel, but that if they cannot afford an attorney, one will be appointed for them. If the court
does not state that counsel will be appointed but merely says that a
legal aid lawyer is available, the effect may not be the same.

*   *   *

On the basis of the above categorization, Zenith was found to
have the highest degree of compliance with *Gault's* mandate. Of the
18 youths in the sample of cases analyzed, 10 (or 56%) were fully
advised of the right to counsel. In Metro, the extent of compliance
was substantially less. Only 2 youths of a sample of 71 (3%) were
fully advised of the right to representation. Gotham was the least
diligent in complying with *Gault's* requirements. In not 1 case
among 59 were the parents and minor adequately advised of their
right to counsel. One of two things happened: Either no mention at
all was made of the right to counsel or there was "partial advice" of
the right, meaning that necessary elements of the warning were
omitted. A case from Metro in which the judge asked: "Mrs.
C_____, did you know that you have a right to have a lawyer?"
illustrates what we have termed "partial advice." The warning,
phrased in the form of a question, was directed solely and explicitly
to the parent, and the judge failed to state that the boy and his parent were entitled to appointed counsel if they were indigent. A
breakdown of the degree of compliance with the right to counsel
for all three cities is shown in Table 2.

Table 2

COMPLIANCE WITH THE RIGHT TO COUNSEL REQUIREMENT

Type of Compliance	Gotham		Metro		Zenith	
	N	%	N	%	N	%
Full Advice	(0)	0	(2)	3	(10)	56
Partial Advice	(9)	15	(46)	65	(7)	38
No Advice	(50)	85	(23)	32	(1)	6
TOTAL NUMBER OF YOUTHS	(59)		(71)		(18)	

N = number of youths.

Thus, a greater attempt at compliance was made in Zenith and Metro than in Gotham. Only one case was found in Zenith where a hearing was held without any mention of the right to counsel, and in Metro, at least some form of advice was given, albeit incompletely, in more than two-thirds of the cases. Gotham, in contrast, emerged as the most resistant to the newly imposed constitutional requirements.[12]

The failure of the courts in Metro and Gotham to comply with the right to counsel requirement cannot be dismissed as a technical matter. In one-third of the sample cases in Metro, and in 85% of the Gotham cases, the error cannot be ascribed to faulty terminology nor even to imperfect comprehension of the rules set out in *Gault*; neither the parent nor the child was informed in any fashion by the courts of the right to retained or appointed counsel. Even in those instances where partial but inadequate advice was rendered, the omission cannot be considered insignificant. Failure to inform the child of the right, or to state that a "free lawyer" is available as a matter of right, is a most critical omission.

Prejudicial Advice

Heretofore, we have been concerned with the relevant legal content of the communication regarding the right to counsel. Successful communication of a message from one person to another depends on many factors other than content of the message itself. Verbal and nonverbal cues may transform a statement's meaning into something altogether different from the actual words used. In considering the extent of meaningful as well as literal compliance with *Gault*, the manner of communication is highly relevant.

Advice of the right to counsel may be rendered in such a way as to encourage the exercise of that right.

* * *

12. It may be argued that Gotham's juvenile court was merely awaiting the anticipated changes in the rules of court. If this is a plausible argument, however, it does not abrogate the authority of the Supreme Court's decision in Gault. Indeed, if anything, it indicated the power of juvenile court tradition in resisting change.

The advice may be essentially neutral in quality.

*   *   *

Conversely, the advice may be given in such a manner as to discourage exercise of the right to counsel.

*   *   *

By failing to respond to the misapprehensions and questions of parties, judges may effectively discourage the use of counsel. Consider the following case from Metro:

> The judge begins by saying, "Mrs. C. . . . . . , did you know that you have a right to have a lawyer?"
> She replied that she "didn't know." She paused, then she said, "Well, Mr. . . . . . [the probation officer] said that it was up to me, and I said that I didn't have any money."
> The judge said, "Well, one thing you have here is all kinds of lawyers." He said that they could get some at the Legal Aid Society.
> The mother replied, "Well, I have one, but he's so expensive."
> And the judge left it at this, and they went ahead and heard the case.

In this case the judge's failure to inform the respondent that the court would appoint an attorney if she could not afford one, taken with his failure to respond to her oblique reference of an inability to pay, militated against exercise of that right. . . .

*   *   *

To avoid delay, a judge may fail to fully advise the child and his parents of their right to an attorney:

> The probation officer stated, "Mrs. G. . . . . . mentioned the fact that she might want to have a lawyer."
> The judge, "Well, we can't have them coming down here at the last minute." The judge then commented about how hard it is to get them down here.

> The mother said something. The judge said, "Have you changed your mind?" The mother replied, "Yes."

Finally, the content of a message may be compromised by the manner in which it is delivered. When rights are communicated to respondents in a rapid fashion, allowing no time for an answer, the communication must be deemed prejudicial. In the following example (a case in Metro) the rapidity with which the information was given plus the obvious desire to hear the case without delay undoubtedly discouraged exercise of the rights mentioned:

> Referee, "You have the right to be represented by an attorney and the right to cross-examine witnesses, and you do not have to say anything, either an admission or denial, if you don't want to. All right, officer, what is the situation?"

"Prejudicial advice" of the right to counsel was found almost uniformly where less than "full advice" of the right was rendered. Only three cases were observed where full advice was given in a manner deemed to be prejudicial, two in Zenith and one in Metro. A complete breakdown reflecting "prejudicial advice" together with "full," "partial," and "no advice," reveals the patterns in Table 3.

Table 3

COMPLIANCE WITH THE RIGHT TO COUNSEL REQUIREMENT*

Type of Compliance	Gotham		Metro		Zenith	
	N	%	N	%	N	%
Full advice	(0)	0	(1)	1	(8)	44
Full advice—also prejudicial	(0)	0	(1)	1	(2)	11
Partial advice	(7)	12	(15)	21	(6)	33
Partial advice—also prejudicial	(2)	3	(31)	44	(1)	6
No advice	(50)	85	(23)	32	(1)	6
Total Number of Youths	(59)		(71)		(13)	

* Percents may not add to 100 due to rounding.

4 Impact on Public Opinion

One of the hoariest and most salient propositions on the functions of the Supreme Court involves "legitimacy." According to Charles Black, Yale law professor and celebrated Court apologist, the mere power of judicial review, as brandished by the Court, confers a stamp of legitimacy upon *all* official acts of government, thereby lending a general air of legitimacy throughout American society.[1] In other words, Black argues that the bald possibility that *any* law can be declared unconstitutional by the Court affords an "air" of legality to *all* acts of American government (that is the envy of people everywhere).[2] His argument is well reasoned at a high level of abstraction, but on closer inspection there is a certain lack of clarity and a distinct paucity of fact. For one thing, what is legitimacy and an air of legality anyway? Next, what conditions in brute reality indicate its existence? What conditions support it at low or high levels? To paraphrase Gertrude Stein's last, last words, modern political science has begun to ask, "What are the questions?" and to expect some exactitude in the asking of them. It is only because political science has matured so that some relevant facts have begun to emerge.

For instance, in order for the Court (acting as an institution) to legitimate anything, its decisions must have visibility. Legitimacy, after

1. Charles Black, *The People and the Court* (New York: Macmillan, 1960), pp. 34 *et seq.*
2. Black believes this "air" possesses a "sweetness" to which Frenchmen are peculiarly unaccustomed. *Ibid.*, p. 35.

all is said and done, must imply a certain level of recognition in the society of specific actions taken by the Court as well as some knowledge about the general power of judicial review. The two studies in this section treat the level of public knowledge about the Court's case work; that is, about its specific decisions or about types of decisions the Court has made. But once the general problem of visibility has been raised, other more detailed questions arise too. What is the exact or approximate size of the community that must be aware of the Court's actions, or what particular segments of the community must have this awareness? The educated? The leaders? Over fifty per cent of the mass? How detailed should their knowledge be about the Court's decisions? How favorably must they view this work? Besides this, in order for there to be legitimacy there must be a certain type or level of public support for the role of judicial review and favorable opinion to the effect that the Court is performing judicial review properly. Again, who or how many must know and approve?

Generally, political scientists are garnering data and analyzing the connection of various factors (such as political culture, the political party identification of respondents, their degree of political alienation, their age, the region of the country in which they live) with their views on (a) specific Court decisions, (b) lines of cases decided by the Court, and (c) the institutional role and function of the Court. The following essays by Kessel and Dolbeare are excellent representatives of some aspects of this major, new line of inquiry.

Mr. Dooley once observed that the Supreme Court watched the election returns. As political science research on popular attitudes toward the Court evolves, the justices may begin to find the results equally worth watching. On second thought, they might find it worthwhile even in its present-day, early stages.

JOHN H. KESSEL

Public Perceptions of the Supreme Court

. . . This paper reports an exploratory study of attitudes about the United States Supreme Court. . . .

*   *   *

A two-stage probability sample was drawn from two state legislative districts, the 32nd and the 43rd, located within the city of Seattle. Taken together, the two districts included upper middle class, lower middle class, and working class residents. In addition, their location adjacent to the University of Washington offered the incidental advantage of easy access for the student interviewers. Four hundred and five interviews were actually completed.

The data reported in this paper are based on 356 of these interviews.

*   *   *

. . . It is clear that our Seattle sample varies from the national sample in important respects. The Seattle sample contains more political independents, more persons with college education, more members of the middle class, and more Caucasians. Hence this paper should be regarded simply as an analysis of the attitudes of persons we happened to interview. This analysis does contain a number of interesting suggestions about what the attitudes of a national popu-

From the *Midwest Journal of Political Science*, 10 (May 1966), pp. 167–91. Reprinted by permission of the Wayne State University Press.

John H. Kessel is Professor of Political Science at Ohio State University.

189

lation might be. These should be read, however, as hypotheses in need of verification, rather than as generalizations which are warranted on the basis of our sample.

I

Just what are the public attitudes about the Court? These attitudes were measured in two ways. The first was an open-ended question (Speaking generally, how would you describe your own feelings about the Supreme Court?) and two associated probes, (Is there anything (else) you particularly like about the Supreme Court? Is there anything (else) you particularly dislike about the Supreme Court?). The answers to these questions were scaled by assigning a $+ 1$ to each positive comment and a $- 1$ to each negative comment, and then calculating a sum for each respondent.

The second means of ascertaining opinions about the Supreme Court was a series of questions about the preferred role of the Court (What do you think the job of the Supreme Court should be? Do you think the Supreme Court is doing this job now?). This sequence of questions was concluded with a standard query about intensity (How strongly do you hold these views? Very strongly? Fairly strongly? Or doesn't this make too much difference to you?). The intensity items were combined with the responses about whether the respondent thought the Court was doing its job to form a Likert scale. . . . However measured, the attitudes were supportive of the Court. . . .

*　　*　　*

The second largest category of supportive responses (9.9% of the respondents) stressed the need for a Supreme Court. Though unable to say why, these persons felt that we had to have one. A machinist put it this way:

> I'd say it has been with us . . . (pause) . . . since government started. It's a useful and necessary part of the government. That's what I'd say off hand.

A smaller group of respondents (4.8% of the total) made the point that the Court was doing its best with a difficult job. . . .

*　　*　　*

The largest number of critical answers were coded under the miscellaneous heading of "other critical comments." This category included 10.4% of the total. On examination, it appeared that many of these answers came from persons who disapproved of Supreme Court holdings. Although they were as well informed as most of the other people we interviewed, many of the persons in this category seemed disturbed about legal complexities they could not understand. An insurance adjuster described his feelings as:

> Generally unfavorable. The outcome as to what is constitutional or unconstitutional depends too much on one individual. The Court recently has been relying too much on technicalities to let the guilty off. One little error and they let a guy go free. In the area of criminal law, they seemed to be concerned with "Did Oswald get a free trial?"! Well, they had enough on him to kill him anyway—so why worry about detail?

*　　*　　*

Nine per cent of the respondents said that they felt the Supreme Court was acquiring too much power or that it was going beyond its proper role. . . .

Another group of critics, three per cent of the sample, felt that the Court was too favorable to some particular class. Sometimes this favored category of litigants was thought to be wealthy, sometimes not. . . .

Finally, a little more than a fifth of our sample (21.4%) was unable to articulate any opinion about the Supreme Court. Nearly two-thirds of these individuals stated frankly that they didn't feel they knew enough to have an opinion. A small businessman who had just bought a new sound truck company admitted:

> I've never given it much thought.

*　　*　　*

Similar characteristics were to be found in the responses to the queries about the preferred role of the Supreme Court. A typical answer to the question "What do you think the job of the Supreme Court should be?" was that of an elderly man:

> To study the law, I guess, and help decide what it should be for everyone.

Most of the answers to this question likewise revealed considerable attitudinal support for the Court resting upon a modest understanding of what the Court actually was about.

The distribution of the answers about the preferred role of the Supreme Court . . . is perhaps significant that taken together they add up to a composite portrait of the tasks which presently concern the Supreme Court. The Court is our tribunal of ultimate appeal. It does interpret the Constitution and the laws according to specified and impartial procedure. And so on. Since the Court is now doing what most of our respondents want it to do, it should follow that most of them will support it. This would suggest that how the Court reaches its decisions may be quite as important in maintaining public support as what it decides.

This is not to say that the content of the Supreme Court decisions is unimportant in shaping the public perception of that institution. While it is true that only a few cases are sufficiently dramatic to rise above the public's threshold of attention, these decisions do stimulate some public discussion. When our respondents were asked what they had read or heard about the Supreme Court during the last year, three-quarters of them referred to Court activity or decisions in four areas: civil rights, prayers in schools, redistricting, and Communists. Civil rights was mentioned by twice as many people as school prayers, school prayers by twice as many people as redistricting, and redistricting by twice as many people as referred to Communists. The exact percentages were civil rights, 42.0%; school prayers, 19.6%; redistricting, 8.0%; and Communism, 4.5%.

This was a bit of luck because the four areas most discussed happened to be the four subjects about which the respondents had been asked to decide "hypothetical" cases. The responses to these queries were related to attitude about the Court. A decision in favor of the public accommodations section, against a required school prayer, for "one man, one vote," and against sending a person to jail simply because he was a Communist was associated with a favorable view of the Supreme Court. The rank-order correlations (Kendall's Tau-b) between these hypothetical decisions and attitudes toward the Court were Heart of Atlanta Motel, .25, Schempp, .14, Wesberry v. Sanders, .12, and Scales, .18.

When the findings about the frequency of discussion of controversial topics are juxtaposed with the tendency to decide hypothetical cases in particular ways, it is possible to conclude something about how each of these decisions contributed to public attitudes about the Court. Civil rights activities are being widely discussed and the activities of the Court are well thought of in this area. The school prayer case and redistricting are being discussed by smaller groups of people and are having less effect on general attitudes about the Court. And while the Court's handling of Communists is being discussed by fewer people than any of the other three subjects, a person who mentions this topic is rather more likely to be critical of the Court.

II

Why do people hold these attitudes about the Supreme Court? What disposes some to have a favorable view of it while others have an unfavorable image? The answer to this simple question is rather complicated. In order to thread our way through the jumble of evidence, we shall confine our attention to a single dependent variable, the respondent's opinion of the Court as measured by the number of positive and negative comments about it, and use a single measure of association, Kendall's Tau-b.

If pure measures of attitudes could be devised, it might be possible to explain attitudes toward the Court on the basis of three independent variables: some measure of liberalism-conservatism, agreement with what the Court has done, and the favorability of communications received about the Court. Or, if one could tap basic attitudes about the cases before the Supreme Court, one might be able to construct an explanation using just these attitudes and what the respondent has read or heard about the Court's activities. This study, however, was not designed in any experimental utopia. We shall have to do the best we can with four independent variables: subjective party identification, support for specific free speech and procedural rights, agreement with four controversial decisions made by the Court, and the favorability of information received about the Court.

*   *   *

. . . Table 1 shows that favorability of prior information—as party identification, support for specific procedural rights, and agreement with Court decisions—did have an effect on attitudes about the Supreme Court.

*   *   *

. . . [H]aving pro-Court attitudes (being a Democrat, supporting 7 to 9 procedural rights, agreeing with 3 or 4 decisions) seems to explain much of what one hears and reads about the Court. At the same time, favorable information makes it less necessary to have such an attitude in order to take a pro-Court position. This implies a circular relationship in which the attitudes of the majority and the communications heard most frequently feed upon and support one another. The minority attitudes (being a Republican, agreeing with 2 or fewer Court decisions) are strong enough to survive in a hostile informational environment, but when persons holding these attitudes do encounter relatively rare anti-Court information, their attitudes are sharply reinforced.

There are several means of noting the joint influence of the four variables. One is to combine classes so that one group has several pro-Court influences. For example, one can create one group made up of Democrats who support 7 to 9 specific procedural rights and who agree with 3 or 4 Court decisions; a second made up of Independents who support 5 or 6 specific procedural rights and who agree with 2 Court decisions; and a third made up of Republicans who support no more than 4 specific procedural rights and who did not agree with more than 1 decision made by the Court. Such a classification of persons who should be pro-Court, neutral, and anti-Court, respectively, produces a Tau-b of .36 when checked against attitudes

Table 1

Independent Variable Party Identification	Attitude about the Supreme Court			
	Strong Supporter (+ 2 or higher)	Supporter (+ 1)	Neutral (0)	Critic (−1 or lower)
Strong Dem	28.4%	22.7%	10.5%	7.1%
Weak Dem	12.5	14.7	18.4	7.1
Independent Dem	20.5	14.7	18.4	13.1
Independent	11.4	13.3	10.5	10.7
Independent Rep	12.5	13.3	14.5	20.2
Weak Rep	10.2	12.0	13.2	15.5
Strong Rep	4.5	9.3	14.5	26.2
	100.0	100.0	100.0	100.0
N	88	75	76	84
Tau-b = .244				
Support for Specific Procedural Rights (McClosky Items)				
Support 7–9 Rights	56.2%	25.6%	26.2%	24.7%
Support 5 or 6 Rights	22.5	37.2	34.2	42.4
Support 0–4 Rights	21.3	37.2	39.5	32.9
	100.0	100.0	100.0	100.0
N	89	78	76	85
Tau-b = .163				
Agreement with Court Decisions				
Agree 3 or 4 Cases	46.0%	30.8%	26.9%	29.6%
Agree with 2 Cases	34.9	39.7	30.8	35.7
Agree 0 or 1 Case	19.5	29.5	42.3	35.7
	100.0	100.0	100.0	100.0
N	87	78	78	84
Tau-b = .144				
Prior Information				
Quite Favorable	35.1%	35.6%	20.0%	7.1%
Favorable	33.3	28.9	24.0	25.7
Mixed	15.8	24.4	20.0	30.0
Unfavorable	12.3	4.4	28.0	20.0
Quite Unfavorable	3.5	6.7	8.0	17.1
	100.0	100.0	100.0	100.0
N	57	45	25	70
Tau-b = .287				

about the Court. This is a higher degree of association than any one of the attitudinal variables produced by themselves.

The difficulty with this approach is that these four variables are somewhat independent of each other. If all Democrats agreed with the decisions of the Court, or if all Republicans were opposed to procedural and free speech rights, it would be easy to divide the world of Court perceptions into liberal and conservative and be done with it. But this is *not* the case. . . .

*   *   *

III

Who are the supporters of the Court? Who are its critics? Which persons are neutral in their opinions of the Court? The most direct answer is that every type of person is to be found in each category. These attitudes were analyzed in terms of a series of demographic variables: age, sex, education, religion, occupation, union membership, social class, income and ancestry. No significant relationships were found. As a general explanation for the existence of these attitudes, a demographic approach is not very powerful.

If, however, we are careful to keep in mind that we are working with weak statistical tendencies rather than with any cause and effect relationships, there are some things which can be noted. The most important findings are presented in Table 2. The effect of age is noticeable in that those under 30 are most inclined to be strong supporters of the Court, while those over 50 are likely to be critical. Men are more likely to be found among the strong supporters or critics of the Court, while women are much more likely to be neutral. Education appears to have a similar, if weaker, effect. Those with college degrees are found disproportionately among those who are strong supporters or critics while those who did not go beyond high school tend to be among those who are neutral or weak supporters.

*   *   *

To the extent that any generalizations can be drawn from these rather weak relationships, there is one theme which runs through

Table 2

OPINIONS OF SUPREME COURT IN TERMS OF SELECTED DEMOGRAPHIC VARIABLES

Demographic Variable	Opinion of Supreme Court			
	Strong	Supporter	Neutral	Critic
Age *				
Under 30	33.3%	26.9%	29.1%	17.6%
30–49	36.6	34.6	30.3	37.6
Over 50	30.1	38.5	40.6	44.8
N	90	78	79	85

$$C = .25, X^2 = 21.806, .20 > p > .10$$

Sex				
Male	55.6%	50.0%	37.5%	55.3%
Female	44.4	50.0	62.5	44.7
N	90	78	80	85

$$C = .14, X^2 = 7.061, .10 > p > .05$$

Education				
Not H. S. Graduate	12.8%	19.4%	14.9%	16.0%
H. S. Graduate	26.7	30.6	31.1	18.5
Some College	24.4	27.8	28.4	24.7
College Graduate	36.0	22.2	25.7	40.7
N	86	72	74	81

$$C = .17, X^2 = 10.006, .40 > p > .30$$

* These data are presented in condensed form in the interests of clarity. The statistics for the data, however, were calculated on the basis of 6 age categories.

the data. This is that the supporters and critics of the Court have more in common with each other than either grouping does with those who take a neutral posture. This holds up when one looks at intensity of opinion. Strong supporters have the same demographic characteristics as strong opponents. Mild supporters resemble mild critics. And so on.

There are exceptions to this. It would be a fairly good bet that a young Jew or a young Italian-American would take a pro-Court position. But a middle-aged man with a college education whose ancestors came from England who had a white collar job and a moderately high income would be likely to have a strong attitude in one direction *or* the other. On the other hand, an older woman with little formal education whose ancestors came from Poland and whose late husband had been a laborer would be likely to lack any firm attitude or, at most, to take a neutral posture. As we read back over these characteristics, the meaning of the differences becomes more obvious. The socio-economic groups who take neutral stances are those who are more isolated from our political culture. Hence, *having an attitude depends on being involved in the political culture while the direction of the attitude depends on the nature of the political environment to which one is exposed.*

If questions can be raised about the weak demographic relationships in Table 2, they can be answered with additional data which support the same conclusions. In Table 3, attitudes about the Court are compared with some measures of involvement in the political culture. We first note that those who have talked about or read about the Supreme Court during the past year are more likely to be found among the supporters or critics of the Court than among those who are neutral. We also see that critics are more likely to have paid some attention to the Court than its supporters. The same thing is true regarding persons who gave some indication in the course of the interview that they were aware of at least one of the four controversial areas in which the Court had been active. A third measure of involvement, intensity of feeling about the Supreme Court, is related to the respondents' comments in a way we have come to expect. Supporters of the Court tend to hold their opinions fairly strongly, more opponents of the Court hold their opinions very strongly; and those who are neutral are also likely not to care too much one way or another. . . .

IV

Now let us recapitulate our major points. Important differences were found between those who had attitudes about the Supreme Court and those who did not. Essentially the differences between those who had attitudes and those who did not were the differences between the politically involved and the politically isolated. Among those possessing attitudes, the direction of the attitude concerning the Court was jointly determined by a cluster of related political attitudes and by

Table 3

OPINIONS OF SUPREME COURT IN TERMS OF POLITICAL INVOLVEMENT

Measure of Involvement	Opinion of Supreme Court			
Read or Heard about Court in Last Year?	Strong Supporter	Supporter	Neutral	Critic
Yes	73.3%	68.5%	45.2%	89.2%
No	26.7	31.5	54.8	10.8
N	86	76	73	83

$$C = .32, X^2 = 36.275, p < .001$$

Heard about Cases Before?				
Yes	70.1%	57.9%	48.7%	78.6%
No	29.9	42.1	51.3	21.4
N	87	76	76	84

$$C = .23, X^2 = 18.187, p < .001$$

Intensity of Attitude about Court				
Very Strong	40.9%	34.2%	17.5%	51.8%
Fairly Strong	48.9	39.7	39.7	32.5
Doesn't Care	10.2	26.0	42.9	15.7
N	88	73	63	83

$$C = .31, X^2 = 36.543, p. < .001$$

Number of Political Activities				
5–6	10.1%	12.8%	3.9%	8.8%
1–4	73.0	61.6	68.8	71.8
0	16.9	25.6	27.3	14.1
N	89	78	77	85

$$C = .19, X^2 = 12.58, p = .05$$

communications concerning the Court. . . . Finally, the over-all distribution of attitudes was favorable to the Supreme Court.

There are important implications in these findings relating to the probability of changes in these attitudes. We have three types of respondents, each of which has rather different characteristics. Let us ask what would happen to each in the event that pro-Court or anti-Court propaganda were directed at them. Supporters of the Court are already receiving a sufficient number of pro-Court communications to maintain their attitudes. Additional pro-Court messages might result in a modest strengthening of their attitudes, but this is about all. Anti-Court communications, on the other hand, are unlikely to come to their attention at all because their attitudes produce such a high threshold of awareness. Identical threshold mechanisms make it unlikely that those who are now neutral in their stance would be aware of either pro-Court or anti-Court propaganda. In addition, their isolation from our political culture makes it improbable that they would have much contact with political communications to begin with. The critic of the Court is not likely to assimilate pro-Court propaganda, but an increase in the frequency with which he encounters anti-Court communications can perceptibly increase the intensity of his conviction. In sum, the minority may become more highly motivated but is unlikely to become a majority.

*   *   *

. . . So there it is. The decisions of the Supreme Court have had more effect on the reputation of the Court than the activities of its antagonists. The attitudes of the majority are favorable to the Court. In this informational environment, such decisions as the Court has been making (or at least the majority of those few decisions which rise to the public's threshold of awareness) are likely to be favorably communicated. To the extent that we can generalize from this study, we can expect a continuing consensus which is supportive of the Court.

This leaves us with two questions. One is the degree to which this Seattle study is an accurate indicator of the national pattern of attitudes toward the Court. Will the national pattern prove to be relatively homogeneous? Or will it prove to be heterogeneous with islands of support in certain parts of the country and centers of opposition located elsewhere? This is most important, and it is clear that we need a good national study of attitudes about the Court as soon as possible.

The other question is whether the joint effect of attitudes and communication here noted will prove to be general. If so, it could offer an explanation of why majorities and minorities on many political issues tend to persist for such long periods of time. Given these kinds of psychological roots, some dramatic new personality or issue or the addition of some new group of citizens is necessary to produce realignment. There are many cases in which realignment is not necessarily desirable. Support for the Supreme Court, for example, provides one anchor for our constitutional system. But if a conscientious minority cannot work in the arena of public opinion with reasonable hope of success, then we must provide them with some alternative way to give vent to their feelings. Otherwise their prospect is one of frustration, which in turn may lead to an embittered isolation or to an eventual explosion. Their feelings are going to find an outlet somewhere, and it is preferable that this expression be legitimate.

KENNETH DOLBEARE

The Supreme Court and the States: From Abstract Doctrine to Local Behavioral Conformity

* * *

Daniel Elazar has suggested a comparative political culture approach to the political behavior of American states and regions.[1] Differences in the political behavior of particular states *as states* have long been observed, of course, and what is distinctive about Elazar's work is mainly the effort to relate the causes, character, and results of these differences to his concept of political culture.[2] In developing his argument, he stresses the existence of distinct but patterned value premises, styles, concerns, and policy products in the politics of various states. The idea is plausible and provocative. Each political culture presumably would be distinctive also in terms of expectations toward courts, the legitimacy of various actions on the part of courts, and the general role of courts and the law within the polity. Such expectations, values, and experience would then also be major factors in shaping responses to Supreme Court decisions within a state.

1. Daniel Elazar, *American Federalism: A View From the States* (New York: Thomas Y. Crowell Co., 1966). See esp. Chs. 4 and 5, pp. 79–140. In speaking of the implementation of constitutional doctrines, he argues: "Although the national constitution may set the standard and the Supreme Court the guidelines, the state governments are left to apply those guidelines within their own boundaries in a manner consonant with their respective political cultures" (p. 7).
2. *Ibid.* Elazar offers no measures and no empirical support for his characterizations, relying chiefly on migration patterns developing out of original settlement differences.

From an unpublished essay by Mr. Dolbeare. Printed by permission.

Kenneth Dolbeare is Associate Professor of Political Science at the University of Washington.

We can hardly expect to assess the relevance of these several dimensions of state political cultures without large-scale attitudinal and behavioral studies. Two primary indicators of the existence and importance of different political cultures may be explored briefly, however, as a means of supporting the utility of this approach. One factor affecting behavioral response to Supreme Court initiatives would be the set of attitudes and expectations which the affected, attentive, and general publics within the states hold toward the Supreme Court and the lower courts as institutions. Another would be the propensity of the people of the state to invoke the processes of courts and law for affecting the behavior of others. In both cases, we shall have to be content with inquiry limited to one or two dimensions of the subject. But the data which are developed in each strongly imply important effects from these aspects of state political culture.

Several recent studies provide some elements of background on public attitudes toward the Supreme Court and lower courts and judges.[3] Public orientations toward courts apparently change slowly over time if at all, as decisions and popular policy preferences (and other factors) interact. At any given moment, however, there is a general level of approval toward the Supreme Court and a set of expectations toward courts in general which form part of the political culture of the state. Two questions immediately arise: do these ratings and expectations vary between states? Do they affect reactions to decisions? Affirmative answers are essential to our thesis.

3. See John H. Kessel, "Public Perceptions of the Supreme Court," *Midwest Journal of Political Science,* Vol. 10 (May, 1966), pp. 167–191 (two-stage probability sample of 356 adults in two state legislative districts of Seattle, Wash., conducted by student interviewers); Kenneth M. Dolbeare, "The Public Views the Supreme Court" in Herbert Jacob (ed.), *Law and Politics in the Federal Courts* (Boston: Little, Brown & Co., 1967) (clustered area probability sample of 627 adults in Wisconsin conducted by the Wisconsin Survey Research Laboratory); Carl D. McMurray and Malcolm B. Parsons, "Public Attitudes Toward the Representational Role of Legislators and Judges," *Midwest Journal of Political Science,* Vol. 9 (May, 1965), pp. 167–185 ("random" sample of 207 white adults in Cape Kennedy area conducted by the Institute of Social Research of Florida State University); Kenneth M. Dolbeare and Phillip E. Hammond, "The Political Party Basis of Attitudes Toward the Supreme Court," *Public Opinion Quarterly* Vol. 32 (Spring, 1968), pp. 16–30. (re-analysis of six national surveys, four conducted by American Institute of Public Opinion, one by Michigan Survey Research Center and one by University of California (Berkeley) Survey Research Center).

The data presented in Table 1 [4] suggest that the answer to the first question is indeed affirmative. Not only do the states involved differ in attitudes toward the Court, but they vary in the extent to which political party identification correlates with ratings of the Court. Other research has indicated that party identification may be the primary cue for attitudes toward the Court; [5] if party plays a different structuring role in different states, there may be several dimensions of linkage to the basic political cultures of those states. There are serious problems of comparability encountered in any present attempt to find data bearing on these questions, and Table 1 has circumvented only some of them. But we may at least aver, in appropriately tentative terms, that there is support for this part of our thesis in what data can be developed short of a major new inquiry.

These findings might have been anticipated; perhaps even more readily predictable are differences between states in attitudes toward particular decisions. Table 2 contrasts responses to the most nearly comparable questions which could be found concerning the recent prayer decisions. The states in this instance were Minnesota and Texas, and they show sharp variation in reactions to the decisions involved. More revealing is the fact that here the variations showed *no* correlation with party identification, or, for that matter, with any other [6] demographic characteristic; other factors in the general political or religious experience of these states will obviously have to be considered in developing a general theory.

The available evidence also suggests an affirmative answer to the second question. Data from Minnesota show dramatically how the action of the Supreme Court may affect policy positions. Respondents in Minnesota were asked *first* whether they favored or opposed prayer at the start of the school day, and after their answers had been recorded, *then* were told that the Supreme Court had ruled the practice illegal and asked whether they liked the decision or not. Table 3

4. Data from the Texas and Minnesota Polls were made available through the courtesy of the Roper Center in Williamstown, Mass. The Berkeley data were specially prepared and made available by the University of California, Berkeley, Survey Research Center, by Mr. Stephen Steinberg, whose assistance was particularly helpful. The Wisconsin data were collected through the facilities of the Wisconsin Survey Research Laboratory, Harry Sharp, director. The assistance of all of these sources is gratefully acknowledged.
5. Dolbeare and Hammond, *op. cit.*
6. The Texas Poll, unfortunately, does not record religion of respondents.

Table 1
"RATINGS" OF U.S. SUPREME COURT

(A) Rating of Job Court is Doing

	Wisconsin,[1] 1966	Seattle, Wash.,[2] 1965	Texas,[3] 1964
Very Good/Good	62%	51%	46%
Fair/Poor	38%	49%	54%
	100%	100%	100%
	N = 625	N = 323	N = 1000

(B) Rating of Job Court is Doing, By Political Party

	United States,[4] 1964		Wisconsin,[1] 1966		Seattle, Wash.,[2] 1965		Texas,[3] 1964	
	Dem	Rep	Dem	Rep	Dem	Rep	Dem	Rep
Very Good/Good	65%	51%	71%	55%	61%	37%	51%	44%
Fair/Poor	35%	49%	29%	45%	39%	63%	49%	56%
	100%	100%	100%	100%	100%	100%	100%	100%
	N = 1314	N = 1052	N = 191	N = 147	N = 152	N = 134	N = 558	N = 77

1. Wisconsin Survey, 1966. Q. How good a job do you feel the U.S. Supreme Court has been doing lately? (Very Good/Good/Fair/Poor/Don't Know). "Don't Know" responses (19% of total) eliminated.
2. See John Kessel, "Public Perceptions of the Supreme Court," *Midwest Journal of Political Science,* Vol. 10 (May 1966) p. 179. Q. Speaking generally, how would you describe your own feelings about the Supreme Court? (Coded into Strong Supporter/Supporter/Neutral/Critic, which have been equated here with Very Good/Good/Fair/Poor for comparative purposes. Nonresponses unspecified, but other indications suggest 10% of total.)
3. Texas Poll, 1964. Q. In general, what kind of rating would you give the U.S. Supreme Court—excellent, good, fair or poor? (Excellent/Good/Fair/Poor/No opinion). "No opinion" responses (15% of total) eliminated.
4. Berkeley Survey Research Center, 1964, South eliminated. Q. The Supreme Court is doing a good job these days. (All agreement responses included under Very Good/Good; all disagreement included under Fair/Poor. Noncomparability acknowledged, data included as the only available national standard.)

Table 2

(A) *Approval/Disapproval of Prayer/Bible Reading Decisions*

	Approval	Disapproval	Don't Know, Don't Care	
Minnesota,[2] 1962	55%	31%	14%	100% (N = 586)
Texas,[3]	28%	60%	12%	100% (N = 1000)

(B) *Approval/Disapproval of Prayer/Bible Reading Decisions,
By Political Party*

	Minnesota, 1962		Texas, 1964	
Response to decisions preventing prayers/ Bible reading in schools	D-F-L	Rep	Dem	Rep
Approve	65	65	34	34
Disapprove	35	35	66	66
	100%	100%	100%	100%
	N = 223	N = 148	N = 599	N = 82

1. The decisions were different although related ones, of course: *Engel v. Vitale*, 370 U.S. 421 (1962) and *Abington Township v Schempp*, 374 U.S. 203 (1963). The differences in response are so substantial, however, that the comparison is worth making. Nor is "approval" of a decision necessarily indicative of anything respecting behavior. Opinion research by political scientists should take care to seek out the prospects of action rather than settling for this indeterminate commercial inquiry.

2. Q. The U.S. Supreme Court has ruled recently that it is not legal to have the school board or any public official or agency prepare one certain prayer for school children to recite in the public schools. Do you like the Supreme Court ruling? dislike it? or don't you care one way or the other? (Like it/Dislike it/ Don't care/No opinion/Other). Minnesota Poll No. 214, 1962.

3. Q. The U.S. Supreme Court has ruled that no state or local government may require the reading of the Lord's Prayer or Bible verses in public schools. What are your views on this? (Approve/Disapprove/Don't Know). Texas Poll, 1964.

shows how the Court's action blurred policy preference; nearly half of those favoring prayer nevertheless "liked" the decision! This effect may be partially attributable to general orientations toward government action, but the implication is strong that it is caused by some form of halo effect from the symbolic image of the Supreme Court.

Table 3

Supreme Court has ruled against it— do you like it or dislike it? [2]	*Should there be prayer in Minnesota schools?* [1]	
	Favor (74%)	Oppose (26%)
like it	44%	89%
dislike it	44%	4%
don't care	12%	7%
	100%	100%
	N = 395	N = 135

Q. 1. In the public schools of some states, the school day is opened with a time for prayer by the children. Do you favor or oppose having a time for prayer as part of each school day in Minnesota's public schools? (Favor/ Oppose/No opinion/Other).

Q. 2. The U.S. Supreme Court has ruled recently that it is not legal to have the school board or any public official or agency prepare one certain prayer for school children to recite in the public schools. Do you like the Supreme Court ruling? dislike it? or don't you care one way or the other? (Like it/Dislike it/ Don't care/No opinion/Other). (Asked immediately after question 1 above.)

We know from the Wisconsin study that persons subscribing to the "myths" of nonpartisan, mechanical jurisprudence are more likely to rate the Court highly than are persons who see the Justices as exercising discretionary, policymaking functions.[7] The extent to which such "myths" are held and the general prestige level of the Supreme Court vary between states; they are background elements of the political cultures of the states which combine with policy preferences and other values to establish the context in which Supreme Court initiatives are received.

*   *   *

The identification and exploration of the varying levels of expectations toward courts which are embedded in the political cultures of the states should be followed by documentation of the relevance of such attitudes to behavior. At present, we have only the hint that propensity to act in opposition to a Supreme Court decision is more

7. Dolbeare, *op. cit.* note 3 above.

a function of a sense of political efficacy than of one's generally unfavorable view of the Court.[8] It seems likely that further research
would show more direct impact of attitudes on behavior, and that
general expectations toward courts have an important structuring
effect on local responses to Supreme Court policy pronouncements.

The second aspect of state political culture previously projected as
relevant to local responses to Supreme Court decisions was the propensity of political actors to employ the law and the courts to gain
their ends. Decisions of the Supreme Court are only rarely self-
executing, and for the most part they must be asserted by litigants in
various ways before they begin to have widespread behavioral impact.
The litigiousness of a state's population then may bear upon the
process of conversion of doctrine into practice; do the states differ in
this respect?

Again, the evidence indicates that they do. . . .

*   *   *

Intrastate diversities make any characterization of the political
culture of "a state" a somewhat tentative enterprise, and there are
additional problems here in the development of empirical measures.
Use of court workload data as a means of assessing litigiousness,
though attractive and practical,[9] is not satisfactory without controlling
for important intervening factors; the workloads of state courts of last
resort are variably affected by the courts' jurisdictional discretion,
and trial court workload may be affected by the availability of
lawyers, the financial capacity of litigants, or other extraneous factors.

*   *   *

. . . Such higher incidence of use of courts is significant in itself,
but it may also suggest further possibilities, such as preference for
courts over open political processes, greater finality for the decisions

8. Dolbeare, *op. cit.* note 3 above.
9. The Council of State Governments, in a series of publications, has provided a potentially valuable source of comparative state data. See, e.g., *Workloads of State Courts of Last Resort* (Chicago: Council of State Governments,
1962).

of courts or a greater role for "legal" rather than "practical" solutions to problems.

These two characteristics of the political cultures of states—images and expectations toward courts, and litigiousness—are by no means a comprehensive catalogue of the court-related aspects of state political cultures. Nor would such factors be the only ones relevant to setting the context of response to Supreme Court doctrine within the states. But they do indicate that such factors are integral to general theories of behavioral response to Supreme Court acts involving social change.

Toward a Theory of Impact:
Theoretical and Methodological Concern

If the social studies are ever to assume the full status of a "science," it will be the result of the development of rigorous theories as a basis for both explaining and predicting behavior. Why? Because it is systematic explanation and prediction that are the hallmarks of any "mature" science. Consequently, it is not surprising to find that many social scientists undertaking systematic behavioral research on the impact of the Supreme Court are also interested in the development of social theory.

At least three distinct terms have cropped up at one time or another as potential candidates for one core concept in a theory of the Supreme Court: *aftermath, compliance,* and *impact.* Aftermath, according to general usage, simply refers to everything taking place after a specified event, direct *and* indirect. The nature and scope of the relationship need not be indicated with much precision and few clues to distinguish the "significant" from the "insignificant" consequences of a particular action are given. For example, suppose a hurricane hits a town and many people are found dead after it passes by. Those who drowned are dead because of it, but what about those who died of heart attacks? And what about the looting— was that "caused" by the storm? And there were large numbers of birds who lost their nests—all directly related to the storm. All of this is in the aftermath. Because of this open-ended and undiscriminating nature of the concept it has not proven to be a viable core for theories in social science—and it probably wouldn't help us too much in studying the effects of Supreme Court decisions.

Compliance, on the other hand, connotes a far more precise set of effects. This term conjures up the notion of why individuals *knowingly obey or do not obey specified rules*. Furthermore, the concept of compliance readily lends itself to traditional philosophical and theoretical concerns. As a matter of fact, a full-blown theory of compliance would be co-extensive with a general theory of social control and social contract. All this is, of course, good. On the other hand, the concept of compliance examines more intently the rule-recipient (he who is faced with the decision of whether or not to comply) than the rule-giver. In a theory of compliance, the conditions and characteristics of the complier or potential complier would be the center of attention. Such a perspective could well be counter-productive to someone interested primarily in the nature and efficacy of only one rule-generating institution, such as the Supreme Court. To take a far-fetched example, if one is interested in the effectiveness of a new type of bomb, one need not bother about developing a general theory of the causes of death by violence.

Also, a focus on compliance as a framework of analysis might lead one to overlook other types of possible responses to the "rule giver." Many theoretically interesting responses to a newly promulgated rule might not appropriately be characterized as compliance or noncompliance, but, for instance, as side-effects or latent functions. Actually, these side-effects or latent functions might easily prove to be of deepest interest to many students of Supreme Court efficacy. For example, one type of response to a high court ruling not easily characterized as compliance would be Congressional efforts to nullify a particular decision by either Constitutional amendment, alteration of Court personnel, or limitation of the Supreme Court's appellate jurisdiction. The point is that these legislative (or executive) challenges to the Court can exist independent of the degree to which the particular decision is complied with by administrators, lower court judges, citizens, etc. So whereas "aftermath" was too broad, perhaps "compliance" is too narrow.

We are left with the third and last candidate, "impact." In many respects it is a compromise, and while it appears to be most desirable—at least for the moment—it also possesses vices and ambiguities characteristic of most compromise candidates. Impact refers to *"all policy related consequences of a decision."* Thus it refers not only to compliant behavior, but to other types of behavior as well, e.g. the response of Congress, etc. It also provides a rough guide to determine the scope and nature of relevant consequences.

Despite these optimistic words, it remains to be seen if a "theory of impact" is conceptually justifiable or empirically possible. It is to this problem that the three articles in this section address themselves. Wasby's piece is excerpted from the concluding chapter of his book, *The Impact of the United States Supreme Court,* in which he attempts to build empirically a "theory of impact." Feeley's piece turns to the conceptual problems inherent in the notion of impact. Becker and Levine's piece deals with a wide-ranging set of issues raised by impact analysis, including whether or not it even should be undertaken. It is, perhaps, appropriate to conclude this volume with these contributions in that they reflect the major theoretical concerns and professional responsibilities of all those deeply involved in trying to help shed needed light on "The Impact of Supreme Court Decisions"—and they are numerous and troublesome.

STEPHEN L. WASBY

Toward Impact Theory: An Inventory of Hypotheses

Stephen Wasby's book, The Impact of the United States Supreme Court, *is perhaps the single major work that explicitly attempts to develop a working theory of the impact of Supreme Court decisions. For this reason alone the book merits attention.*

Most studies of the impact of the high court's decisions are not theoretically oriented. Instead they are simply case studies of particular decisional consequences. Thus, the task of moving toward an inductive social theory of impact and compliance is more than a little challenging. Nevertheless, with the help of a carefully conceived initial framework and a lengthy and thorough review of all the major studies of the impact of decisions of the Supreme Court, Wasby has moved forward in our quest for some theory, no matter how reluctantly and tentatively. By combing numerous studies, he has inductively generated a number of low and middle level generalizations that are warranted by the scanty data available. Such an effort is the first crucial step in the development of an empirically based social scientific theory. Additionally, his hypotheses are organized so that many of them are logically related to, or derived from, others. Such interrelationships meet still one more key test for the proper development of a theory.

We would like to call the reader's attention to the fact that Wasby called his concluding "findings" an "inventory of hypotheses" rather than a "propositional inventory." What is important about this distinction? It implies that many of the generalizations are tentative, impressionistic, frequently based upon tenuous evidence or inference

Excerpt from Stephen L. Wasby, *The Impact of the United States Supreme Court* (Homewood, Ill.: The Dorsey Press, 1970) excerpt from pp. 246–268. Stephen L. Wasby is an Associate Professor of Political Science at Southern Illinois University.

214

and, in short, in dire need of future testing and refinement. Thus, approach them with caution. Still, their tentativeness should be regarded as a special challenge to the reader of this collection of studies in that the various reports in this volume offer a considerable basis for that future "testing and refinement." To what extent do the studies in this book either support or weaken various propositions Wasby has put forth? Our readers are invited to assume the role of social scientist: they can utilize the data of the empirical studies to support, disprove, or modify some of Wasby's forty-one hypotheses listed below. We wish them luck.

THE EDITORS

I. CHARACTERISTICS

1. A line of cases will have greater impact than a single case.

2. A decision in which precedent is overruled will create more resistance than one in which there is no overruling.

3. Noncompliance will be greater when there is an economic component than when there is not.

4. Decisions invalidating procedural defects are more frequently evaded than are decisions on substantive law.

5. Where the basis for a decision is made clear, compliance will be greater than when it is not made clear.

6. Continued denial of *certiorari* with respect to a given subject will shift activity from the judicial system to other political arenas.

7. Attempts to curb the Court are less likely to be successful when intensely held economic or civil liberties interests are involved than when federal-state relations or separation of powers questions are decided by the Court.

8. The broader the decision, the greater the impact and the broader the noncompliance.

9. Compliance will be more immediate when courts provide clear guidelines than when they do not.

10. The greater the technicality of the language of a decision, the smaller the impact.

11. Ambiguity in Supreme Court rulings decreases compliance.

12. Where there is no clear agreement on the meaning of a decision, compliance is less than where there is such agreement.

13. Noncompliance will be greater when dissenting and/or concurring opinions exist than in unanimous decisions.

14. The broader the scope of a holding, the more difficult evasion becomes.

15. A Supreme Court decision based on the Constitution will receive less attack and greater compliance than a decision grounded on statute, the Court's supervisory authority, or other bases.

II. COMMUNICATION

16. The greater the number of channels through which decisions are reported, the greater the impact.

17. Information about the specifics of how to comply with a decision will bring greater impact than general discussion of a case.

18. Reporting of immediate negative reaction tends to increase noncompliance.

III. POLITICAL ENVIRONMENT

19. If the relevant social policy is backed up by a strong political majority, judicial decisions in accordance with it are readily acceptable.

20. The greater the number of levels of government or the number of people affected, the greater the noncompliance.

21. Compliance is more likely to be delayed if resistors see a chance of victory in reversing the Court than if they do not.

22. Where it is unclear that the Supreme Court would now follow a prior decision, compliance with that decision will decrease.

23. Friction between parties or between factions of parties increases noncompliance and action directed at reversal of the Court's decisions.

24. A decision will be more likely to bring action if it disturbs the balance between interests than if it affects an interest without affecting others.

25. The President's ability to oppose the Court by himself is far less than if he and the Congress are acting in concert.

26. Groups with broad policy concerns are more likely to be activated by Court rulings than are groups with narrower concerns.

27. Attempts to reverse the Court will be more frequent when it

is felt the Court has misinterpreted the intent of another branch than when this is not the case.

IV. FOLLOW-UP

28. Impact will be greater when efforts are made to follow up a decision than when such efforts are not made.

29. Where past decisions have not been enforced, resistance to present decisions will be less great than where they have been enforced.

30. Failure to obtain reversal of disliked decisions will give rise to attacks on the Court for later decisions.

31. Compliance is more likely when some reviewing body is available to those complaining of noncompliance.

32. Units of governments are less likely to comply with court rulings than are individuals.

V. THOSE RESPONDING

33. Judges are more likely to follow Supreme Court opinions than are other government officials.

34. Federal court judges are more likely to comply with Supreme Court rulings affecting the states than are state court judges.

35. Lawyers are more likely to comply with Supreme Court decisions than are nonlawyers.

36. The greater the discretion of local officials, the lower the compliance with Supreme Court rulings.

VI. BELIEFS AND VALUES

37. The Court's legitimacy is increased when people agree with its specific rulings.

38. Belief in judicial neutrality and belief that judges only find rather than make law increase acceptance of decisions.

39. Those who consider the Court's authority legitimate will be more likely to comply with its rulings than those who do not.

40. Greater information about Court decisions brings greater disapproval.

41. Support of the Supreme Court is not dependent on knowledge of particular rulings of the Court.

MALCOLM M. FEELEY

Power, Impact, and the Supreme Court

INTRODUCTION

Within the past few years students of the Supreme Court have begun to move away from the formal analysis of constitutional law decisions and begun to explore the consequences and impact of these decisions. Even more recently this interest has tended to swing away from descriptions of impact and compliance toward a concern with the development of explanatory theory. This interest is probably best expressed in some of the works of Krislov,[1] Wasby,[2] Becker,[3] and Levine.[4] Each of these scholars has not only analyzed the impact of particular decisions but also discussed theoretical frameworks in which to characterize the related problems of compliance and impact. The purpose of this paper is to consider some of the implications of these recent expressions of interest in theory building, examine some of the conceptual and methodological problems inherent in such a theory of impact, and then offer an alternative perspective for research, that of public policy analysis.

While there has been considerable concern with the social and

1. Samuel Krislov, "The Perimeters of Power: Patterns of Compliance and Opposition to Supreme Court Decisions." Paper presented at the annual convention of the American Political Science Association, 1963.
2. Stephen Wasby, *The Impact of the United States Supreme Court* (Chicago: The Dorsey Press, 1970).
3. Theodore L. Becker and James Levine, "Toward and Beyond a Theory of Supreme Court Impact," *American Behavioral Scientist* (1970), pp. 561–73. Reprinted in this book, pp. 232–246.
4. James P. Levine, "Methodological Concerns in Studying Supreme Court Efficacy," 4 *Law and Society Review,* (1970), pp. 583–92.

Malcolm M. Feeley is Assistant Professor of Politics at New York University.

psychological conditions under which individuals comply or do not comply with the law, the major focus of attention in impact research has been on the institutional strengths and limitations of the Supreme Court. Thus, for example, both Wasby and Levine have begun to explore the basis for the Court's efficacy by examining the institutional and symbolic conditions that produce compliance to its decisions. Both explicitly and implicitly much of their discussion is modeled on Richard Neustadt's analysis of Presidential power. Their use of this model seems particularly appropriate, since Neustadt's thesis is that the major weapon of the President is the "power to persuade," a power long recognized as the major (if not sole) source of power possessed by the Supreme Court, an institution possessing neither purse nor sword. Wasby is optimistic about the possibility of building on Neustadt's framework, and notes that many of the generalizations specifying conditions under which the Court is likely to receive high compliance to its decisions are similar to those Neustadt offers in his discussion of the conditions under which Presidential orders are likely to be "self-executing." Thus, for example, he quotes a section from *Presidential Power* which lists the conditions under which Presidential orders were found to be "self-executing," i.e. received prompt and complete compliance:

> At least five common factors were at work. On each occasion the President's involvement was unambiguous. So were his words. His order was widely publicized. The men who received it had control of everything needed to carry it out. And they had no apparent doubt of his authority to issue it to them.[5]

Wasby then goes on to quote discussions by Suchman et al,[6] LaFave,[7] and Krislov,[8] on compliance to Supreme Court decisions in which each investigator reiterates variations on Neustadt's points, but with specific reference to the Supreme Court, not Presidential power.

What all this adds up to is that some scholars have realized that

---

5. Wasby, *op. cit.*, p. 267.
6. Edward Suchman, *et al.*, *Desegregation: Some Propositions and Research Suggestions* (New York: Anti-Defamation League, 1958), p. 39.
7. Wayne LaFave, "Improving Police Performance through the Exclusionary Rule: Part II," *Missouri Law Review*, Vol. 30 (Fall 1965), p. 567.
8. Samuel Krislov, *The Supreme Court in the Political Process* (New York: Macmillan, 1965), p. 136.

Neustadt's model or generalizations can be extended to other realms of authority, and that it invites explicit attention to the concept *power* as a theoretically useful concept in analyzing the nature of the high court's impact. Once this relevance is established, however, two questions immediately arise: (1) What is the precise relationship between impact and power? and (2) Is a power-impact framework helpful in producing a "theory" of impact?

Turning to the first question, I think that the terms "impact" and "power," as they are used generally in the social science literature, are closely related if not interchangeable. Perhaps the most well-known recent definition of political power is Robert Dahl's definition: "A has power over B to the extent that he can get B to do something he would not otherwise do."[9] The term impact, as it has been used in the studies of the Supreme Court, seems also to fit within the spirit of this definition. Substitute "Supreme Court" for A and the relevant actors (i.e. lower courts, policemen, school superintendents, etc.) for B, and the basic structure of impact analysis has been stated.[10]

In general, careful analysts of the concept of power have tended to be pessimistic about the prospects of developing any type of rigorous theory of power. Speaking of its utility William Riker stated: "My initial emotion, I confess, is that we ought to banish it."[11] R. H. Wagner, in a perceptive analysis of the concept, is also pessimistic about its theoretical usefulness: "While indispensible as an abbreviation of complex phenomena, [power] does not unambiguously refer to anything, and therefore is not likely to play a major part in any useful theory."[12] Without going into an exhaustive cataloguing of all the problems inherent in the notion of power, there are several conceptual and methodological issues particularly applicable to the analysis of Supreme Court impact that I would like to examine here. The hope is that such a discussion will contribute, if

9. Robert Dahl, "The Concept of Power," 2 *Behavioral Science* (1957), pp. 201–15. See also his discussion of power in chapter five of *Modern Political Analysis* (Englewood Cliffs: Prentice-Hall, 1963).

10. Indeed Wasby has explicitly recognized this connection, and begun to explore some of the implications in his book. See Wasby, *op. cit.*, pp. 35–37.

11. William Riker, "Some Ambiguities in the Notion of Power," 58 *American Political Science Review* (1964), pp. 341–49, 49.

12. R. H. Wagner, "The Concept of Power and the Study of Politics," in R. Bell *et al.*, *Political Power* (New York: Free Press, 1970), pp. 3–12, 11.

not to a theory of impact, at least to a better understanding of the nature and limits of the high court's powers.

THREE PROBLEMS WITH POWER AND IMPACT

(1) One difficulty with the concept of power is termed the *comparability problem*.[13] Posed in its simplest form this notion questions the possibility of ever developing a rigorous theory of power because of the difficulty—if not impossibility—of making comparisons about the magnitude of power among various types of relationships. For example, Alfred might be successful in talking his boss into allowing him an extra two days of paid vacation. Likewise Alfred might successfully seduce Betty despite the fact that she had promised herself never to sleep with someone she did not know well. Clearly, Alfred has affected the behavior of both his boss and Betty, but it would be foolish to attempt to specify in which of the two situations he had exercised the greater power, or for that matter in unequivocally determining if power had in fact been exercised. This is the problem of comparability: unless there is a clear unit of power or some other translator and indicator of the magnitude of power, it is impossible to make meaningful systematic comparisons between two sets of actions.

Translated into analysis of Supreme Court impact, it would be difficult to compare the Court's power or impact in different types of cases. Can anyone assert with confidence that the Court has had greater "impact" in the reapportionment decisions (in that there was relatively quick and complete compliance to court orders) than it has had in the school desegregation cases (from which followed much deliberateness and little speed)? Or is it just the reverse in that the former actions resulted in some redrawing of a few boundaries and replacement of a few elected officials while the latter sparked a profound social movement?

One scholar, James Levine, has been particularly sensitive to the problem of comparability, suggesting that as a first order of priority "it is essential that scholars be more precise in conceptualizing the dependent variable [impact] . . . so that we can stop putting apples

13. See Dahl, "The Concept of Power," *op. cit.* See also Levine, "Some Methodological Concerns . . . ," *op. cit.*

and oranges into the same basket."[14] Like most good advice, no one seems to be following it, no doubt because there seems to be no clear way to proceed. Even the most mathematically sophisticated of the power approaches—game theory—is plagued by the comparability problem. Therefore it is not surprising to find the more open-ended and inductive discussions of power and impact to also suffer the same fate.

(2) The second problem involves *causal analysis* and the related problem of *spurious correlation*. That most discussions of power possess implicit assumptions about the nature of causality has been carefully explicated in a number of discussions by Herbert Simon and William Riker.[15] This same problem also faces students of impact, and any theory of impact must deal with it. Thus far two notions of causality have been identified in the social sciences. One is termed the "recipe" idea of causality, the other is that of "necessary and sufficient conditions." The former notion suggests that "causes" are statements about rules of manipulation, or recipes (e.g. if you provide A, then B will occur). For example, one might say that the Supreme Court "caused" state legislatures to reapportion. Aside from not being a repeatable type of event, and hence somewhat *theoretically* barren, such a statement of causality has a profound weakness: it assumes as fixed (or otherwise ignores) all other possibly relevant variables. The point is that other variables may also contribute to the "effect" and that these variables or conditions might easily be overlooked or ignored if one tends to focus exclusively on the consequences or "impact" of a single variable.

An alternative notion of causality centers on "effects." That is, by regarding "cause" as a set of necessary and sufficient conditions for an event to occur, an elaboration of the necessary and sufficient conditions would include a complete listing of *all* the factors required to bring about an event. This almost invariably means a shift from a concentration on a single variable, which is particularly compatible with the recipe notion, to a set of elements, which implies a full explanation, and a complete theory.

This analysis poses a serious dilemma for theoretically oriented

14. Levine, "Methodological concerns . . . ," *op. cit.,* p. 590.
15. Herbert A. Simon, "Spurious Correlation: A Causal Interpretation," reprinted in R. Bell *et al.* (eds.), *op. cit.,* pp. 194–201. See also William Riker, *op. cit.*

students of the Supreme Court, or any other institution or actor for that matter. That is, once one focuses on that single institution in order to identify and measure its "impact" or "power," he is likely to embrace a recipe notion of causality which severely limits, if not renders completely impossible, the possibility of the development of a *theoretical* explanation. On the other hand, if one embraces fully the search for the necessary and sufficient conditions for an event to occur, the preoccupation with a single variable, e.g. the Supreme Court, will almost invariably be abandoned and replaced by a concern with the set of factors "causing" outcomes. In short, if one pursues the path of tracing the impact of a single variable, he tends to abandon the hopes of developing a full, theoretical explanation of an event, but if he pursues the course of developing a full and theoretical explanation, he is likely to abandon or at least diminish his focus on the single variable which initially piqued his curiosity.

There is a related problem that requires at least brief mention here, that of *spurious correlation*. In its simplest form, a spurious correlation between two variables is an apparent relationship that stems from the fact that each of them is related to a third factor, but not necessarily to each other. For example, there might be a high correlation between A and C such that some type of "meaningful" or causal relationship between the two might be inferred. However, if a third variable, B, is introduced, a spurious relationship would be identified if this "relationship" between A and C was due to both of their being related to B, and *not* to each other.

For example, much heat and occasionally some evidence has been generated in the argument that police "effectiveness" has been curbed by the Warren Court's decisions dealing with right to counsel and search and seizure. Nation-wide figures on the decreasing conviction and clearance rates after *Miranda* have been cited as evidence substantiating this claim. However, before a convincing case can be made, other factors must be considered. For instance, other possible explanations for this "relationship" include: improved crime reporting systems, increases in certain types of crimes, crowded court calendars, etc. Before anything meaningful can be attributed to this simple correlation, the alternative explanations must be explored and rejected to guard against a spurious interpretation of the data.

A recipe notion of causality, as is found in most impact studies of the Supreme Court, is particularly susceptible to the fallacy of spuriousness. Why? Because a preoccupation with a single independent variable is particularly likely to result in the failure to search out diligently other possible "causes" of the observed "effects." There is a tendency, an all too natural one, for a researcher to become satisfied and search no further once he has identified a "relationship" between two variables and provided himself with a plausible argument with which to "confirm" it. It is not surprising, therefore, that spurious relationships go unchecked from time to time. The possibilities of not identifying spurious relationships in the social sciences is further enhanced by the facts that: (a) the basis of identifying relationships in the first place is frequently impressionistic and vague; (b) many relationships are at best only indirect; and (c) time. As the time span between the supposed cause and effects is lengthened, the possibilities of spuriousness is likely to increase.

One Supreme Court-related illustration of the type of problem I am raising here can be found in the attempt to identify the impact of the Supreme Court's celebrated decision, *Brown v. Board of Education*.[16] Some scholars assign a great impact to the decision; other considerably less. Was, for example, the Court's decision a decisive factor in the formation of the civil rights movement or of subsequent civil rights legislation? Or was it even a significant factor in the decision to desegregate the public schools of St. Louis? Topeka? Widely ranging interpretations have been put forth by various scholars. Given the several problems listed above, it is not surprising that one finds such differences in interpretation of the impact of a particular event, or that histories of the same events are constantly being rewritten.

(3) A third problem with power and impact, and I think the most important although least considered one, is termed the *law of anticipated reactions*. This "law" has plagued students of power generally, and as will be seen, presents a particularly knotty problem for students of any institution possessing a high degree of legitimacy, such as the Supreme Court. But while it does present a complicating factor, it also sheds a clarifying light on one important but gen-

16. 347 U.S. 483 (1954).

erally ignored dimension of the impact and function of the Supreme Court and the institution of law in general.

The law of anticipated reactions holds, as Friedrich has reminded contemporary political scientists, that an actor's behavior can be altered as a result of his anticipation of another's interests.[17] To return to Dahl's A and B, it holds that B can anticipate A's interests and consequently feels constrained by them and acts accordingly, even though there is no outward appearance of relationship or command by A. So in a sense there is an effect, B's "altered" behavior, without any cause, i.e. A's "command." This sophist's logic can easily be overcome, but the conceptual and methodological problems associated with identifying such types of relationships are enormous. This fact of life has stymied more than one political theorist and contributed significantly to more than one scholar's desire to banish entirely the concept of power from systematic political theory.

Of the three sets of problems with power, this "law of anticipated reactions" seems to be the most interesting with respect to the impact of the Supreme Court. Following Weber, Friedrich has argued that to a large extent "authority," i.e. legitimate power, is the ability to have people anticipate interests and act accordingly without having to rely on explicit communications and the concomitant threat of sanctions.[18] Clearly, the Supreme Court is an institution enjoying a particularly high position of legitimacy within American society. For this reason, therefore, we could expect that anticipated reactions would account for some substantial portion of the total impact of the Supreme Court.

Furthermore, the very nature of law and legal reasoning insures that the law of anticipated reactions would characterize some important segment of the high court's impact. By this I mean that the questions, "Is it constitutional?" and "What is the Court likely to do?" are frequently asked by legislators, executives, and policy-makers at all levels of government, and are also answered by the same policy-makers or their legal advisers without having to resort to an actual *test* of the Court's reaction. Role playing, reading between the lines of the Court's decisions, and determining the direc-

17. Carl Friedrich, *Constitutional Government and Democracy* (Boston: Ginn, 1946), pp. 589ff.
18. *Ibid.*, 590.

tions and implications of the Court's actions are all ways of anticipating its responses and likely responses to particular situations. The extent to which one's behavior is affected by such actions can be labeled as conforming to the law of anticipated reactions.

Almost invariably the design of "impact studies" has ignored this type of phenomena and has focused exclusively on the "aftermath" of the high court's decisions. Few of the systematic studies of impact have been explicitly concerned with the nature and scope of anticipated reactions, despite the fact—as I contend—that it constitutes a major segment of the Court's power on the American political process.[19] Clearly, one factor contributing to such oversight is the difficulty if not impossibility of systematically identifying anticipated reactions and adjustments. The canons of experimental design simply do not provide convenient rules for such problems. Perhaps the best one can hope for is the identification of occasional illustrative examples. Also, however, I suspect that such oversight is due in part at least to the domination in the social sciences of an Austinian conception of law, a view that emphasizes the "command" of the official and the subsequent reaction by the subject. As one moves away from this conception of law to one emphasizing a system of rules with a "life of their own," the importance of "anticipated reactions" is likely to increase and become more obvious. Until such time, it is likely that a very important aspect of the impact of legal institutions will continue to be overlooked.

AN ALTERNATIVE PERSPECTIVE:
PUBLIC POLICY ANALYSIS

So far the criticism of the desire to construct a "theory" of Supreme Court impact has dealt almost exclusively with the ambiguity of the term impact. There are, however, additional concerns which must be dealt with. By and large they raise the continuous controversy over the desired level of generality in social science theory-building.

Presumably any theory should serve at least the following func-

19. One exception is Stephen Wasby's discussion of anticipated reaction in his book, *The Impact of the United States Supreme Court, op. cit.,* pp. 35–38. Unfortunately, however, his subsequent analysis of impact does not return to this interesting and elusive problem.

tions: (1) provide a set of generalizations which ideally should take the form of "universalistic laws," (2) offer a framework for inter-relating these laws, and (3) point out new directions for research. Of these the first and second are the more important. Putting these criteria to test, the questions posed by impact analysis—and empirical research generally—are to what extent can generalizations based on the examination of a single institution, e.g. the Supreme Court, actually allow one the means by which to generate anything approaching "universalistic laws"? Second, is it useful to attempt to develop a "theory" of impact for a single institution? In both cases, the response is negative. The very emphasis on a single institution, rather than on a general process, considerably limits the scope of inquiry and the level of abstraction and generality. While one certainly can make interesting statements about the impact of a particular decision, such generalizations are of a rather low theoretical level. In a sense, such an inductive approach—if extended—would require the development of a "theory" of each separate institution, and in many ways contribute to fragmentation rather than integration of knowledge.

An alternative, more generalized level of analysis is suggested by the questions, "What are the *social functions* of law? and "Why do people *comply* with legal rules?" In both these questions a *general process* is invoked and the analysis of a particular institution would be used as only one of a number of data sources. Consequently, answers to these questions framed in general terms are more likely to begin to contribute to the development of a theory of behavior, although—as indicated in the discussion of causality above—they would tend to lead *away from* detailed and explicit analysis of a single institution.

I am not proposing, however, that either theoretical or empirical analysis of the Supreme Court's impact be abandoned. Rather what I am suggesting is that the search for a *theory* of impact of the high court be abandoned and replaced by a more generalized perspective and (perhaps) a less ambiguous central concept. On the other hand, empirical analysis of the conditions and consequences of Supreme Court actions is of course appropriate and desirable, but probably ought to be termed something less than a quest toward a theory. The Court, clearly an important American institution, ought to receive

the careful scrutiny of concerned scholars, and the consequences of
its decisions should be described and traced as thoroughly as possible.

A more modest and, I think, useful framework in which to place
the study of the high court's impact is offered by public policy
analysis. While this field, or more properly term, is rather new, essentially it is nothing more than the tracing of policy-relevant consequences of official decisions.[20] In pursuing this task, research is
not likely to be "pure," in that in accounting for the consequences
of particular policies, explanations are apt to cut across traditional
disciplinary boundaries and draw from a wide variety of theories.
It is essentially *applied* rather than *theoretical* research. That is,
public policy analysis attempts to provide answers for specific, immediate questions rather than develop rigorous theories about generalized processes. While examples of the two types of research often
merge, the distinction is nevertheless important. The former is more
likely to be directed toward the evaluation and assessment of the
performance of the particular institution in a particular setting, give
considerable attention to the combination of particularistic and idio-
syncratic historical factors, and to be coupled with an analysis of a
variety of other possible alternatives which might have been followed.
The latter, on the other hand, is not so much concerned with the
specific outcomes in a particular setting as it is with the general
process, and it is not so much concerned with *immediate* prediction
as with *general* explanation of a process.

SUMMARY AND CONCLUSIONS

This paper has examined some of the major problems of constructing
a theory of the impact of the Supreme Court. The term impact was
considered as a possible candidate for a core concept in such a theory
but was found wanting on several counts. They included the problem caused by the lack of comparability, the ambiguity stemming
from the incomplete and unarticulated notions of causality implicit
in the term, and the dilemma of the "law of anticipated reactions."
In addition the level of generality in the analysis of the Court's im-

20. See, for example, Austin Ranney's excellent collection of articles dealing
with public policy analysis in his edited volume, *Political Science and Public
Policy* (Chicago: Markham Publishing Co., 1968).

pact was considered and also found wanting. Lastly the empirical study of Supreme Court impact was identified with the general field of public policy analysis, examined in light of the distinction between applied and theoretical research, and I argued that it was more appropriate to consider impact analysis as a type of applied public policy analysis. It is hoped that this discussion, while certainly not providing a framework for impact analysis, has at least clarified certain basic problems and begun to link impact analysis with the much larger field of public policy analysis.

JAMES P. LEVINE
AND THEODORE L. BECKER

Toward and Beyond a Theory of Supreme Court Impact

The purpose of this paper is to explain why the Supreme Court has had limited effects on American society, to suggest some means by which the Court's influence can be increased, and to raise some questions about the proper role of social science in this endeavor.

REASONS FOR SUPREME COURT INEFFICACY

Lower Court Autonomy

It is often presumed that the hierarchical organization of the American judiciary centralizes much lawmaking authority within appellate courts and that trial courts generally defer to the Supreme Court in deciding cases of constitutional law. The operation of this role constraint on lower courts is illustrated by the Indiana Supreme Court's reaction to Henry Miller's *Tropic of Cancer,* which was involved in a local obscenity case. After expressing distaste for the book, the Indiana court deferred to the authority of the superordinate court and reversed the conviction.

> Regardless of our personal opinion on this matter both as to the law and the facts, we are bound as judges of this Court, under the oath we took, to follow the Constitution of the United States, as interpreted by the Supreme Court of the United States, and that Court, in our opinion has determined the issue in this case.[1]

1. Cuffel v. State, 215 N.E. 2d 36 (Indiana, 1966).

Reprinted from *American Behavioral Scientist,* Volume 13, Number 4 (March/April 1970), pp. 561–573, by permission of the Publisher, Sage Publications, Inc.

James Levine is Associate Professor of Political Science at CUNY-Brooklyn College. Theodore L. Becker is Professor of Political Science at the University of Hawaii.

However, the "trickle-down" theory is at best a very rough first approximation of reality. First of all, there is no solid evidence showing that most trial judges actually feel obliged to follow Supreme Court rulings if they are opposed to them. And unless the duty to comply is internalized, there are few means available to appellate courts to keep lower courts in line, since only a very small proportion of cases are ever appealed. Because the threat of reversal is fairly hollow, the trial judges can act independently with impunity.

Indeed, there are some data which suggest that lower courts frequently apply standards decidedly at variance with those articulated by the Supreme Court. For example, in Betts v. Brady,[2] (since overruled by Gideon v. Wainwright[3]), the Court ruled that defendants in noncapital cases were entitled to state-appointed counsel if special circumstances were present making it impossible for the defendant to represent himself adequately. However, in only 11 out of 139 state appellate cases concerning this issue were special circumstances found (Lewis, 1964: 151). In 1961, the Pennsylvania Supreme Court actually denied a plea for legal aid from an eighteen-year-old boy with an IQ of 59, equivalent to a mental age of nine.[4] Since Betts v. Brady was a landmark case, this smacks of outright defiance of the Supreme Court.

Many institutional features of the judicial system provide ample opportunity for inferior judges to legitimately ignore, modify, or evade high-level policy formulations (see Murphy, 1959). First, lower courts have the authority to make crucial findings of fact which can only be partially controlled by appellate courts. Second, since the fact constellations of any one case are never *exact* replicas of those of other cases, lower courts can often distinguish away alleged precedents ordained on high. Third, the verbiage of Supreme Court language can be manipulated, with favorable sentences elevated to the status of a "holding" which is binding and unfavorable words dismissed as "mere dicta." Fourth, state courts can often insulate themselves from Supreme Court review by grounding their decisions in state law. Thus, judges who want to be obstructive have adequate tools at their disposal.

Another impediment to Supreme Court efficacy is the very nature

2. 316 U.S. 455 (1942).
3. 372 U.S. 335 (1963).
4. Commonwealth ex rel. Simon v. Maroney, 405 Pa. 562 (1961).

of most decisions. The Court is often either ambiguous or divided on policy matters, which gives lower courts encouragement to go their own way. Because compromise and negotiations are frequently necessary to obtain the support of most of the Justices (or even a bare majority) behind one opinion (Murphy, 1964: ch. 3), the resulting document is often beset with confusion providing lower courts with few guidelines to decide run-of-the-mill cases. If the Justices persevere and hold out for clearly written principles, the result is often a very split Court and the continuing possibility, of which lower courts are aware, that small changes of personnel will alter the balance on the Court and change its direction. There seems to be an inverse relation between the *clarity of holdings* and the *size of the Court majority*, so Justices must often choose between two routes to ineffectiveness. Chief Justice Earl Warren obtained unanimity in Brown v. Board of Education, but the price may have been the now infamously vague "all deliberate speed" mandate. On the other hand, when Warren in 1966 did spell out precise rules for police interrogations in Miranda v. Arizona,[5] only five Justices subscribed to his majority opinion and four Justices dissented. The Court, like others, may not be able to have its cake and eat it, too.

Even when a united Court is committed to some specific policy, the physical burden of handling a constantly increasing number of appeals often prevents them from periodically reinforcing this commitment and supervising implementation. The Court, for example, terminated its approval of the usage of the due process clause of the Fourteenth Amendment to invalidate economic legislation as early as the 1930s, but Paulsen (1950) has shown that lower courts continued to declare statutes unconstitutional on that basis for many years. Given its limited resources of time and manpower, the Court is simply unable to do much spotchecking of the lower courts except in issue areas of the highest priority.

Finally, linear trends are not characteristic of Supreme Court policy-making. The voting equality cases are atypical, what with the Court from 1962 to 1967 declaring 31 out of 32 instances of alleged malapportionment unconstitutional. Usually the Court exhibits occasional fluctuation or vacillation as it has done in the right to privacy cases. Such equivocation is probably seized upon by lower

5. 384 U.S. 436 (1966).

courts who oppose the general directions being taken and used to retard policy changes at the trial court level.

Elite Unresponsiveness

Of more concern than lower court compliance with the Supreme Court is the conduct of presumably affected people who never get into the court at all. The real test of the Court's potency are the changes voluntarily initiated by those elites, public and private, whose activities are similar to those declared illegitimate by the Court. Due to the inertia which propels many organizations, there is a natural tendency to carry on established routines and disregard Court holdings that rock the boat. This is especially so where the Court strikes at central practices of the institution and where policy changes are perceived by those in control as being dysfunctional to primary objectives.

Thus, those who operate the criminal courts, which are usually oriented toward conviction (Blumberg, 1967), react negatively to court decisions extending defendants' rights, which would have the effect of turning a fairly efficient bureaucratic process into a time-consuming and nonproductive adversary system. Similarly, officials in the Selective Service System are unlikely to respond positively to judicial restrictions on draft board procedures which would curtail the rapid mobilization of military manpower. Indicative of this is General Hershey's recent disavowal of a federal court declaratory judgment ruling that it was illegal to speed up inductions of draft protestors.

Because no general announcements of policy are communicated to affected parties, it is quite frequent that authorities remain totally unaware of new responsibilities required of them and new norms governing their behavior. Barth found that district attorneys in Wisconsin are very ill-informed about current obscenity rulings (Barth, 1968), and Rabin's (1967) interviews with Selective Service personnel showed that they were oblivious to United States v. Seeger[6] which broadened the legitimate bases for conscientious objection. In a similar vein, Krislov (1968: 194) has pointed out that police train-

6. 380 U.S. 163 (1965).

ing conferences pay virtually no attention whatsoever to development in civil liberties law.

There is frequently a high personal utility to willful noncompliance. Sometimes it is simply good politics to defy Court decisions, as the fortunes of George Wallace and Lester Maddox have dramatically demonstrated. In other cases the payoffs are even greater, as when the policeman in high crime districts obtains greater physical security by shortcutting the requirements of due process in enforcing the law. Muir's (1962: ch. 4) study of educators' reactions to the school prayer decisions points out a less tangible benefit resulting from resistance to the Court: the maintenance of social relationships and the approval of associates. In short, elites often see it in their own self-interest to turn their backs on the Court.

Since the judiciary really lacks the sanctions to coerce compliance, elites often see few risks ensuing from disobedience. Positive programs involving the allocation of considerable economic resources are often required to implement Court doctrines, and judicial enforcement machinery is largely limited to negative instruments such as injunctions and acquittals. Both the cost of litigations and the prerequisites of court utilization (e.g., establishing standing, showing a real case and controversy, actually violating a law) minimize the force of judicial controls. Moreover, the decentralized and uncoordinated nature of many institutions regulated by Supreme Court decisions (such as school boards, police departments, and welfare agencies) magnify the scope of the enforcement problem. The attorneys general of the states supposedly have the authority to spur compliance, but Krislov (1959) and others have shown that they also often have political disincentives to act vigorously. To offend local norms and opinion can be political suicide.

The beneficiaries of Supreme Court policies are often either ill-equipped or unwilling to pressure elites to comply: It is often insular minorities who are supported by the Court, and they lack the resources—the funds, personnel, organization, and information—to mount a cause at the local level. The poor are hardly in a position to push for their constitutional rights to equal governmental treatment.

Also, the cost of pushing compliance usually outweighs the limited satisfaction of having one's interest vindicated. Parents may be irritated by Bible-reading in their children's classrooms, and public employees may be troubled by compulsory loyalty oaths, but the intensity of their grievances is insufficient to motivate them to act. For criminal defendants, the price of insisting on the right to appointed counsel may very well be harsher treatment by the court and stiffer sentences. It is normal for persons to try to maximize their utilities, and fighting for constitutional rights is often just not worthwhile.

Consequently, the deck is rather stacked against widespread voluntary implementation of Supreme Court policies. Institutions such as Congress, with its control over the public fisc, and the executive, with its massive bureaucracy, are in a far better position to promote social change on more than a token basis. For example, it was not until the United States Commissioner of Education started a systematic campaign to enforce the Federal Aid to Education Act of 1965, which prohibited funding of segregated schools, that any serious progress was made toward desegregation of schools in the deep South. Without political action in other quarters, the hands of the Supreme Court are likely to be tied and the status quo ante will probably remain.

Public Unawareness

Although the Supreme Court has the inherent capacity to mold its decisions into powerful political symbols, the empirical evidence on symbolic effects of decisions is still meager. Hyman Sheatsley (1964) anlayzed survey data on changes in attitudes toward desegregation from 1942 to 1964 and concluded that the Brown decision had radically accelerated the shift towards acceptance of desegregation. More recently Dolbeare (1969: 185–187) found that the "halo effect" caused by the Supreme Court's virtuous image caused people to applaud the Court's banning of public school prayers, even though they had previously approved of schoolhouse religion. Since political leaders do respond to public moods and sentiments, these kinds of consequences can be important in the formation of public policy. However, there is a missing link in the above line of argument: the communication processes between the Court and the public. Judicial symbols must be widely diffused to be effective, and the findings of survey research are beginning to unfold massive public ignorance of Supreme Court decisions (Dolbeare, 1967). News coverage of the Court is generally sketchy and frequently either misunderstood or distorted, with major decisions often relegated to back pages or summarized in a couple of column inches (for all but assiduous and devoted readers of the *New York Times*. See Newland, 1964). If the Court is to be a catalyst of major social change, it must reach beyond the legal community (which remains largely untouched anyway) and into the general community.

INCREASING THE SUPREME COURT'S IMPACT

To increase the Court's impact, some traditional practices should be abandoned as quickly as possible while new approaches and procedures are adopted and applied—with imagination, flexibility, and boldness. Since the social isolation treasured by most of the Justices mutes the Court's voice in national politics, we urge, as a start, that the Court give up this haughty posture and begin making serious attempts to relate to the American public.

Some innovations might necessitate legislative action, but others could be instituted by the Court itself, thereby obviating resort to the booby-trapped trail through the legislative obstacle course called Congress. Let us take a candid look at how the Court clues us all in on what it has decided in camera. Its "streamlined" method is rooted in practices developed under Forefather John Jay, as modified by that other great modernist, Forefather John Marshall, as well as by other radical proceduralists. Of course these jurisprudential giants of yesteryear were acquainted, to a degree, with the political system as it existed in their heyday. But need we emphasize that the times, they have a-changed? In today's world, the medium is the message, and the medium that the Court chooses to pass its word is drab, dreary, and humdrum. Verbatim reading of opinions by the Justices to handfuls of court observers and the doling out of advance sheets to lawyers and libraries are that medium. Small wonder that so few get the message!

We are certain that a multitude of arguments, mostly mired in tradition, can be mustered to applaud this musty arrangement. However, if we may be so brash, as political scientists currently interested in a more effective Court, we would suggest a vast array of changes in the props of the setting on opinion day. For one thing, there is surely no reasons, in this, the age of McLuhan, to categorically exclude television from the court chambers. In our era of mass communications, it is almost anachronistic that the Court has shunned the tube for as long as it has. We are well aware, of course, that if the Justices were to perform before the cameras as they now do in the flesh, there is little doubt that their Nielsen ratings would set record lows. Justice Black's ponderous performance on a recent network television interview does nothing to dispel this suspicion.

But can there be any question about the fact that one reason the Court receives so little popular support for important decisions is that the public simply does not comprehend what the Court has said and why the Justices believe their view to be proper? Since television networks donate free time to the President to express his views in news conferences and through prepared speeches, it would seem that they could be convinced (or forced by law) to open their facilities once a month to the Court for a professionally designed program describing and dramatizing what it is that the Court has decided and spelling out the justifications for its policies.

True, this might be nudging the judiciary into the realm of theatrics. But so what? And true, this might compel the Court to employ a staff that would include television or movie directors, actors, and technicians, in order to produce short vignettes about what the Court finds offensive in the actions of some officials and what the scope of its rulings really are. In doing this, the Court will be assuming one of its basic responsibilities; it will be taking a direct hand in creating an illuminating presentation that could truly educate the public on constitutional politics. Years ago, Eugene Rostow (1952: 203) characterized the Justices as "teachers in a vital national seminar" about fundamental political principles, but it is a sad fact that few Americans are enrolled in the course. The Court has ignored its pedagogical functions and has passed the buck to woefully inadequate sources of information, such as harried newspaper reporters, copy editors, and headline writers pressured by deadlines into frequently misinterpreting and malinterpreting.

It is sometimes written that the Presidency became the political power into which it has evolved as the President became aware of the role of mass media in gaining grassroots support. FDR's fireside chats were a significant device that aided President Roosevelt in consolidating the coalition so essential to his continuation in office through four elections. Several Presidents since have managed to use television, in particular, to their own political advantage so as to maximize the chances for getting favored policies accepted by large segments of the citizenry. The Court's refusal to admit this to itself and its continued abhorrence of this most significant of media may well undermine its remaining vestiges of influence. One can hardly understand or respect even the most eloquent of orators if he speaks only into a paper bag. Only the orator hears a resonance of the beautiful rhetoric; others hear muffled sounds.

Aside from recognizing this failing, there are changes in staffing that the Justices should consider. After all, it is rather absurd to pretend that the only help the Court needs is that of its law clerks and its secretarial and administrative staffs. Neither these people nor the Justices themselves qualify as experts in political analysis or in the arts of public relations and political pressure. How long must we wait until the common knowledge among us that the Court is a political institution is translated into meaningful reforms in how the Court acts in the political system?

For instance, it is well known that the Court frequently runs into stiff opposition from Congress. There have been many studies that detail the hatred and defiance among members of the Senate and the House of Representatives that the Court has triggered by some of its most recent decisions (see, for example, Beaney and Beiser, 1964; Nagel, 1965). But what is worse still is that the Court is frequently misunderstood by even its staunchest supporters who, on the basis of the idle conjecture and often amateurish speculation, bear the onerous burden of communicating accurately to their legislative colleagues the precise holding of the Court and the political and legal reasons behind the Court's decision. What possible benefit can be gained in allowing this fumbling and groping to continue? Whom are we kidding? Whom is the Court fooling? Surely the Congress is not (comprised of), a naive clique of legal positivists who believe *en masse* that the Court *finds* the law a la Lord Coke. They recognize that a host of extra legal factors influence the Court's decision as well as we do. Why, then, don't we do for the Court that which we have done for administrative agencies (like the Pentagon) and furnish the Court with a group of political scientists, lobbyists, and public relations men to plead its case before Congress? These men could also assist the Court in moulding and writing opinions that would hold down potential irritation levels of Congress (and the President) thus enhancing the chances of maximum compliance.

As to the political scientists on an expanded Supreme Court staff, their role would be far more than simply figuring out political ploys and tactics on the Hill. Indeed, the time has come (if not gone) when the Court must officially recognize the need for developing a large store of data on success and failure in implementing its announced law at all levels of government. It would seem to be the proper place, in our scheme of things, to sponsor these studies through the Court itself. As the first section of this paper shows clearly enough, political scientists are already deeply committed to a search into what conditions foster (or undermine) compliance with Supreme Court decisions. As this area of study grows, and as theory begins to take shape, it would seem the height of folly for the Court to dwell in ignorance of the findings as well as of expert advice from political scientists interested in a more effective Supreme Court.

WITHDRAWING SCIENTIFIC SUPPORT

This leads us into the final point we wish to make in this paper. It is a difficult one, and one that plunges us deeply into thorny dilemmas about the appropriate role of empirical scientists assisting those who hold the reins of power.

We have been reminded of late of the naivete of many nuclear physicists, in the early and mid-forties, concerning the uses to which their knowledge and expertise would be put by our government. This blindness has been dramatized by a play entitled *In The Matter of J. Robert Oppenheimer* (presented at New York City Lincoln Center's Vivian Beaumont Theatre during the 1968–1969 season). According to the testimony given at Oppenheimer's security hearing, many of these scientists refused to believe that the bomb would actually be used against the Japanese people. This belief was firm enough to resist change despite the fact that the military had several of these very same scientists (including Oppenheimer) working on problems of heat and blast effects on a variety of Japanese cities!

Transposed to studies of the Supreme Court, the problem presents itself thusly: we must be alert constantly to future changes in our political system and its processes and consciously determine the point at which we should withdraw scientific support of governmental policies once we believe them to be inimical to political values that we cherish. To fail to see this as a problem would be immoral and irresponsible.

It is easy for many of us who consider ourselves to be a shade of liberal (or even a tint of conservative) to rail at the mosaic of non-compliance with Supreme Court decisions. After all, the Supreme Court is the duly constituted final arbiter of a wide variety of federal and constitutional questions and issues. When it speaks, its words are the *supreme law* of the land. And law must be obeyed. Therefore, as scientists, we can plunge in without any reluctance and treat the malady of defiance. Right? Wrong.

That was the error of the nuclear physicists who trotted gallantly out in quest of the secret of the atomic bomb. But, as many of them discovered later, and as many other scientists who have been employed by the American military-industrial complex have learned more recently, they were utilized to achieve ends that they came to consider evil, unjust and wrong. At some earlier point, they may have had a bargaining position that might have allowed them, as citizens—with power (scientific knowledge)—to influence processes and policies. But they were dazzled by a golden ideological haze that convinced them that American power could only be used for good. Only at a point too far removed, and after the fact, did they come to their normative senses. We must begin to think about this problem now, in all areas of the study of government and politics, and that would certainly include our potential use to the Supreme Court as political scientists and as political advisors.

We do not wish to belabour this point, but there is a thick and durable smog of nonsense that cloaks the actual functioning of the Supreme Court of the United States. The basic function of the Court is surely not the one we find so consistently uttered by much of the political-legal community in this day and age. For liberals, all too often, the Court is pictured as some eternal fortress, of sorts, against encroachments on the democratic process and on individual liberties. To one degree or another, the Court is seen by prominent experts as being an important factor in expanding our freedoms and in developing legal guidelines for expanding our democratic base. And, of course, in a legal sense, and to some degree of political reality, it has had this function of late on the American scene. Our point is that this is more an accident of history and a result of particular personnel than it is an inherent function of the Supreme Court.[7]

Who in their right minds could believe that the United States Supreme Court, or any other high court for that matter, is anything other than an *un*democratic institution? Despite rationales to the contrary we have no serious structural democratic checks by the populace directly as they exist in Australia and Japan. Of course our Court's judges, as an enlightened and benevolent aristocracy, have had strong democratic and liberal ideals and thus have made decisions that are *pro*-democratic and *anti*-police state. But, and this is critical, there is no guarantee that such a status-quo-oriented, elite-staffed institution will continue to decide as it has in the last decade or so. We must remember that the same Court produced the Dred Scott Decision.[8]

Suppose, for example, President Nixon and his successor—say, a President Agnew—get another twelves years in the White House. Suppose they manage to select an overwhelming number of highly reactionary justices. Suppose the court of Chief Justice Warren Earl Burger reverses precedents (with some relish) and tries to implement a personal policy preference of seriously curtailing the protections of the Fifth Amendment. Suppose, even, that the Supreme Court becomes more police-state oriented than many high police administrators and that the latter, contrary to the Court's mandates, devise ingenious plans for evasion, avoidance, and defiance? Thus we might find career bureaucrats trying to sabotage what some people fear as being imminent on the horizon, that is, a drastic "turn to the right." What then for those among us who would be working out a theory on the impact of the Supreme Court? Should we continue to work it out? Should we continue to advise on how the Court can be most effective? The problem that we must ponder is again to set forth

7. For the fullest argument along these lines, see Becker (1969: ch. 5). A more cursory treatment of this point can be found in Becker (1967).
8. Dred Scott v. Sanford, 19 Howard (U.S.) 393 (1857).

specific criteria by which changes in our system and its process and policies should force us to withdraw scientific support, *as a profession!*

This should be debated in our classrooms, in our literature, and at our conventions—local and national. It would be tragic for social scientists to ignore this issue much the same as it was overlooked by the nuclear physicists in the forties and the entire scientific community in the fifties and sixties. After all, we have their lesson to learn from and we are, or should be, *political* scientists.

CONCLUSION

In an age of almost incomprehensibly rapid changes, institutions which fail to keep pace are bound for oblivion. Miller's (1968: ch. 6) ominous predictions about the coming "desuetude" of the Supreme Court may prove to be correct unless the Court adjusts its strategies and tactics. Theodore Roosevelt is alleged to have urged nations seeking world power to speak softly and carry a big stick. To which we add, those who lack big sticks, like the United States Supreme Court, had better learn to yell loudly, plead fervidly, and act shrewdly. The Court's strength is in its symbols; it should make the best of them.

Lest we conclude on a self-righteous and self-assured note, it must be admitted that we of the academy will take *some* of the blame for the tragically wide gulf between the ideals of constitutional doctrine and the reality of political life. Having criticized the Supreme Court for blindly staggering in the dark and cloistering itself inside the marble palace, we must also point a guilty finger at the discipline of political science for failing to light the way and for taking refuge in the ivory tower. Both our research and our teaching have only very recently been directed to the empirical study of institutional practices and their social consequences, which is one area where we *ourselves* can aspire to make a political impact.

Finally, now that increasing attempts are being made to devise more refined theory and collect better data on the impact of the Supreme Court, let us not make the grievous error of being indifferent to the real danger of having our knowledge used for malevolent purposes. If and when the day should come that the Supreme Court becomes repressive, inhumane, and unjust in its policy-making, we may have a political obligation to confound their efforts by quashing our inquiries and withdrawing our counsel. It is not too early to ponder these disturbing possibilities and perplexing dilemmas; 1984 is only fifteen years away.

REFERENCES

BARTH, T. (1968) "Perception and acceptance of Supreme Court decisions at the state and local level." J. of Public Law 17: 308–350.

BEANEY, W. M. and E. N. BEISER (1964) "Prayer and politics: the impact of Engel and Schempp on the political process." J. of Public Law 13: 475–503. (Reprinted on pp. 24–38 of this book.)

BECKER, T. L. (1969) Comparative Judicial Politics. Chicago: Rand-McNally.

——— (1967) "Judicial structure and its political functioning in society." J. of Politics 29: 302–331.

BLUMBERG, A. (1967) Criminal Justice. Chicago: Quadrangle.

DOLBEARE, K. (1969) "The Supreme Court and the states: from abstract doctrine to local behavioral conformity," in T. Becker (ed.) The Impact of Supreme Court Decisions. New York: Oxford Univ. Press.

——— (1967) "The public views the Supreme Court," pp. 194–212 in H. Jacob (ed.) Law, Politics, and the Federal Courts. Boston: Little, Brown.

HYMAN, H. and P. SHEATSLEY (1964) "Attitudes toward desegregation." Scientific Amer. 211: 16–23.

KRISLOV, S. (1968) The Supreme Court and Political Freedom. New York: Free Press.

——— (1959) "Constituency versus constitutionalism: the desegregation issue and the tensions and aspirations of Southern attorneys general." Midwest J. of Pol. Sci. 3: 75–92.

LEWIS, A. (1964) Gideon's Trumpet. New York: Vantage.

MILLER, A. (1968) The Supreme Court and American Capitalism. New York: Free Press.

MUIR, W. (1962) Prayer in the Public Schools. Chicago: Univ. of Chicago Press.

MURPHY, W. (1964) Elements of Judicial Strategy. Chicago: Univ. of Chicago Press.

——— (1959) "Lower court checks on Supreme Court power." Amer. Pol. Sci. Rev. 53 (December): 1017–1031.

NAGEL, S. (1965) "Court-curbing periods in American history." Vanderbilt Law Rev. 18 (June): 925–944.

NEWLAND, C. (1964) "Press coverage of the United States supreme court." Western Pol. Q. 17 (March): 15–36.

PAULSEN, M. (1950) "The persistence of substantive due process in the states." Minnesota Law Rev. 34 (January): 91–118.

RABIN, R. (1967) "Do you believe in a supreme being—the administration of the conscientious objector exemption." Wisconsin Law Rev.: 642–684.

ROSTOW, E. (1952) "The democratic character of judicial review." Harvard Law Rev. 66 (December).

For Further Reading

BOOKS:

Berger M. *Congress v. The Supreme Court*. Cambridge: Harvard University Press, 1970.

Blaustein, Albert P., and Clarence Clyde Ferguson, Jr. *Desegration and the Law: The Meaning and Effect of the School Segregation Cases*. New Brunswick, N.J.: Rutgers University Press, 1957.

Carmen, Ira. *Movies: Censorship and the Law*. Ann Arbor: University of Michigan Press, 1966.

Hill, Roscoe, and Malcolm Feeley (eds.). *Affirmative School Integration*. Beverly Hills: Sage Publications, Inc., 1968.

Jackson, Robert. *The Struggle for Judicial Supremacy*. New York: Knopf, 1941.

Johnson, Richard. *The Dynamics of Compliance*. Evanston, Ill.: Northwestern University Press, 1967.

Krislov, Samuel. *The Supreme Court and Political Freedom*. New York: Free Press, 1968.

Krislov, Samuel, et al. (eds.). *Compliance and the Law*. Beverly Hills: Sage Publications, Inc., 1972.

Kurland, Phillip. *Politics, the Constitution, and the Warren Court*. Chicago: University of Chicago Press, 1970.

Lytle, Clifford M. *The Warren Court and Its Critics*. Tuscon: University of Arizona Press, 1968.

Miller, Arthur Selwyn. *The Supreme Court and American Capitalism*. New York: Free Press, 1968.

Milner, Neal A. *The Court and Local Law Enforcement*. Beverly Hills: Sage Publications, Inc., 1971.

Mitau, G. Theodore. *Decade of Decision: The Supreme Court and the Constitutional Revolution, 1954–1964*. New York: Charles Scribner's Sons, 1967.

Muir, William K., Jr. *Prayer in the Public Schools: Law and Attitude Change.* Chicago: University of Chicago Press, 1967.

Murphy, Walter. *Congress and the Court.* Chicago: University of Chicago Press, 1962.

Murphy, Walter. *Wiretapping on Trial: A Case Study in the Judicial Process.* New York: Random House Inc., 1965.

Nagel, Stuart. *The Legal Process from a Behavioral Perspective.* Homewood, Ill.: Dorsey Press, 1969.

Peltason, J. W. *Fifty-eight Lonely Men: Southern Federal Judges and School Desegregation.* New York: Harcourt, Brace & World, 1961.

Pritchett, C. Herman. *Congress Versus The Supreme Court.* Minneapolis: University of Minnesota Press, 1961.

Pritchett, C. Herman and Alan Westin (eds.) *The Third Branch of Government: Eight Cases in Constitutional Politics.* New York: Harcourt, Brace & World, 1963.

Randall, Richard S. *Censorship of the Movies: The Social and Political Control of a Mass Medium.* Madison: University of Wisconsin Press, 1968.

Sarratt, Reed. *The Ordeal of Desegregation: The First Decade.* New York: Macmillan, 1971.

Scigliano, Robert. *The Supreme Court and the Presidency.* New York: Macmillan, 1971.

Shapiro, Martin. *The Supreme Court and Administrative Agencies.* New York: Macmillan, 1968.

Smith, Bob. *They Closed Their Schools: Prince Edward County, Virginia, 1951–1964.* Chapel Hill: University of North Carolina Press, 1965.

Wasby, Stephen. *The Impact of the United States Supreme Court.* Homewood, Ill.: Dorsey Press, 1970.

ARTICLES:

Barth, Thomas E. "Perception and Acceptance of Supreme Court Decisions at the State and Local Level," *Journal of Public Law,* Vol. 17 (1968), pp. 305–50.

Behan, T. R. "The Post-Warren Freedom Survey: Report No. 1," *American Bar Association Journal,* Vol. 56 (January 1970).

Dolbeare, Kenneth, and Phillip Hammond. "The Political Party Basis of Attitudes Toward the Supreme Court," *Public Opinion Quarterly,* Vol. 31 (Spring 1967), pp. 16–30.

8413

Katz, Ellis. "Patterns of Compliance with the Schempp Decision," *Journal of Public Law*, Vol. 14 (1965) pp. 396–405.

Miller, Arthur S. "On the Need for 'Impact Analysis' of Supreme Court Decisions," *Georgetown Law Journal*, Vol. 53 (1965) pp. 365–401.

Miller, Arthur S., and Alan W. Scheflin. "The Power of the Supreme Court in the Age of the Positive State: A Preliminary Excursus," *Duke Law Journal*, Vol. 1967, pp. 273–320.

Mollan, Robert. "Smith Act Prosecutions: The Effect of the *Dennis* and *Yates* Decisions," *University of Pittsburgh Law Review*, Vol. 26 (June 1965), pp. 705–48.

Murphy, Michael J. "The Problem of Compliance by Police Departments," *Texas Law Review*, Vol. 44 (1969), pp. 939–46.

Patric, Gordon. "The Impact of a Court Decision: Aftermath of the McCollum Case," *Journal of Public Law*, Vol. 6 (Fall 1957), pp. 455–64.

Petrick, Michael J. "The Supreme Court and Authority Acceptance," *Western Political Quarterly*, Vol. 21 (March 1968), pp. 5–19.

Sayko, Andrew F. "The Impact of the Supreme Court Section. 103 Cases on the Standard of Patentability in the Lower Federal Courts," *George Washington Law Review*, Vol. 35 (May 1967), pp. 818–27.

Sorauf, Frank J. "*Zorach v. Clauson:* The Impact of a Supreme Court Decision," *American Political Science Review*, Vol. 53 (September 1959), pp. 777–91.

Stumpf, Harry. "The Political Efficacy of Judicial Symbolism," *Western Political Quarterly*, Vol. 19 (June 1966) pp. 293–303.

Way, H. Frank, Jr. "Survey Research on Judicial Decisions: The Prayer and Bible Reading Cases," *Western Political Quarterly*, Vol. 21 (June 1968), pp. 189–205.